I0866678

THE OBSESSIONS OF GEORGES BATAILLE

SUNY series in Contemporary French Thought

David Pettigrew and François Raffoul, editors

THE OBSESSIONS OF GEORGES BATAILLE

Community and Communication

Edited by

Andrew J. Mitchell

and

Jason Kemp Winfree

SUNY PRESS

Published by
State University of New York Press, Albany

Printed in the United States of America

For information, contact
State University of New York Press, Albany, NY
www.sunypress.edu

Production by Eileen Meehan
Marketing by Michael Campochiaro

Library of Congress Cataloging-in-Publication Data

The obsessions of Georges Bataille : community and communication / edited by Andrew J. Mitchell and Jason Kemp Winfree.
p. cm.
Includes bibliographical references and index.
ISBN 978-1-4384-2823-9 (hardcover : alk. paper)
ISBN 978-1-4384-2824-6 (pbk. : alk. paper)
1. Bataille, Georges, 1897–1962. 2. Communities—Philosophy. I. Mitchell, Andrew J., 1970– II. Winfree, Jason Kemp.

B2430.B33954O26 2009
194—dc22 2009000584

10 9 8 7 6 5 4 3 2 1

Contents

List of Illustrations

Editors' Preface

Shifting from criticism to autobiography, theory to fiction, blending philosophical reflection with lived experience, the work of Georges Bataille (1897–1962) is notoriously difficult to classify. Bataille is often mentioned in contexts related to surrealism, psychoanalysis, poststructuralism, postmodernism, and deconstruction; but he is less often carefully read. Considered as a sociologist, an art historian, a theorist, a pornographer, a novelist, Bataille seems to haven fallen short of philosophy, at least in the strictest sense, and this even by his own admission and in spite of his impact on major philosophical figures of the twentieth century and beyond. Foucault, Derrida, Blanchot, Lacan, Kristeva, Baudrillard, and Nancy, among others, all owe a significant debt to the place of Bataille in their formation. While there have been attempts to show the philosophical capacities and consequences of Bataille's thinking before, the present volume differs from these by its focus on the joined issues of community and communication and by insisting on the importance of these issues for contemporary (post-Heideggerian) continental philosophy.[1] The chapters contained here are written by scholars from diverse fields, but they share one thing: an understanding of Bataille's relevance for philosophy, a sense that Bataille's writing has a unique capacity to respond to the philosophical questions that dominate our contemporary horizon.

In first formulating this project, the editors imagined how they would respond to the questions that would inevitably attend a book treating Bataille from a philosophical perspective. Regarding the book's contents, we envisioned a chain of terms, apparently substitutable for one another, as precise as they were unwieldy: "It's about community, that is, communication, that is, politics, or rather, sovereignty, that is, death, Nietzsche and Jesus . . . well, it has to do with things." Readers of Bataille are no doubt familiar with the difficulty. In the opening "Preface" to *The Accursed Share*, Bataille himself expresses this same concern. After proposing and then withdrawing the suggestion that his endeavor be understood as a contribution to political economy, he asks: "[H]ow can we measure up to the universe if we content ourselves with the slumber of conventional knowledge?" (OC 7: 21/AS 1: 11). The problem is not only *that* the scope of Bataille's interest—here nothing less than the universe itself—exceeds the restrictions that enable the formation, codification, and establishment of knowledge. It is rather at once a problem of *how* and *why* they do so and *what happens* in the wake of this. So Bataille adds immediately for the sake of clarification: "If one has the patience, and courage, to read my book, one will see that it contains studies conducted according to the rules of a reason that does not relent, and solutions to political problems deriving from a traditional wisdom, but one will also find in it this affirmation: '*that the sexual act is in time what the tiger is in space*' " (OC 7: 21/AS 1: 11–12). It is relentless in its rigor, yes, but relentless too in its affirmation—wild, intense, obsessive.

Like the tiger in space, Bataille's work submits everything in its horizon to total reconfiguration: values, things, histories, practices, ideas all lose their neutral and relative autonomy, their discreteness and authority, new relations surface, and they are joined in the face of exuberant life. And like the sexual act, Bataille's work expends itself, peeking and falling, resting and exploding, collecting and losing itself. The work is constantly driven into unfamiliar territory, unfamiliar forms of expression, reaching for everything, searching everywhere, like someone possessed. The universe, the slaughterhouse, asexual reproduction, the Marshall Plan, prehistoric art, solar energy, whores, Descartes, communism, ascesis, laughter—each of these, and more still, is a site of entry into the excessive movement of expended energies, a privileged point of access to the pressing question of what we are and how we live.

Bataille's willingness to transgress the conventions of academic writing even in his most schematic works opens the issues of his concern to the illumination and ventilation of what has been excluded from disciplinary discourse (be it sociological, philosophical, biological, political, etc.). Such a "method" serves as an antidote and corrective to contemporary manners of thinking that have become overly cautious and disciplinarily restrictive. In a tepid age where *interdisciplinarity* is the new buzzword, Bataille's work stands as a testament to what interdisciplinary study can yield if pursued without regard for institutional forms of normalization and acceptance. In all its splendor, crudity, innocence, speculation, violence, madness, and truth, Bataille's work exemplifies the danger and the courage that this practice demands.

When Jean-Luc Nancy turned to Bataille in *The Inoperative Community* (first published in the journal *Aléa* in 1983), he did so hoping to find a still undiscovered resource for thinking the question of the political (21 below). And indeed Nancy found in Bataille, at the very least, a provocation and starting point for considering community, the sociality of our being with one another, in terms outside the requirements and economy of production, but equally outside the Heideggerian *Mitdasein* and the deferrals of deconstruction. Maurice Blanchot's response to Nancy's work, *The Unavow-*

able Community (also published in 1983), emphasized the recalcitrance of Bataille's obsession with community to conceptualization (even in terms of the negligible *désoeuvrement*) but also insisted upon the concreteness of Bataille's vision as the reason for that resistance and difficulty. This exchange reoriented an entire generation of continental thinkers, not only to the issue of community, and not only to Bataille, but to the rigorously elusive and heterogeneous character of Bataille's work, to the contestation at the heart of community and the impossible at the heart of communication. On the twenty-fifth anniversary of Nancy and Blanchot's exchange, the provocation of Bataille for a thinking of community remains undiminished. Indeed, the issue of the being and meaning of community reaches its burning point in Bataille's work in ways still not exhausted by the intervening years.

The current volume takes its point of departure from the force of Bataille's work in these contexts. In doing so, community and communication do not indicate two arbitrary themes among others but stand out as the privileged and omnipresent foci subtending Bataille's work, obsessions just as much as they are discrete points of topical interest. Bataille shows that an adequate articulation of community is only possible on the basis of a contradiction, or better, a contestation between opposed tendencies, here a drive towards sovereignty, on the one hand, and a seeking out of fusion, on the other. He also shows the only thing worth communicating is the incommunicable itself. What are the consequences of this thought? Where does it lead? Whence its necessity? What are its limits? The essays collected in this volume respond to these questions, and they do so from the recognition that to encounter Bataille's work is to encounter an obsession of unparalleled affirmation.

Notes

1. See Leslie Anne Boldt-Irons, ed., *On Bataille: Critical Essays* (Albany: State University of New York Press, 1995), which examines Bataille's work from a number of perspectives, some philosophical, some literary, and Scott Wilson and Fred Botting, ed., *Bataille: A Critical Reader* (Oxford: Blackwell, 1998), which gathers together a number of articles by leading figures of twentieth-century French thought on an even wider variety of topics. More recent works of note in English include Shannon Winnubst's anthology, *Reading Bataille Now* (Bloomington: Indiana University Press, 2007); Allan Stoekl's *Bataille's Peak: Energy, Religion, and Postsustainability* (Minneapolis: University of Minnesota Press, 2007); and Michel Surya's *Georges Bataille: An Intellectual Biography* (London: Verso, 2002).

Acknowledgments

The editors would like to thank Stuart Kendall for his assistance in selecting the essays by Bataille included in this volume and for favoring us with the careful work of their translation. We would also like to thank Christine Irizarry for her more than generous contribution to the refinement of the translation of Nancy's "Confronted Community." A grant from California State University, Stanislaus, supplemented the translations, as did funding from the Foundational Fund of the philosophy department at CSU; we are grateful to both. Kim Collins, art-history librarian at Robert W. Woodruff Library, Emory University, was instrumental in gaining the permissions for the images reproduced in this volume, and we are thankful for her work. Support for image reproductions was provided by *Fröhliche Wissenschaft* (www.froehwiss.org). We would also like to express our gratitude to Jane Bunker of SUNY Press and our series editors for their immeasurable patience with this venture.

Key to Abbreviations

The works of Georges Bataille are cited parenthetically in the text according to the following abbreviatory schema. References are given first to the French original followed by English translations, where applicable. Modifications of translation are indicated throughout by "tm," modifications of emphasis by "em."

AM *The Absence of Myth: Writings on Surrealism*. Edited and translated by Michael Richardson. London: Verso, 2006.

AS 1 *The Accursed Share: An Essay on General Economy*. Volume 1: *Consumption*. Translated by Robert Hurley. New York: Zone Books, 1991.

AS 2 *The Accursed Share: An Essay on General Economy*. Volume 2: *The History of Eroticism*. Translated by Robert Hurley. New York: Zone Books, 1993.

AS 3 *The Accursed Share: An Essay on General Economy*. Volume 3: *Sovereignty*. Translated by Robert Hurley. New York: Zone Books, 1993.

BR *The Bataille Reader*. Edited by Fred Botting and Scott Wilson. Oxford: Blackwell, 1997.

CH *The Cradle of Humanity: Prehistoric Art and Culture*. Edited by Stuart Kendall. Translated by Michelle Kendall and Stuart Kendall. New York: Zone Books, 2005.

CS *Le Collège de Sociologie (1937–1939)*. Edited by Denis Hollier. Paris: Gallimard, 1979. *The College of Sociology*. Edited and Translated by Denis Hollier. Minneapolis: University of Minnesota Press, 1988. Cited by French/English pagination.

E *Erotism: Death & Sensuality*. Translated by Mary Dalwood. San Francisco: City Lights Books, 1986.

F "Friendship." *Parallax* 7: 1 (2001): 3–15.

G *Guilty*. Translated by Bruce Boone. Venice, CA: Lapis, 1988.

I *The Impossible*. Trans. Robert Hurley. San Francisco: City Lights Books, 1991.

IE *Inner Experience*. Translated by Leslie Anne Boldt. Albany: State University of New York Press, 1988.

L *Lascaux or the Birth or Art*. Translated by Austryn Wainhouse. New York: Skira, 1955.

LE *Literature and Evil*. Translated by Alastair Hamilton. London: Marion Boyars, 1993.

MM *My Mother*. In *My Mother, Madame Edwarda, The Dead Man*. Translated by Austryn Wainhouse. London: Boyars, 1989.

OC *Œuvres complètes*. 12 vols. Paris: Gallimard, 1970–1988.

ON *On Nietzsche*. Translated by Bruce Boone. New York: Paragon House, 1992.

TE *Tears of Eros*. Translated by Peter Connor. San Francisco: City Lights Books, 1989.

TG *The Trial of Gilles de Rais*. Translated by Richard Robinson. Los Angeles: Amok Books, 1991. Note: variant printings of this edition count four fewer pages through page 67 and six fewer thereafter.

TR *Theory of Religion*. Translated by Robert Hurley. New York: Zone Books, 1992.

US *The Unfinished System of Nonknowledge*. Edited by Stuart Kendall. Translated by Michelle Kendall and Stuart Kendall. Minneapolis: University of Minnesota Press, 2001.

VE *Visions of Excess: Selected Writings, 1927–1939*. Edited by Allan Stoekl. Translated by Allan Stoekl, with Carl R. Lovitt and Donald M. Leslie, Jr. Minneapolis: University of Minnesota Press, 1985.

EDITORS' INTRODUCTION

Community and Communication

This collection of essays is occasioned in part by the renewed interest in the thought of Georges Bataille signaled by Jean-Luc Nancy's *Inoperative Community* and Maurice Blanchot's response to that work, *The Unavowable Community*.[1] The titles that organize their exchange situate Bataille with respect to the problem of community he so radically and scandalously pursued and that he opened in ways still not exhausted. In the face of an entire set of tired contemporary invocations of "community" in the service of global capital and power—the world community, the intelligence community, the business community—Bataille's thought stands as an outrage if not a crime. But it is no less an affront to the progressive or utopian revolutionary desire for the restoration of a lost social order, one that would heroically or salvifically put an end to the ostentatious expenditures of capital. For it is not an extant community to which one belongs or from which one receives one's meaning that is invoked by Bataille; he privileges no nation, religion, or ethnicity. Rather, what is most exceptional in this thinking of community resists conceptualization as positive appropriation, and it is this that leads Nancy to speak in terms of "inoperativity" and Blanchot to intimate the "unavowable," even where these formulations falter or say too much. As these determinations attest in all their care and difficulty, Bataille's obsession with community is an attraction to what the concept of 'community' has never been able to grasp.

Not only Bataille's interest in community but the entire effort of his thought is dedicated to a presentation of the force and value of what he calls "unemployed negativity" (OC 5: 369/G 123). An undoing of the work of totalization (*l'oeuvre*), it is unemployed negativity to which Nancy's formulation ultimately gestures in the attempt to articulate a social bond not subject to recuperation, accumulation, or production.[2] Inoperativity, worklessness, idleness (*désoeuvrement*)—these require a sense of community no longer concerned with achievement, the production of itself through works or ideology, or the reproduction of itself through education. And for this reason, the language of inoperativity gestures toward what it can hardly contain: "Beware not to elevate community in any way," Nancy reminds himself in light of Blanchot's response, "even under the designation 'inoperative' " (25 below).

For his part, Blanchot emphasizes the need to understand Bataille not only in terms of inoperativity but also in terms of the unavowable, what cannot be affirmed, what must remain hidden. And this has to be taken in the still more specific sense of the shameful or clandestine, that which remains unmentionable, like an illicit affair or an illegitimate child. The unavowable is thus impossible for any community defined in terms of transparency of self and other, for any community that is in itself and for itself a whole, equally determining and determined by the presence of its members. The unavowable is impossible, not just because what is hidden cannot be appropriated and put to work, but because it carries with it a sense of transgression against the conservative forces of the established order, a taste for the inappropriate and improper, a desire not for recognition, but for expenditure, consumption, and ruin. If inoperativity designates the ontology of a social bond not subject to the work of sublation and formation, the unavowable names the dangerous movement of loss and resistance that bond carries in its attraction, obsession, and contact with what is other.

It is thus difficult to hold together the thought of community in Bataille's work, let alone hold it open, since it constantly presses toward that which eludes appropriation and resists positive discursive articulation. Community names not so much a unified field or concept for Bataille as it does an obsession, one he pursues in multiple ways, addressing differences that can hardly be said to constitute the same phenomenon. Hence we find community articulated both externally and internally, objectively and subjectively, ontologically and politically, and each of these distinctions is itself often subject to disruption and collapse by the analyses Bataille sets forth. Schematically, though, Bataille's work on community can be divided into three parts. There are, first of all, the explicit calls for community, which belong to Bataille's association with Acéphale and the College of Sociology.[3] Respectively, these consist of articulations of Bataille's desire for contestatory creativity in the face of political disaster and endeavors to pursue a knowledge of the violent emotional bond that enables the organization of expenditure for the sake of war and the decimation of life. This volume contains one such call, Bataille's previously untranslated address to Acéphale from the spring of 1937, "What We Have Undertaken" (OC 11: 559–63/189–95 below). Second, the concern with community also has a place in Bataille's exposition of the logic of transgression and expenditure, which articulates the ontological principle of excess in economic terms. And there is, finally, the sense of community related to what Bataille calls "inner experience," the excess that I am in my improbability, insufficiency, and communication with others. The affirmation of chance, the community of lovers, and the role of fusion all have their place here. It is also here that Jean-Luc Nancy's "Confronted Community," newly translated for this volume, hesitates to follow Bataille, emphasizing instead the need for a sense of the political alert to the philosophical difficulty of plurality.

The divisions between these approaches to community have often been portrayed as indicative of a shift away from the political to a more personal realm, or as an evasion of political-historical imperatives in favor of detached analyses affirming the inevitability of evil. At the same time, according to the same division, Bataille has been criticized on both counts of flirting with fascism. In light of this, it is helpful to begin with a brief account of how the work from the period of Acéphale and the College of Sociology prefigures the work on inner experience and general economy, attending above all to the "Programme (Relative to *Acéphale*)" from April 1936, roughly cotemporary with the first drafts of *Inner Experience* and the work on expenditure.[4]

The "Programme" begins with the call to form a community, and it casts this task in terms of contestation, indeed destruction. Item 3 of the "Programme" reads: "Assume the function of destruction and decomposition, but as accomplishment and not as the negation of being" (OC 2: 273/BR 121). Undoubtedly, what renders this destruction an accomplishment is its unwillingness to submit to the dominant order of Western life at the time, when the homogenizing forces of society were reaching a state of political and historical crisis, but for which there was no political solution. The destruction of the dominant order that dulls life and lays it to waste is thus a refusal of servility and as such can be likened to the second of Zarathustra's "Three Metamorphoses," where the lion smashes values thousands of years old and in doing so overcomes the burden of the camel. Bataille's refusal thus has no place in the established political order whose discourse is prefigured by those who already belong and already have a voice, prefigured by powerful values of inclusion and exclusion that serve productive accumulation. So Bataille insists, "When we speak to those who want to hear us, we do not essentially address their political finesse. The reactions we hope for from them are not calculations of positions, nor are they new political alliances. What we hope for is of a different nature" (OC 1: 402/VE 161).[5] That is, at issue in the call for community is an entirely different way of being, one that is necessary lest we cease to exist altogether. Bataille calls this new way of being "universal community," and its possibility is bound up with the radical resistance he proposes at the time. Item 7 of the "Programme" states this in unequivocal terms: "Fight for the decomposition and exclusion of all communities, national, socialist, communist or churchly—other than universal community" (OC 2: 273/BR 121). The call for community is not a struggle against this or that oppressive social system, then, but paradoxically, a call for the destruction of community in any recognizable sense. Community is as much—indeed, more—a heterological operation as it is an end or a goal. It is anarchic rather than utopian.

Coterminous with Acéphale, the College of Sociology served as another forum through which Bataille pursued the question of community, although in an entirely different register. The College devoted itself to an exposition of the heterological, which Acéphale sought to carry out and live, and which Bataille understood as operative but co-opted in the psychological structure of fascism. Although not belonging to the College strictly speaking, "The Notion of Expenditure" (1933) also stems from the endeavor of the College, articulating as it does the necessary principle of expenditure for all living systems, bridging the gap between the work of Acéphale and the slightly later work on general economy. Reiterating the College's central interest in collective states of excitement, Bataille interprets these states in terms of the nonproductive expenditure of energy, "the need to destroy and lose," or in other words, "the constitution of a positive property of loss" (OC 1: 310/VE 122). The central concern of the College thus leads Bataille to an ontological exposition of general economy: excess as the principle of being. This most fundamental ontological fact is attested to almost everywhere (from the radiance of solar energy to torture practices) and everywhere also avoided, suppressed by the social systems that nevertheless require the prodigal expenditure of the energies they cannot productively use. Taking up just this point, David Allison's "Transgression and the Community of the Sacred" shows how Bataille's thinking of transgression (building upon the analysis of labor and the sacred found in sociologists like Emile Durkheim and Roger Caillois) not only disrupts the social order but also serves to sustain and strengthen it. The insight concerning the cooperation between the social order and transgression, rooted in the work on general economy, thus refers back to the contestatory call issued by the "Programme" noted above, as a way of carrying through an attack upon the forces of social homogenization through analysis of their most fundamental mechanism. It is an attempt to elevate and carry through the political concerns of the College by way of fundamental ontology, an exposition whose force Bataille took to be "the shame of a generation whose rebels are afraid of the noise of their own words" (OC 2: 273/BR 121). And it is an endeavor Bataille carried through to the very end, as Marc Froment-Meurice shows in his essay on the excesses of Gilles de Rais, whose gruesome deeds place him among those privileged examples of "war, cults, [and] the construction of sumptuous monuments" (OC 1: 305/VE 118) already mentioned in the early essay on expenditure.

According to the classic conceptions of communal formation, from Plato and Epicurus through to social contract theory, community arises in order to meet the basic needs of human beings, the preservation of individual lives and the propagation of the species. At the basis of communal life as such lies a principle of insufficiency, one rooted in need. Freud rightly exposes the inadequacy of such an account, emphasizing the necessity of *eros* as well as *ananke* in the formation of social life, and Bataille shares that corrective when it comes to an account of community in any traditional sense. Yet he also insists beyond Freud that still another deficiency plagues the classic conception of community, and it is Bataille's originality here that has most invigorated recent discussions of the topic. For Bataille, the insufficiency of individual life is not just that of a self-enclosed subject that seeks the assistance of others in order to preserve its being. Instead, insufficiency is an opening to the world, a surface of contact with what is other, where one's being spills outside itself. Finitude does not consist in a limit that encircles but in the fact that I cannot be so encircled, the fact that I am not an enduring totality. To be finite is thus to be uncontained, outside of oneself in the catastrophe of utter abandon, which Bataille paradoxically calls "inner experience." As a result, insufficiency does not name the fact that I cannot subsist on my own, the fact that I am dependent on the cooperation and self-restriction of others. No, all this is an evasion, repression, or denial of what I fundamentally am, a lacerated being, one whose limit constitutes an opening to the outside. This is the fundamental ontological fact of excess: "A being that isn't cracked isn't possible" (OC 5: 259/G 23).

The contestation of homogenizing social forces emphasized in the earlier work is ultimately grounded in this ontology, and not in an effort or program or task. This is because, as Bataille puts it, "[T]he total improbability of my coming into the world poses, in an imperative mode, a total heterogeneity" (OC 1: 89–90/VE 130).[6] The heterogeneous is thus a contestation that arises from, or rather as, the insufficiency of existence itself. This being dislocates itself from service to the homogeneous, restricted world of work (a world itself dedicated to the production of works) because it dislocates itself from itself, because it is utterly without foundation and origin. It is a being shot through with chance, born in the improbability of luck, risked in its very structure. Insufficiency thus names the cracked character of being as well as its being without ground or reason. And that is to say, it no longer answers—indeed, never did, never could—to the fundamental structure of meaning through justification. It the face of such demands, it is utterly unaccountable and unaccounted for, absolutely unjustified, and its lack of justification constitutes its sole authority. This is what Bataille means when he says, "Inner experience is a movement in which man contests himself entirely," existing and persisting through and as this challenge (OC 5: 431/IE 179). The contestatory character of insufficiency, the loss of authority that now becomes authoritative, is the only thing that counts.[7] What appears from within the requirements of justification as a loss of ground, intelligibility, and form is just inner experience, excessive finite existence in its undeniability and strange insurmountability, existence in its tendency toward the outside.

Just as the contestation of community proposed by Acéphale must appear from within the unquestioned dominant social order as a rogue element or terrorist threat, so must the excess of finite existence appear within the demands of the philosophical tradition and its requisite self-knowledge as irrational and deformed. But what is unaccountable from the point of view of knowledge is, lived from within, exhilarating and free. There are thus differences among the question belonging to the accountability of discourse, the work of critique, and the ecstasy that is the putting-into-question of everything. That is why Bataille insists, "In the end only chance has the possibility of disarming," leaving us open in all our vulnerability and nakedness (OC 6: 123/ON 103; tm). For my improbability, my insufficiency, hence my very existence is nothing more than this chance. In the insufficiency of my existence I am lucky, "a direction of being required by the eagerness of its own movement," like the fall of dice (OC 1L 90/VE 131). Of course, I know that I do not know how or why I came to be, but that is different than the astonished, "How improbable my existence is!" I know as well that I will die, but that is not the same as dying, where I say, "Take my hand, I don't want to die alone." I do not know how we came to meet, how or why I came to love you, but this alone counts: "I love you so much I can't live without you! Your happiness is my joy, your sorrow is mine." Thus, at the limit of discursive thought experience tends not only toward the outside, toward death; it also tends toward contact with another, toward community. Indeed, so much that "[t]here cannot be inner experience without a community of those who live it" (OC 5: 37/IE 24). Inner experience requires a community of chance, a community of lucky beings drawn together, bound together in their excessive movement, in their fall away from themselves. This, then, is "where" community is located: in the chance movement of insufficiency; in the openness that my being *is* in exceeding the requirements of homogenization, preservation, and justification—in the movement outside oneself, which falls in love, dies, laughs, cries, mourns, celebrates, suffers.

The metaphysics of substantial subjectivity is at once a metaphysics of the thing, of the self as thing that wills and the world as a totality of things to be used. In his essay, "The Horror of Liberty," Stuart Kendall shows how not only does the debt to this metaphysics show up in the political hegemony of capitalism, but it also grounds the project of communism and its radical equality (shedding light on Bataille's 1948 response to the problem of communism, "The Political Lie" (OC 11: 332–38), included in this volume). Bataille's thinking proposes, by contrast, a subjectivity offered to the world rather than dominated by the principle of utility, and Kendall argues that this constitutes the basis of an ethics. Correlatively, in his essay, "Of Goods and Things," Chris Gemercak develops the question of ethics in Bataille's treatment of community in terms of the ethos attentive to the vicissitudes of the insufficiency and chance that contests the substantial self, an intimacy that reconfigures our relation to ourselves, others, and the world.

Bataille's development of the community of chance as the expression of inner experience tends in two directions, the community of lovers (or closed community) and fusion (or formless community). In both cases, the specification of the ontological principle of insufficiency is characterized by a particular mode of resistance to forces of homogenization. Lovers are exemplary, however, because of the way they give expression to the desire of chance. Only a chance being could fall in love, propelled by the anarchy of its desire. To fall in love is to be lucky, to find oneself delivered over to another being that is subject to the same excessive movement and to find one's desire and ecstasy confirmed in contact and contagion with the other. Lovers' love is the exponentially compounded inertia and expenditure of a wounded, lacerated, cracked being; it is the exposure of one life to another, the disappearance of one opening in another, the overlapping of one wound upon another, the penetration of one orifice by an other. And it is obsessive, driven beyond itself without reason, satisfied by nothing short of total possession, consumption, and loss. The rest of the world pales in comparison to the beloved who shares her pain, her joy, and her body with me, so lovers' love is sacred. They love without respect for the rest of the world, whose tasks and efforts are cheated and disregarded in favor of wasting the day in bed. Lovers express the movement toward the outside in its momentum and obsession, its luck and its pleasure. "To be with life as you are with a wife, a girlfriend, when making love, drinking, laughing, being attentive, affectionate, even a little eccentric, never purer than when 'doing it' " (OC 5: 296/G 57). Community is obsessive, desirous, and compulsive. It is the passion, violation, and possession of contact and contagion.

What distinguishes the community of lovers is thus not just its closed and elective character, its exclusion from the world of production and preservation, but the intensity of contact. For Bataille, the orgasm, laughter, and tears serve as privileged moments of that intensity. The community of lovers passes into the territory of a more general community, indeed, general almost to the point of utter nondistinction. With the sudden bursting forth (*jaillissement*) of chance, exposure and penetration pass indiscernibly into one another. "Each isolated existence," writes Bataille, "emerges from itself in a sort of easy flash: it opens itself at the same time to the contagion of a wave which rebounds, for those who laugh together become like the waves of the sea" (OC 5: 113/IE 95). Elsewhere, Bataille develops this image in terms of water in water, thus, neither distinguishable nor indistinguishable, both fused and diffused. Here, then, fusion cannot mean identification, nor can it signify a self-evident field of unity. Undoing the identity of unity and the unity of any identity, fusion and diffusion are indistinguishable without being the same. All of this is to say, the movement to the outside tends toward a contact and contagion that is uncontainable, finite without limit: "They are no more separate than are two waves, but their unity is as *undefined*, as precarious as that of the agitation of the waters" (OC 5: 113/IE 95–96; em). This community is formless.

It is no doubt in this respect that the following summative statement must also be understood: "What fusion brings into me is *another* existence" (OC 5: 391/G 141). Fusion is neither the result of appropriation nor an expropriation of oneself into identity with the world. In laughter we do not identify with others, but we are suspended together without distinction, I in you, you in me, carried beyond ourselves. In tears we embrace one another, emptying ourselves in an expenditure that exceeds our identity or difference. In orgasm we come together. This is what Bataille means when he insists, "In experience there is no longer limited existence. There a man is not distinguishable in any way from others: in him what is torrential is lost within others" (OC 5: 40/IE 27). My chance, my passion is not even really mine but delivers me over to what is other, another that ignites my passion, intensifies it, but in no way sublates it and puts it to work. If today the theme of community has any importance in the face of the expansion of global capital and processes of homogenization, in the face of tepid and insipid invocations of community by power or those seeking power, it is because community names the obsessive and passionate desire for the outside, the desire for contact with what is other, and the desire to be other than that which the social order makes us. It is because the obsession with community communicates the danger, attraction, and hope of a new way of being.

※ ※ ※

In the preface to *Inner Experience,* Bataille speaks of how the various instances of expenditure he traces throughout the book "defined of themselves a law of communication regulating the play of the isolation and the dissolution of beings," and it is indeed isolation and dissolution that establish the parameters of Bataille's thinking of communication (OC 5: 11/IE xxxiii). But this does not mean there are substantial isolated beings in existence prior to a communication that would then dissolve the distance between them. Rather these beings are already given over to the vicissitudes of communication as evidenced by the nakedness of their appearing in the world. Existence is exposed and as such always already communicative, always already reachable and addressable, always already reaching out. Consequently, communication does not name for Bataille a transmission passed between the two poles of sender and recipient, each of which would precede the communication. Rather, "*existence is* communication" as it finds itself overstepping its own bounds, transgressing itself, reaching toward the other: "everything in me gives itself to others!" (OC 5: 115, 151/IE 98, 130).[8]

The dispossession of self intrinsic to communication likewise prevents communication from becoming a matter of knowledge or an issue in epistemology as typically understood. According to such a view, to know is to possess knowledge of something. But once the known is possessed and internalized, the relation to what lies beyond the self is severed and our contact with the outside regulated and neutralized. Through knowledge we do indeed come to possess the thing but at the expense of no longer finding ourselves possessed and arrested by it. We cling to a relic and our ecstasy gives way to stasis. Thus, for Bataille there is an irreconcilable difference between "the desire to appropriate unto oneself and the opposite desire to communicate" (OC 5: 165/IE 142). From communication as a relation that eschews the appropriation of knowledge, from communication as an ontological rather than epistemological concern, it follows that, strictly speaking, I will not know what is communicated. I will not be able to, for the finitude of the subject in this case does not consist in the self-enclosure requisite for the possession of knowledge, but in exposure and opening to the outside. Communication in the most fundamental sense is thus a matter of nonknowledge, an expropriation of the self without the security or certainty or regularity of knowledge. "I give myself to non-knowledge (this is communication)," says Bataille (OC 5: 65/IE 51). In his essay, "Contact and Communication," Alphonso Lingis takes his point of departure from this insight, exploring the ways in which contact with beings unlike ourselves constitutes a fundamental communication that both violates the integrity of our bodies and makes possible rational discourse, which is so often mistaken for the basis rather than the consequence of communication.

Breaching the self-possession of Cartesian subjectivity and its prized self-certainty, insufficiency, rupture, and wound open us to a world beyond our grasp or control. Communication is thus risky through and through: " 'Communication' cannot proceed from one full and intact individual to another. It requires individuals whose separate existence in themselves is *risked*" (OC 6: 44/ON 19). With life at stake in communication (*"All communication participates in suicide"*; OC 6: 49/ON 26), it is surely an easy step to the dialectic of master and slave, but here Bataille is interested instead in a sovereignty without mastery. He is indefatigably alert to the "project" character of the Hegelian dialectic, that it seeks its own completion in absolute knowing. Bataille does not merely reverse the Hegelian reversal of lordship and bondage but contests its fundamental principles: productivity and recuperation of self. In contrast to Hegel's treatment of the dialectic of "the master (the law, the sovereign) and the slave (the man enslaved by work)," Bataille writes in *Literature and Evil*, "Sovereignty . . . is the object which eludes us all, which nobody has seized and which nobody can seize for this reason: we cannot possess it, like an object, but we are doomed to seek it" (OC 9: 305/LE 193–94). Hence, "sovereignty must inhabit the realm of failure" (OC 9: 306/LE 194). Where Hegel celebrates the slave as the true sovereign, he does so on the basis of the slave's accession to absolute knowing, which is always self-knowledge, even if merely implicit. By contrast, the true sovereign does not need the security of this certain knowledge, which carries the possibility of a recuperation of oneself in the self-possession of a knower who would know itself knowing itself, but embraces the risks of communication and self-abandon all the more unrestrictedly.

Precisely because communication is risk, sovereignty is not an established state of being, nor something arrived at by holding oneself back. Communication does not risk a being that would otherwise be complete or finished but completes the insufficiency of the one who communicates by ensuring its contamination and contact with what is other. Since communication is not a possession, but a relation of exposure and abandon, sovereignty, too, is nothing that might be appropriated and achieved: "Never can we *be* sovereign. But we distinguish between the moments when fortune lets us glimpse the furtive lights of communication and those moments of disgrace when the mere thought of sovereignty commits us to seizing for it like a positive benefit" (OC 9: 306/LE 194). To seize at sovereignty is to forego communication in order to appropriate. Communication is a giving, a giving oneself over to what is other, what attracts and beckons one, such that "[t]here is no difference between this powerful communication and what I call sovereignty" (OC 9: 313/LE 201). Simply put, "Sovereignty is NOTHING" (OC 8: 300/AS 3: 256).

While communication undoes any purported isolation of the subject, it runs the risk of leading to a complete dissolution of the self. Indeed, Bataille's emphasis on the fusion of subject and object—" 'Oneself' is not the subject isolating itself from the world, but a place of communication, of fusion of the subject and the object" (OC 5: 21/IE 9)—or on the indistinguishability of self and other—"there is no longer a limited existence. There a man is not distinguished in any way from others" (OC 5: 40/IE 27)—might seem to suggest that he thinks communication is a form of identificatory union between opposed parties. We have indicated above how such a reading mistakes nondetermination for identity, but it is also the case that communication as fusion requires difference. In an appendix to *Guilty*, for example, treating of the relation between communication and laughter, Bataille speaks directly to the point: "these [communicative] contacts are *heterogeneous*. What fusion brings into me is *another* existence (it brings this other into me as *mine* but at the same time as *other*); and insofar as it's a transition (the contrary of a state) and in order to be actually produced, fusion requires heterogeneity" (OC 5: 391/G 141).[9] Bataille's conception of 'fusion,' then, is not the result of either an appropriation of the other or an expropriation of oneself into identity with the world but the introduction of something other at the core of the self. Fusion is not something that communication must avoid but is instead synonymous with it. Cast in terms of fusion, communication comes to name the indigestibility of the other, the persistence of the foreign at the heart of the same. If fusion brings the other "into me," it must always be remembered that this "me" is always already outside of itself. Bataille thus takes existence for "the movement of painful communication which it is, which goes no less from within to without, than from without to within," that is to say, as a permeability of self and other, of subject and object (OC 5: 138/IE 118). If the outside is on the inside, and what is inside is on the outside, then the very idea of the self as a simple enclave distinct from the world must be abandoned. Fusion does not entail a homogeneous field merging together self and world, but to the extent that it emphasizes the ineradicable rupture of the foreign that cracks open identity, it names the inappropriable porousness of contact. Karmen MacKendrick addresses just this heterogeneous fusion in her essay, "Sharing God's Wounds," on communication with God as an infinite other, a communication that shows itself in the excess of a wound (stigmata).

Discursive communication utilizes language as a means for the achievement of some ulterior goal, and communication in the strictest sense is no such utilitarian project. The irreconcilable difference noted above, between the desire to appropriate and the desire to communicate, can also be put in terms of the difference between weak and powerful communication, profound and discursive communication: "What I wanted: profound communication between beings to the exclusion of the links necessary to projects, which discourse forms" (OC 5: 109/IE 92).[10] To be sure, discursive communication renders us understandable to one another, but that is also to say ever more assimilable to one another (in an assimilation to sameness that should not be mistaken for the sovereign moment of fusion so attractive to Bataille). By contrast, profound communication occurs precisely when these attempts at creating banal commonalities fail: "Communication in my sense of the word, is never stronger than when communication, in the weak sense, the sense of profane language or, as Sartre says, of prose which makes us and the others appear penetrable, fails and becomes the equivalent of darkness" (OC 9: 311/LE 199). It is precisely when the transparency of utilitarian language or discursive thought fails, then, that real communication takes place. Or more precisely, through this darkness that interrupts identification, "powerful" communication opens onto the impenetrable: "there is a fundamental distinction between *feeble communication*, the basis of profane society (of active society—in the sense in which activity merges with productivity) and *powerful communication* which abandons the consciousnesses that reflect each other, to that impenetrability which they 'ultimately' are" (OC 9: 312/LE 200). This impenetrable is nothing simply or immediately given; it stands to be gained in the risk run by sovereignty. To reach what is impenetrable, the self must expose itself to violation. Penetrated by the other, its being is no longer in tact in such a way that it could be transparent to itself. And instead of being present to itself with the clarity and distinctness of self-knowledge, it runs up against what is utterly foreign to it. At its very core, the impenetrable wells up within it, as if granted by its exposure to the outside. And yet, I myself do not even know what is impenetrable in me. This density of the impenetrable is the counterpart of exposure: I offer myself wholly to the other in sovereign abandon, and the other fails to seize me as something to be possessed and known. As such, we make contact outside the demands of recognition and acknowledgment. We come to share out a strangeness or alterity that is nothing possessed, but that resides between us, with us in the world. Existence is "shared between the impenetrability of ourselves and that of the world" (OC 9: 311/LE 199; tm). In "Bataille: Discerning Edges in the Art of Lascaux," a meditation upon Bataille's treatment of the caves of Lascaux, Edward S. Casey brings together reflections upon the nature of edge and line as fundamental to art with the way in which the artwork calls forth a community, not only among people, but among humans and the earth as well. Communication is nothing other than such a shared experience.

In *Literature and Evil* (1957)—a work that itself could stand as a treatise on communication[11]—Bataille repeatedly casts this exposition before the other as explicitly and ineluctably moral. Bataille's treatment of the (sovereign) morality of communication also explains why language, despite all his reservations concerning its limitations, is nonetheless able to communicate the incommunicable. The morality of communication follows from the fact that feeble communication, in the attempts to accommodate ourselves to the world and the world to ourselves, belies a deeper accord: "This incessant effort to situate ourselves in the world with clarity and distinction would be apparently impossible if we were not first bound to one another by the feeling of *common subjectivity*, impenetrable in itself, and for which the world of distinct objects is impenetrable" (OC 9: 311/LE 199). Such a feeling of common subjectivity is possible only in tandem with the persistence of our differences from each other and never as a bridging of the gap between us. As Bataille notes in *Erotism*, "This gulf exists, for instance, between you, listening to me, and me, speaking to you. We are attempting to communicate, but no communication between us can abolish our fundamental difference" (OC 10: 18–19/E 12). The separation itself allows for common experience: "It is a deep gulf, and I do not see how it can be done away with. None the less, *we can experience its dizziness together*" (OC 10: 19/E 13; em). Such a feeling is not the possession of any single individual but accessed only through the sovereign refusal to objectify or to sever the radiant excesses of another.

Sovereign self-limitation is the focal point of Bataille's reading of Genet (the closing chapter of *Literature and Evil*, which is equally a reading of Sartre's reading of Genet and thus a reading of philosophy's attempts to read literature), where it is expressly cast as moral: "The Evil required by sovereignty is necessarily limited. Sovereignty itself limits it. It sets itself in opposition to all that enslaves it in as far as it [sovereignty] is communication. It opposes itself with that sovereign instinct which expresses a sacred aspect of morality" (OC 9: 315/LE 203). This self-limiting characteristic of sovereignty is perhaps what is most at odds with the popular caricature of Bataille as excremental hedonist. Sovereignty cannot be reduced to a formula of maximized satisfaction or maximized destruction through evil, for in that case (the case of Genet), "Evil becomes a duty, just as Good does" (OC 9: 300/LE 187). Such a stance would remain paradoxically utilitarian even in its quest for destruction, whereas "Only a morality of communication—and loyalty based on communication—goes beyond utilitarian morality" (OC 9: 309 n./LE 207, n. 44). Loyalty names at once the fact that existence is never isolated, that there are always others, that these others are under no necessarily binding obligation to me, and that I offer myself wholly to them nonetheless. Loyalty means opening oneself to betrayal, in the language of Genet. But Genet's mistake is to make a project of betrayal as a way of demonstrating his superiority to and independence from all others. He seeks a sovereignty that would only be for himself: "he has not seen that sovereignty involves the heart, it requires loyalty and, above all, communication" (OC 9: 304/LE 192). Genet consequently suffers from what *Inner Experience* diagnoses as egotism, "the indifference to communication" (OC 5: 50/IE 38). Genet remains isolated, "He never yielded completely to the irrational impulses which unite beings, but which unite them on the condition that they shed the suspicions and diffidence bred in the difference between each being" (OC 9: 315/LE 203). The morality of communication thus opposes the diffidence and indifference of the isolated ego with a groundless and limitless loyalty. Morality as loyalty demands the promise *to not be oneself*, but to remain true to the heterogeneous other within and without. "Communication requires loyalty" (OC 9: 171/LE ix).

Communication communicates the incommunicable (there is nothing else to communicate). This impenetrable incommunicable is nothing that I retain as a private possession. Communication is not a mutual recognition that the impenetrable cannot be communicated, a recognition that could rest secure in the knowledge that we each possess what the other cannot have. Such a view still bases itself on the enclosed subject. Instead, our "private" experience is shared from the outset and thus inherently moral. This is what Bataille's "theory" of communication struggles to articulate, and it is what distinguishes Bataille's views from those of philosophy's arch representative in literary matters, Jean-Paul Sartre: "Only a morality of communication—and loyalty based on communication—goes beyond utilitarian morality. But for Sartre, communication is not a basis; if he sees its possibilities it is through the opacity which beings present to each other. For him, it is the isolated being that is fundamental, not the multiplicity of beings in *communication*" (OC 9: 309 n./LE 207 n. 44).

Genet and Sartre alike show the extent to which literature all too easily serves the homogeneous order of isolated beings, even in its apparent resistance to everyday banality and its discursive order. And as with literature, so too with poetry: "It has almost always been at the service of the great systems of appropriation," Bataille says, tending toward "any one of a number of aesthetic homogeneities" (OC 2: 62/VE 97). If literature or poetry is to amount to something more than advertisement, their communication must be born of contestation. Undoubtedly, it is this insight that leads Bataille to title as *The Hatred of Poetry* (1947) what is later published as *The Impossible* (1962). The earlier title failed in that it appeared to make poetry the object of hatred, while it intended to insist that poetry, at its best, is the product of hatred, born in the refusal to submit to the social and discursive homogeneity that deadens communication of the impossible. If discourse neglects the ungraspable or impenetrable part of existence, as Bataille claims it does—"Although words drain almost all life from within us . . . there subsists in us a silent, elusive, ungraspable part. In the region of words, of discourse, this part is neglected" (OC 5: 27/IE 14)—this still does not mean some other mode of expression would be able to seize it. It means, rather, that expression must work otherwise, establish a different relation between itself and its object, writer and reader. Given the limits of discourse as Bataille diagnoses them, then, this alone explains why he bothers to write at all. His own communication is situated at the point where the demand for loyalty meets imperative revolt.

With respect to poetry, Bataille clarifies the matter saying, "Poetry had no powerful meaning except in the violence of revolt" (OC 3: 101/I 10). For this reason, it falls to poetry, but also to literature, to approach this elusive unknown through an interruption of discursive language, through a resistance to the homogeneous order that effects profound communication and the dissolution of isolated existence.[12] The poet sacrifices the word in its utilitarian function: "Of poetry, I will now say that it is, I believe, the sacrifice in which words are victims. Words—we use them, we make of them the instruments of useful acts. We would in no way have anything of the human about us if language had to be entirely servile within us. Neither can we do without the efficacious relations which words introduce between men and things. But we tear words from these links in a delirium" (OC 5: 156/IE 135).

Thus, when the poetic word is "detached from interested concerns" (OC 5: 157/IE 135), it too is opened beyond itself and released from servility to egoistic demands or imposed duties. In poetic language, the impenetrable ungraspable is no longer neglected, but neither is it objectified or possessed. Instead, the poetic attempt at articulation hews the word from silence, letting it be shaped by the silence of profound communication. No rules can be given for how the poet proceeds here, for it is precisely a matter of overstepping the rules in an exposure of self, of creating oneself as author in this negotiation with the silent other. This means that "poetry is, necessarily, no less silence than language," where the poet surrenders the word to this silence as what lies beyond the word's own spoken or written expression (OC 5: 41/IE 29). Even poetic language cannot hope to seize or adequately evoke the ungraspable. Sovereignty is failure, as we have seen, and the anguished attempt to let the heterogeneous shape the word, if only via the word's relation to silence, is doomed to a failure that discourse avoids. But therein lies the profound communicability of poetic language, as failure communicates what the smooth functioning of feeble communication cannot: sovereignty. "Literature is communication: a sovereign author addresses sovereign humanity, beyond the servitude of the isolated reader" (OC 9: 300/LE 188). Reader and writer both suppress their isolated being in order to join in communication: "However this may be, even if an apparent absurdity results from this process, the author was there to suppress himself in his work, and he addressed the reader, who read in order to suppress himself—or, if we prefer, to render himself sovereign through the suppression of his isolated being" (OC 9: 301/LE 188–89). Speaking to this point and linking the concern for communication with that of community, this volume includes in its appendix Bataille's "Silence and Literature" (OC 12: 173–78), a review of Blanchot's *récit*, *When the Time Comes*, developing the problem of writing and sovereignty in relation to silence.[13]

At different times discursive, literary, poetic, confessional, the totality of Bataille's work is surely best described by what Kalliopi Nikolopoulou calls, following *Inner Experience*, "dramatization." If words fail to capture the ungraspable, heterogeneous, impenetrable, this is not to say that in such a failed attempt communication would no longer be at play. It is only to say experience is not reducible to conceptual determination, to discursive linguistic articulation, that it requires above all another direction of expression. Dramatization thus responds to the experience that changes those it puts in play. And it is in this light that we must in part understand Bataille's communication of his own thought and those who read him. "Thus we are nothing, neither you nor I," writes Bataille, "beside burning words which could pass from me to you, imprinted on a page: they are addressed to you, you will live from having had the strength to hear them" (OC 5: 111–12/IE 94). The aim of this volume is to remain loyal to that thought, in all its heterogeneity, all its impossibility.

Notes

1. Jean-Luc Nancy, *La communauté désœuvrée* (Paris: Christian Bourgois, 1986); *The Inoperative Community*, ed. Peter Connor, trans. Peter Connor, Lisa Garbus, Michael Holland, and Simona Sawhney (Minneapolis: University of Minnesota Press, 1991); Maurice Blanchot, *La communauté inavouable* (Paris: Minuit, 1983); *The Unavowable Community*, trans. Pierre Joris (Barrytown, NY: Station Hill, 1988).

2. In fact, Nancy credits Blanchot with the formulation of inoperativity, noting at the same time the proximity to Bataille, almost as if from Bataille, as he puts it ("The Confronted Community," 22 below).

3. Both a journal and a group, *Acéphale* was organized by Bataille following a break with Breton and surrealism. The journal lasted from June 1936 through 1937 (with an anonymous issue published in June 1939). Contributors included Pierre Klossowski, Jean Wahl, and André Masson (who illustrated the publication), among others. Literally meaning "headless," *Acéphale* was interested in harnessing the vital forces of human life, their violence and their contagion, in opposition to those modes of life that subordinate the human to its rational capacities. In the "Programme" published in the journal, *Acéphale* advocated the destruction of community in any traditional sense and aimed at a more universal articulation and experience human life. Little is known about the group *Acéphale*, since its members were sworn to secrecy. Still, it was centered around rituals, secret meetings, and the prospect of human sacrifice. For an account of the significance of this, see Maurice Blanchot, *The Unavowable Community*, 13–15.

In 1937, the journal *Acéphale* published the declaration of the College of Sociology. The College was to pursue an ontological and sociological knowledge of the radical energies the secret group aimed to harness and to do so in opposition to the political monopolization of life. Membership in the two groups was not simply overlapping, however. The College included the active participation of Roger Caillois, Michel Leiris, Pierre Klossowski, and Alexandre Kojève. Other notable attendees included Sartre, Walter Benjamin, and Claude Lévi-Strauss. See also Stuart Kendall, "Editor's Introduction," to Georges Bataille, *The Unfinished System of Nonknowledge*, ed. Stuart Kendall, trans. Michelle Kendall and Stuart Kendall (Minneapolis: University of Minnesota Press, 2001), xi–xliv, xiii–xiv; and Denis Holier, "Forward: Collage,"

The College of Sociology, ed. Denis Hollier (Minneapolis: University of Minnesota Press, 1988), viii–xxix.

4. Georges Bataille, "Programme (Relative to *Acéphale*)," OC 2: 273/BR 121.

5. Georges Bataille, "Popular Front in the Street," OC 1: 402–12/VE 161–68.

6. Georges Bataille, "Sacrifices," OC 1: 89–96/VE 130–36.

7. "The paradox in the authority of experience: based on challenge, it is the challenging of authority; positive challenge, man's authority defined as the challenging of himself" (OC 5: 19 n./IE 7 n.).

8. Expressed in a Heideggerian register, "communication is a phenomenon which is in no way added on to Dasein, but constitutes it" (OC 5: 37/IE 24).

9. It is no coincidence that Bataille employs a language of mediation and transmission, of waves and undulation, in considering human existence. In a recurrent motif of *Inner Experience*, Bataille thinks this communicative identity as analogous to the tenuous and shifting identity of waves in the ocean: "[T]hey are no more separate than are two waves, but their unity is as undefined, as precarious as that of the agitation of the waters" (OC 5: 113/IE 95–96).The idea that our difference would be a formal difference amidst the same material is announced at the outset of the section 'Communication' in *Inner Experience* and prefigures the biological explorations of later works like *Erotism*. The opening of the section is worth quoting at length: "From one single particle to another, there is no difference in nature, neither is there any difference between this one and that one. There is *some of* this which is produced here or there, each time in the form of unity, but this unity does not persevere in itself. Waves, undulations, single particles are perhaps only the multiple movements of a homogeneous element; they only possess fleeting unity and do not break the homogeneity of the whole." The groups constituted from numerous single particles alone possess this heterogeneous character which differentiates me from you and isolates our differences in the rest of the universe (OC 5: 110/IE 93).

10. Since communication is not the transmission of a verbal message for Bataille, he emphasizes the role of silence in communication, "Profound communication demands silence" (OC 5: 109/IE 92), as well as the use of disciplinary techniques for achieving such silence, signal among them, yoga (see OC 5: 28–31/IE 15–18). The recently translated "Method of Meditation" develops these ideas further, where Bataille states his desire to interrupt the easy flow of language, "I want to find that which reintroduces—in a point—the sovereign silence that interrupts articulated language" (OC 5: 210/US 90).

11. Understanding the "evil" of the title to refer to the need for sovereign existence to overstep the external and artificial constraints imposed upon it by society, it is nonetheless *Literature and Evil* where Bataille most strongly emphasizes the inherently moral aspect of sovereignty.

12. On the identification of poetry and literature, see *Literature and Evil*, "*Literary* communication—which is such in so far as it is poetic—is the *sovereign process* which allows *communication* to exist, like a solidified instant, or a series of instants, detached both from the work and from the reading of the work" (OC 9: 300–01/LE 188).

13. Maurice Blanchot, *Au moment voulu* (Paris: Gallimard, 1951); *When the Time Comes,* trans. Lydia Davis (Barrytown, NY: Station Hill, 1985).

CHAPTER ONE

The Confronted Community

Jean-Luc Nancy
Translated by Jason Kemp Winfree

The history of philosophical texts concerning community in the 1980s deserves to be written with precision, since it is, among other histories (only more so), revealing of a profound movement of thought in Europe at that time—a movement that still carries us, although in a context that has become very different, one in which the motif of "community" now, instead of coming to light, seems to sink into obscurity (especially at the time I am writing these lines, in mid-October 2001). In *The Inoperative Community* I evoked the beginning of this history, but in a manner too brief. Thanks to the occasion of this preface, I return to it here with the distance of time, which allows a better understanding.

At the same time, the heavy context to which I am referring—madness and sectarian wars of all kinds and all "worlds" (ancient, new, third and fourth, north and south, east and west)—perhaps renders useful recalling a movement that only raised the thought because it pertains first of all to existence.

※ ※ ※

In 1983 Jean-Christophe Bailly proposed a topic for a forthcoming issue of the journal *Aléa* that he was then editing for the publisher Christian Bourgois, which he formulated as "community, number."

The perfectly realized ellipsis of this expression—which Bailly, skillfully as always, proffered with as much assurance as elegance—took hold of me from the instant I received the invitation to contribute to it, and I have admired its relevance ever since.

At the time, the word *community* was unknown to the discourse of thought. It had come to be all but reserved for the institutional use of the "European community." Today, almost twenty years later, we know to what extent this use ignores the very concept it employs, and this as well is relevant to the question of community such as it leaves us haunted, deserted, or embarrassed. Whether or not one knew it then, the word and its concept were caught in the snare of the Nazi *Volksgemeinschaft*, the "community of the people" in its well-known sense. (In Germany, in fact, the word *Gemeinschaft* still sparked a strong reflex of hostility on the left, and the German translation of my book in 1988 was treated as Nazi by a leftist journal in Berlin. By contrast in 1999 another journal, appearing in the former East Berlin, spoke of my book in a positive manner under the title "Return of Communism." This double anecdote seems a good summary of the amphibology, the equivocation and perhaps the aporia, but also the obstinate and not necessarily obsessive insistence, that the word 'community' itself brings with it.) Furthermore, the socialistic confidence that remained, no matter its extent or shape, kept its affection for the word *communism* (as long as one retrieved its first exigencies, of course, against real communism, which had long been unmasked).

Now, 'communism' points to an idea and a project, whereas 'community' seems to note a fact and a given. 'Communism' declares itself in favor of a 'community' that is not given but that it gives itself as a goal. And in Bailly's expression I immediately heard the question, what *is* it about community? Indeed, I heard it as a question tacitly substituted for that other one, which asks: Which communist, communitarian or communal project? What about it? Indeed: What is its being? And what ontology accounts for that which the word *common* indicates, a word that is well known but whose concept may have become uncertain?

The concept itself demanded consideration, and such as it was the invitation showed some restraint from the order of the *project* in general. (Bailly comes from an insistent—if not extreme—political left, but not communist in the sense of party.) The mere foregrounding of the word posed it as a program for analysis and probable problematization.

Number too was unexpected, but in a different way. It called to mind not only the remarkable multiplication of people in the world, but something like the effect or qualitative corollary of this, that is, a multiplicity escaping the assumptions of unity, a multiplicity changing gears and intensifying its differences, dispersing into small groups, and even into individuals, multitudes, or populations. Here 'number' meant diverting, yet returning to, what had been "the masses" or "the crowd" in many prewar—and postwar from still another angle—analyses (see Le Bon, Freud, and so on). And we did know how various forms of fascism had a way of handling the "masses," while various forms of communism had a way of handling the "classes"—the historic mission of the one and the other fixed, set, arrested.

The formula could therefore be read as a dazzling summary of the problem that we had inherited as that of "totalitarianism(s)," now a problem no longer directly posed in political terms (as if it were a problem of "good government"), but in terms that had to be understood as ontological. Indeed, what is community if number becomes its only phenomenon—or even the thing-in-itself—and if there isn't any "communism" or "socialism," either national or international, that any longer supports even the slightest figure or the least form, the least identifiable schema? And what is number, then, if its multiplicity no longer stands for a mass waiting to take shape (formation, conformation, information), but stands for itself, as it were, in a dispersal that one wouldn't know whether to designate as a dissemination (a seminal exuberance) or a kind of crumbling (a sterile pulverization)?

※ ※ ※

It so happened that when Bailly suggested this topic, I was finishing a year-long course dedicated to Bataille considered from a political angle. I was researching, very precisely, the possibility of a hitherto unheard-of resource that would avoid fascism and communism as much as democratic or republican individualism (more recently the term *citizen* has sought to answer the same problem, albeit making scarcely any progress with it). In fact, it was in Bataille's work that I was searching because I already knew that the word and the motif of community circulated there—and the motivation of this search was also the one articulated by Bailly (who knew Bataille, of course, though he did not mention him). The index of this research, for both no doubt, meant positing the problem at first neither directly nor exclusively in a political way, yet without a clear awareness of the stakes: before or in retreat of the "political," there was *this*, that is to say, something "common," some "togetherness," and something having to do with "number," and we no longer know at all, perhaps, how to think this order of the real.

The seminar had left me dissatisfied. Bataille had not made it possible for me to touch on a new and unprecedented politics. On the contrary, in many respects he had made political possibility as such even more remote. In his postwar writings, and up until the end, he had turned away from the political atmosphere of his prewar thinking. Similarly, he had discarded any rivalry with sociology as "science," as well as any attempt to create a group or *collège*. It was no longer a question of a "sacred sociology" that would retrieve from various forms of fascism their drive and "activist" energy, wherein he had seen their primary strength. This heterological agitation had miscarried, and the war, which concluded with the victory of the democracies, left those political projects in the shadows instead of exposing and bringing to light their ecstatic force.

And further, just as Bataille made of "sovereignty" not a political but an ontological and aesthetic or ethical concept (as one would say today), so too he came to consider the strong bond of community—passionate or sacred or intimate—as reserved for what he named "community of lovers." The latter came, therefore, to be contrasted with the social bond as its countertruth. That which was supposed to structure society—even in the guise of a transgressive breach—was set outside society in society, in an intimacy out of reach for politics.

I seemed to recognize an aspect of something that throughout this period everyone was obscurely beginning to establish: the unhitching of politics and being-in-common. But on both sides—that of a community of intense intimacy, and that of a society of an extensive and homogeneous bond—Bataille's point of reference appeared to me in the following way: the desired position (whether reached in love or relinquished in society) of a community as an assumed interiority, as the self-presence of a realized unity. It seemed to me therefore necessary to analyze this presupposition of community—even if it was clearly designated as the impossible and thus turned into a "community of those who are without community" (I quote this expression from memory, without knowing today if it is from Bataille or Blanchot. I have decided to write these lines without consulting the relevant passages, and I am leaving some space for memory, which alone can give back the movement then followed and imprinted in me; rereading it all would require me to rewrite history).

And so the thought imposed itself upon me, one that was drawn out across the philosophical tradition, reaching all the way up to its Bataillean overflowing and excess (and earlier still, in that of Marx, no doubt). A representation of community in which the reflection on "totalitarianism"—which marked everything in those years, which required that everyone catch their breath—led me to give it this essential character: community realizing itself as its own proper work [*oeuvre*]. By contrast, what the difficult, worried, and in part disastrous thinking of Bataille invited one to think—with it but beyond it—I thought I could term "inoperative community" [*communauté désoeuvrée*].

"Inoperativity" [*désoeuvrement*] was taken from Blanchot, standing in the closest proximity to Bataille and to the community or communication between the two men called "friendship" and "infinite conversation." From this most singular, silent, and to some extent secretive communication, a word came that helped me to cast the dice again and restart the game.

The years that followed went on to show how much an interest the motif of community aroused, thus replayed a first time and also how much it became necessary to try to qualify once again this region of man or being that no communist or communitarian project could any longer sustain. To qualify this region in a different way meant to say: let us no longer qualify it by itself; let us leave behind the tautology in which community is made substance and value in itself as such (and without doubt still designated in a more or less Christian way, as primitive community of apostles, religious community, church, communion—the origins of Bataille are in fact quite clear in this regard). After Blanchot's book and mine, a series of works thematizing and qualifying community came out—and this goes on to this day, but in a context in which a kind of "communitarianism" has been reinvented in the United States, requiring a separate examination.

※ ※ ※

Blanchot wrote *The Unavowable Community* in response to the article I published under the title "The Inoperative Community" and while I was already working to extend it into a book. His response stunned me, at first because the attention that Blanchot signaled in this manner demonstrated the importance of this motif not only for him, but through him for all those who felt an imperious, even violent, need to start back to work on that which communism had concealed as powerfully as it had revealed it: the instance of the "common"—but also its enigma or difficulty, its ungiven and unavailable character, and thus in this sense the least "common" in the world . . .

But what further stunned me was the fact that Blanchot's response was at the same time an echo, a resonance, and a retort, as well as a reservation and in some respects a reproach.

I have never quite clarified this reservation or this reproach—neither in writing, nor for myself, nor in my correspondence with Blanchot. I mention it here for the first time, on the occasion of this preface.

I did not do so since I felt myself neither capable (and no more so today) nor authorized to elucidate the secret that Blanchot clearly designates in his title—and even in his text since he speaks toward the end of an "unmentionable," "unavowable" death given in love, of a love given in death (and this very thing itself is not avowable even when it is said).

Indeed, the unavowable secret pertains to this (which nevertheless does not contain it): at the point where I attempted to bring to light the "work" of community as the *death sentence* of society, and correlatively to establish the need for a community refusing to make itself (into a) work, thus preserving the essence of infinite communication (communicating an "absent sense" to itself, to speak with Blanchot again, and the passion of this ab-sense, or the passion in which this ab-sense consists)—at this very point, then, Blanchot spelled out, or rather gave a signal of the unavowable. Juxtaposed yet also opposed to the "inoperative" in the title of my essay, his adjective invites one to think that beneath the worklessness of inoperativity (*désoeuvrement*), something—an unavowable work—is at work nonetheless.

What it gives to be thought (and once again I am writing without rereading anything; I am writing not in order to resolve anything, but to draw the attention of future readers) is that the community of those who are without community (all of us, henceforward), that is, the inoperative community, will not be revealed as the unveiled secret of being-in-common. And consequently, it cannot be communicated, even though community is the common itself, indeed, because it is so.

Instead, this community makes this secret graver, aggravates it, emphasizing the impossibility or rather interdiction of acceding to it—or further, that to do so is subject to inhibition, shyness, or shame (all these accents do appear in Blanchot's text, I believe).

What is unavowable is not unsayable. On the contrary, the unavowable is continually said, or speaks itself, in the intimate silence of those who cannot avow it though they may have the ability to do so. I imagine that Blanchot would want to *intimate* to me this silence and what he says: he wanted to prescribe it to me and make it enter my intimacy, as intimacy itself—the intimacy of a communication or of a community, the intimacy of a manner of quiet *work* better concealed than any disengaged inoperativity, making it possible and necessary but without allowing oneself to dissolve in it. Blanchot asked that I not stop with the negation of communal community and that I think farther than this negativity, toward a secret of the common, which is not a common secret.

※ ※ ※

I have not gone farther, until now, to resume this analysis, as I could have done specifically by responding in my turn to Blanchot's text. I have not done so in my few letters to him, since letters should not be mixed up with texts; there is an appropriate order for texts to communicate among themselves. (Moreover, what is a *correspondence*? What kind of *co-* or *com-* is engaged here?) And I have not done it in an essay either, since as far as the order of my work properly speaking is concerned, I have not pursued this vein or theme of the word 'community.'

Little by little I have preferred replacing it with the awkward expressions *being-together, being-in-common,* and finally *being-with*. There were reasons for these shifts and for resigning myself to this awkwardness, at least temporarily. I could see from all sides the dangers aroused by the use of the word 'community': its resonance fully invincible and even bloated with substance and interiority; its reference inevitably Christian (as in spiritual, fraternal, communal community); or more broadly religious (as in Jewish community, community of prayer, community of believers, or '*umma*), as it is used to support an array of so-called "ethnicities." All this could only be a warning. It was clear that the emphasis placed on this necessary but still insufficiently clarified concept was at least, at this time, on par with the revival of communitarian trends that could be fascistic.

I therefore preferred to concentrate my work around the "with": almost indistinguishable from the *co-* of community, yet it carries with it a clearer indication of the spacing at the heart of proximity and intimacy. "With" is plain and neutral: neither communion nor atomization; just the sharing/dividing [*partage*] of a place, at the most, contact: a being-together without assemblage. (In this sense, it is necessary to push even farther the analysis of *Mitdasein* left suspended by Heidegger.)

⁂ ⁂ ⁂

All this may lead me toward Blanchot's book again. This new edition is my first opportunity. As if Blanchot, across the years and other signs exchanged, were cautioning me: "Watch out for the unavowable!" I think I hear it to say: Beware not to elevate community in any way, even under the designation "inoperative." Or else, follow even further the indication of this word. The worklessness of inoperativity comes after the work's operativity, but it comes from it. It is not enough to keep society from making itself into a work in the sense demanded by nation-states, or parties, or churches (universal or autonomous), assemblies and councils, peoples, companies, or fraternities. It is also necessary to think that there has already existed, always already, the "work" of community, that is, a sharing operation, which will always have preceded every singular or generic existence; a communication or contagion without which there could not be (in the most absolute manner) any *presence* or *world*, since each of these terms carries with it the implication of a coexistence or a cobelonging—this "belonging" doing nothing but belonging to the fact of being-in-common. Between us (between all of us together and as distinct sets of togetherness) there has been already a common thing shared, which is nothing but its sharing-out, but which in doing just this makes to exist and touches this existence itself, which is the exposition of its own proper limit. This is what has made us "us," separating and bringing us nearer, creating proximity through the space *between us*—"us," remaining in the great indecision where this collective or plural subject stands and stays condemned never to find its *own* proper voice.

What has been shared? Probably something—the "unavowable," then—that Blanchot points to in the second part of his book and in the very fact that in this book he pairs some reflections about a theoretical text with others about a tale of love and death. In both cases Blanchot writes relating them, and he writes his relation to these texts, which he also relates to one another in this way. He keeps the two texts distinct, it seems to me, by offsetting one with a negative consideration of "inoperativity," whereas the other would give access to a community, albeit one that is not "worked" or "achieved" ["*oeuvrée*"], but one that is carried out in secret (an unavowable secret) in the sharing out of an experience of limits: the experience of love and death, of life itself exposed to its limits.

Perhaps he is saying—and this is what a rereading must search for—that these two ways of acceding to the essence without essence of "community" intersect somewhere, between the two parts of the book as between the order of the social-political and the order of the passionate-intimate. Each part would be necessary to think the enigma of intensity, bursting forth and loss, or the abandon that at once makes possible both plural existence (birth, separation, opposition) and singularity (death, love). But the unavowable is always implied in birth and death, love and war.

The unavowable designates a shameful secret. It is shameful because under two possible figures, that of *sovereignty* and that of *intimacy,* it engages a passion that can only be exposed as the unavowable in general: confessing to it would be unbearable while at the same time it would destroy the force of this passion. But without it we would have already renounced any kind of being-together, which is to say, being itself. We would have renounced that which, according to the order of a sovereignty and an intimacy withdrawn in abyssal discretion, brings us into the world. For what puts us into the world is also what at once carries us to the extremes of separation, finitude, and the infinite encounter where each collapses in the contact with others (thus also with oneself) and with the world as the world of others.

Unavowable is thus a word that here mixes indiscernibly modesty [*pudeur*] and shamelessness [*impudeur*]. Shamelessly it announces a secret; modestly it declares that the secret will remain secret.

The one who is silent about this knows in this way what is not said. But this knowledge is not to be communicated, being itself at the same time the knowledge of communication, whose law is bound to be noncommunicative since it does not belong to the communicable order, without being for all that ineffable: but it opens every spoken word.

※ ※ ※

At this point, I will conclude by returning to the event that today (let me date it again, in this month of October 2001) spreads across the world and particularly the Western world and its edges, its borders, both internal and external (if external ones still exist), taking on all the characteristics of an outbreak of passions. It goes without saying that the figures of passion—be it that of an omnipotent God or a Freedom no less theological—and the expressions of their confrontation, both cover and reveal all we know about extortion, exploitation, and manipulation, along with their deployment by the contemporary movement of the world. But it is not enough to remove the masks, even if that is necessary first of all. One must also consider that these figures of passion have not incidentally come to occupy an empty space: this place is that of community's truth. The appeals to a wrathful God, or the statement *In God We Trust*, instrumentalize a desire, an anguish of being-together, and they do so in parallel ways. They once more involve the making of a work—all at once a heroic gesture, an imposing spectacle, and some insatiable trafficking. In doing so, they give the assurance that the secret is revealed while continuing to dazzle.

We still have not gone far enough in thinking the inoperativity of community, nor in what constitutes the possibility of sharing a secret without divulging it: of sharing it precisely in not divulging it to ourselves, among ourselves.

In the face of these monstrosities of thought (or "ideology"), confronting each other for no less monstrous stakes of power and profit, there is a task: to dare to think the unthinkable, the unaccountable, the intractable of being-with, but without subjecting or submitting it to any hypostasis. This is not a political or economic task, but even graver, and it eventually rules, at the limit, both politics and economics. We are not in a "war of civilizations"; we are in an internal fissure or tear unique to that civilization which both civilizes and barbarizes the world in the very same movement, for it has already touched on the extremes with its own logic: it has given the world over entirely to itself; it has handed the human community entirely over to itself and to its secret without god and without commercial value. This is what one has to work with—with community facing off with itself, with us confronting us, the *with* confronting the *with*. Confrontation no doubt pertains essentially to community: that is to say, all at once a confrontation and an opposition, a coming before oneself so as to challenge and test oneself, so as to part within one's being a gash that is also the condition of this being.

※ ※ ※

The first version of this preface stopped here. I finished it on October 15, 2001. Now I am resuming it four months later, in February 2002. Indeed, the movement that carried me away from Blanchot's book and toward it—starting from a question about community and moving toward a way of thinking no doubt destined to free itself from the "question" itself—could not be stopped. It seems to me on the contrary still more obvious that we will continue to be carried by this movement as long as a hitherto unheard-of "community" has not found its place among us (among and between all of us, but who are we? One people or several, one continent or several, one world?), admitting that elsewhere this community could be nothing except the one in which or from which we are already gathered, since all our divisions, all our hesitations and questions that are justified when it comes to the theme "community" cannot prevent *us* from being in *common*—all of us, whoever we are, and whatever the nature of this given fact, which cannot be forestalled. "Community" is given to us, that is to say, a "we" is given to us before we can articulate a "we" and still less justify it.

I will go a little further from this point: the sudden offensive strike that has taken on a stunning figure with the collapse of the symbol of global commerce (and therefore of exchange, of relations, and of communication) presents itself, or wants to present itself, as a religious confrontation, with fundamentalist monotheism, on the one side, humanist theism, no less fundamentalist, on the other. Theology of the Absolute against the theology of the Enlightenment, one would have said in Hegel's day. Religion seems to entail the communitarian motif, and in such a way that there would be no community except with religion (in fact, since the Greeks, then the Romans, and then Rousseau, it seems that we will have been on the lookout for a "civil religion" and wished for such a possibility, though it has always been fragile and fading away more or less rapidly in the end). Reciprocally, it seems that all a religion can do is assemble a community, especially in monotheism (*synagogue, church, umma* are the three-pronged names of this assemblage). This reciprocity is so present in our Western culture that one is always sent back to the etymology of "religion" as *religare*, meaning "to link," "to tie by a bond." And we also speak readily of a "social bond" (Rousseau, again, already used this expression).

Yet it is established that this etymology is not exact, that the Romans themselves knew another one, and that the recourse to the idea of a bond has at least been reinforced by Christianity. The other etymology refers to *relegere* in the sense of "to collect" or "take in," to bring back to oneself for a scrupulous examination. We can draw two consequences from this set of facts.

On the one hand, community thought as bound by a transcendent or mystical bond and the bond itself thought as reunion lifted into a unity (of which one of the forms inspired by the Romans has been the bundled *fascio* of fascism) do represent communitarian being as the mystery of a union, an incorporation, and even a fusion. Being-in-common presupposes a common being, a grounding foundation, a principle, and an end where the "members" find their meaning and truth. But one must also understand that this community, as the paradigm of a modern way of thinking, entails within its religious determination the tendency to efface religion properly called to the benefit of a celebration of community itself as the living body of this unity. It works here as in the entire so-called process of "secularization." The social body takes on the function of the mystical body, and the sovereign (the people) takes on the identity of the divine or of Christ. This communitarian theology, latent even up to Marx, points both to a shift and to an occultation. The mystical element moves into a civic element—but the civic element remains hindered and even stunned by its own mystical character. Hence the failure of any sort of civic religion, whatever they may have been; hence democracy's muted or avowed anxiety with regard to its grounding in the concept of 'sovereign people.' For what concerns us here, we can say that the religious interpretation of community fails to translate into politics, but on the contrary separates the political from the theological and in an atheological milieu (such as our republican one) points to a void, a vacancy, or an enigma, at the place where an enlightening mystery was to offer itself: common intimacy itself or the tying of bonds are obscured in the exact measure that they claim to be revealed.

On the other hand, there also seems to emerge a second characteristic that leads back to the other sense of "religion." As Emile Durkheim put it (the founder, if not of the word, at least of the thing called "sociology," knowledge of social being as such), contracts presuppose something other than themselves. Contracts presuppose not only the possibility of entering them but also the disposition to do so and the energy that such a commitment demands. Such dynamics call for trusting, confidence, that is, anticipating that others will be committed. Confidence is faith put together: it is the faith or fiduciary quality that the contract presupposes in its very idea, which is to say, in the idea of its validity and contractual strength.

The "other thing" that contracts take for granted is of the order of "faith." Faith has nothing to do with belief in the sense of a weak or presumptive knowledge. Faith is not of the order of knowing but rather of adhering or participating (one could term it the order of *methexis* rather than *mimesis*, if it is possible to disjoin the two). As Valéry puts it, "Society functions in a fiduciary way—it presupposes a credo or credit." But this "credo or credit" is the act of a belief that is placed in nothing other than society itself. Affiance (*fiance*) is con-fident (*con-fiance*) because it has confidence in the *co* of coexistence; or rather, the *co* is possible only as affiance in itself. Now, the *co* by itself is nothing, except the act of this trusting confidence.

This second direction brings us nearer to the second sense of *religio*. Here the enigma of the common no longer figures as a mystery to reveal or on the contrary to protect behind some mysticism. The enigma has to do with the secret of confidence; this secret is confidence itself, in which affiance and co-indefinitely presuppose one another. *Religio*, then, inasmuch as it is scrupulous, is the way to hold back before this secret—to observe it and keep it—since it is the incommunicable secret of what first of all engages, assures, and risks some communication, whether this communication is economical, technical, linguistic, affective, or sexual. (No doubt it is all that at once, with varying proportions of each kind.)

Put in still other terms: *cum* in *confidentia* does not really designate "with" but it has the value of a prefix signifying something accomplished or completed (as in *conspicio* or *conficio*): *fides*, or *fiducia*, is accomplished to the end, it gives itself or surrenders itself without reserve. In fact, it has to become involved in this manner; if it did not do so, it could not even begin. Confidence or trust that is limited or mitigated presupposes the possibility of unlimited confidence. The latter, in its turn, presupposes among the "faithful" (between the "fiancés") a proximity that one should be able to term "unlimited" when it is in fact, and exactly, the proximity on the limit that separates them absolutely—the body, death, one's unassignable "self." So the extreme intensity of *fides* is identical to the proximity of *cum* in the sense of "with," and the former communicates where the latter maintains the irreducible parting that the "with" implies in its own structure.

So we are redirected anew toward Blanchot's text. The secret is unavowable because it is incommunicable. But it is unavowable and not just incommunicable. If it were only incommunicable, it would be a mystery reserved for some divinity floating outside of the common and concealed under the veil of a prohibition. As unavowable, it is of the order of what is effective and well known by those who take part in it—well known by all of us and evident in its own way, manifest in all our communications, our commerce, our contracts, and our sexual intercourse. The secret demands some reserve and modesty because it touches on our nudity and our intimacy. Just as there is no greater trust than when one bares oneself in all one's nakedness, delivering oneself to love or medical treatments, so too there is no confident trust that does not bare itself, that is not denuded. It bares that which of the common is not given, or rather, this: that the common is not given, is nothing, is not a thing, but that which makes possible in engaging itself, in trusting itself to itself—which is not given. I am rereading Blanchot's text now: "[T]he strangeness of what couldn't be common is what grounds this community—forever provisional and always already deserted."

This strangeness is not a mystery, nor is it a negativity (death is not present here as negativity but as the effectivity of strangeness). This strangeness is the affirmation of naked confidence, of confiding nakedness—exposed, exhibited, fragile, uncertain, but also, precisely, *exposed*, shown, manifested, in its disconcerting and troubling strangeness, the strangeness of the most ordinary encounter as much as of the most unavowable bond.

CHAPTER TWO

The Contestation of Community

Jason Kemp Winfree

> But because thou art lukewarm, and neither cold nor hot, I will vomit thee out of my mouth.
>
> —St. John, The Apocalypse

> To be sure, nobody who really thinks about history can take politics altogether seriously.
>
> Susan Sontag, *Regarding the Pain of Others*

"Form a community creative of values, values creative of cohesion" (OC 2: 275/BR 121). So reads the first line of Bataille's "Programme (Relative to *Acéphale*)," written on April 4, 1936—the publicized program of a community, an effort, or a bond that remains to this day largely secret.[1] According to Blanchot, Acéphale was the only group that mattered for Bataille, who continued to see in it, long after its disappearance from the scene in 1939, an extreme possibility and point of attraction.[2] And yet, in spite of this, whatever else it was, Acéphale was insufficient, and along with it the call to form a community it announced. Empirically, this insufficiency is evidenced by the fact that Acéphale lasted only three and half years and was coterminous with other endeavors, notably the College of Sociology, which gave an altogether different expression to Bataille's obsession with community, addressing what Bataille and Caillois called "sacred sociology." While Acéphale concerned the formation of community, the College of Sociology occupied itself with the knowledge of the emotional bond described by Bataille as a "communifying movement," the force that binds the individual to others, transforming it and the group into something else, something uncontainable and excessive to the profane order and its regulation, conservation, and preservation of life. The obsession with community in Bataille's work can thus be divided, heuristically at least, between a practice and a knowledge, or better still, between a revolutionary practice and a theoretical inquiry, a heterogeneous zone of disruption and a homogenous understanding directed toward an account of the heterological itself. The *Somme athéologique*—which begins during this same period and is comprised primarily of *Inner Experience*, *Guilty*, and *On Nietzsche*—exhibits the valences of the heterological endeavor organized with respect to the issue of community in a particularly acute manner, mingling practice and knowledge, tearing the works apart, and presenting that rupture. Acéphale, the College, the *Somme*—three sites of Bataille's obsession with community, three points of access to an impossible watchword.[3]

The Impossible Program: Against Community

As Bataille's invocation of community received renewed attention during the 1980s, the religious dimension of his thought was emphasized, and it was juxtaposed with a purportedly growing occlusion of political concern.[4] Undoubtedly, Bataille's own statements support that general impression, both within Acéphale and the College (not to mention the diverse texts comprising the *Somme*, apparently withdrawing from the political problems of the war altogether into a space of personal anguish). And yet, what is meant by Bataille's own characterization of Acéphale as religious has as little to do with religion in any common sense as it does politics in its everyday meaning. Just three weeks after the publication of the program cited above, Bataille writes in "The Sacred Conspiracy," published in the first issue of *Acéphale*: "WE ARE FEROCIOUSLY RELIGIOUS and, to the extent that our existence is the condemnation of everything that is recognized today, an inner exigency demands that we be equally imperious. What we are starting is a war. It is time to abandon the world of the civilized and its light. It is too late to be reasonable and educated—which has led to a life without appeal. Secretly or not, it is necessary to become completely different, or to cease being" (OC 1: 443/VE 179). Because it is explicitly mentioned, it is tempting to take the religiosity of the statement as self-evident. However, nothing is further from the truth. For what alone is unmistakable here is the ferocity of the articulation—fierce not because it is designated so, but because of its mood, urgency, and pronounced combative character. It is the force of contestation that is unmistakable in these lines, and it requires and effects a radical abandonment of that category of value that defines and justifies both religious and political discourse: education. Bataille's concern here is not for the sake of a common good, already determined in advance and without question in the direction of upbuilding and formation, the good of the social order and the fulfillment of individual talent in its service. His concern here is rather a question of life and death. And there is a profound sense that life has been dulled, deadened, and muted by the social bonds common to and developed through the communal or social forces of religion and politics alike, forces of normalization, security, and the accumulation of wealth. Bataille's call to form a community is at once and unequivocally a call for the destruction of community in any traditional sense. It is a call to do away with the bonds we most readily and thoughtlessly define as communal. Item 7 of the "Programme" reads: "Fight for the decomposition and exclusion of all communities, national, socialist, communist or churchly—other than universal community" (OC 2: 275/BR 121). It is a call for revolution.

From the vantage point of apologists for capital or bourgeois democracy (and is there really a difference?), there could be no distinction between these demands and those of militant revolutionaries, be they communist, socialist, or anarchistic. For Bataille, however, the need to become completely different, or cease being, requires a break from the formative dimension of revolutionary activity, its participation in congresses and talks, its displacement of debate from the space of the streets to the hallways of negotiation. The entire force of revolutionary creativity rests for Bataille in the emotional bond that wells up within the masses as refusal, the atmosphere of hope and rage that swells like an uncontainable wave. The need to become completely different requires the abandonment of political process—defined as it necessarily and inevitably is by those who already have a voice—but not political practice. It is a refusal to concede that political thought and action must occur within the sphere of established discourse, which begins with distrust, "a complete lack of confidence in the spontaneous reactions of the masses," and which in this way, at just this point, unites militant revolutionaries and bourgeois intellectuals alike. Thus, Bataille can say at once, "It is necessary to produce and to eat: many things are necessary that are still nothing, and so it is with political agitation" (OC 1: 403/VE 162).And at the same time: "When we speak to those who want to hear us, we do not essentially address their political finesse. The reactions we hope for from them are not calculations of positions, nor are they new political alliances. What we hope for is of a different nature." What Bataille hopes for is an affirmation of the bond that does not belong to discourse, production, or accumulation; a confrontation with the impotence perpetuated by traditional social structures of nationality, religion, party, and the like; a mobilization of hope and rage incomprehensible and irresponsible to everyone who tethers the question of the political to the axis of security. It is a contestation of the "morally empty and materially miserable life" perpetuated and sustained by institutional structures of power and their widespread internalization (OC 1: 402/VE 161).

Undoubtedly, the "Programme" is destined to fail, if it really is a program at all. Item 3 highlights this difficulty, stating, "Assume the function of destruction and decomposition, but as accomplishment and not as the negation of being" (OC 2: 275/BR 121). The demand not only poses insurmountable structural difficulties of understanding: how destruction could be deprived of its negative work, how it could be taken as an achievement in any positive sense. It also articulates a real political problem. Contributing nothing worthy or capable of appropriation by the established order—that of discourse, the accumulation of wealth, the value of security, and so on—it beckons its own destruction. For it addresses itself solely to the raw violent drives society either represses or sublimates. What is more, not only does the "Programme" addresse itself to those drives, but it also gives them expression, and it deploys them in its very call. Its call to affirm crime is itself criminal.[5] Its refusal to calmly suffer for a placid future, its rejection of all political projects that sacrifice the present for an indefinite and impossible end, its demand to "[c]onsider the world to come in the sense of reality contained as of now, and not in the sense of a permanent happiness which is not only inaccessible, but hateful"—in each of these affirmations, this project tears itself apart as project. What looks like a program is in fact a heterological operation, one that deploys the form of program to effect a cut with everything every program supposes. Community is not an idea or concept, an aim or goal, nor is it an extant dimension of social reality. It is a declaration of war.

Sacred Sociology and the Genesis of the Ontological Task

Throughout Bataille's writings from this period there is a strong sense of crisis, one that has at least three aspects and that leads to the program of research undertaken by the College of Sociology, the purportedly exoteric manifestation of Acéphale's esoteric interest. I remark on these crises at this point not only because they constitute the conditions that necessitate the explicitly ontological direction undertaken by the College, the endeavor of sacred sociology, but also because this program bares on the issue of community and Bataille's powerful and idiosyncratic development of it. Like the impossible program described above, which pushes the very notion of project to its breaking point, the ontological task that takes community as its object struggles against ontological totalization and requires an altogether new conception of the ontological—an ontology of insufficiency rather than ground.

There is, first of all, the crisis of the war itself. The "Declaration of the College of Sociology" from October 1938, signed by Bataille, Caillois, and Leiris, reads: "The College of Sociology sees its specific role to be the assessment, without indulgence, of the collective psychological reactions aroused by the imminence of war, which when the danger was over, fell too quickly into what must rightly be called restorative oblivion, or else turned into rosy, almost comforting recollections in a complicitous memory" (CS 100/44). At the same time that it denies itself to be a political organization, then, the College nevertheless not only defines itself in relation to the war but also explicitly addresses what would typically be taken as political problems in this context, or at least concerns with immediate political import, the formation of memory, and the force of forgetting. What is more, while the College clearly defines itself in relation to Mauss, who in confrontation with Marxist economic analysis emphasized the "cohesion of primitive" cultures,"[6] Bataille's trajectory during this period focuses this research in part through a series of analyses bearing on overtly political events and figures. While Caillois addresses festivals and "animal societies," and Klossowski speaks of Sade and tragedy, Bataille concerns himself with the structure of democracy, Hitler, fascism, and the function of armies. In the context of the war, observations that the army "parades itself before others and offers itself for their admiration" and "even claims to be the embodiment of their existence and their fate" are not neutral, even if they are not political in the strict sense of party affiliation or position, even if they avoid indulgences, as stated in the "Declaration." But even the "Declaration" itself is not neutral, its language indicting those who in the aftermath of immediate danger "too quickly" forget, or seek "rosy" "comfort" in "complicitous" memory, decrying the return of homogeneous forms of existence.

More narrowly construed, the crisis that motivates Bataille during this period is what he calls, just three years prior to the formation of the College, and that no doubt conditions that formation, "a serious crisis of the entire Left." Part of that crisis is articulated above in the condemnation of militant revolutionaries in the same breath with bourgeois intellectuals, Bataille's scathing critique of their mutual lack of confidence in the masses, and the way that distrust expresses itself through membership in an oppressive and exclusive community of discourse. Beyond this obviously political failure, though, the Left is handicapped by its own success, the accomplishment of its economic analysis, and its nevertheless limited results (OC 1: 408/VE 166). Although undeniable with respect to the economy of production and its necessary class division, the Marxist analysis cannot account for the drives or desires that play out across the system of exchange it so eloquently and decisively elaborates. Nor can it account for the various formations that arise in the aftermath of its dissolution. The rise of fascism exhibits these limits, according to Bataille, since the persistence of irresolvable conflict between Italian capitalists and workers indicates that the unity achieved by fascism "is located in its actual psychological structure and not in the economic conditions that serve as its base" (OC 1: 367/VE 157). The character of this psychological structure requires analysis the Left cannot provide, beholden as it is to *this* side of production. And along with the emotive force that binds the energies of fascism, the analysis must extend to the "emotions that give the masses the surge of power that tear them away from the domination of those who only know how to lead them on to poverty and to the slaughterhouse" (OC 1: 409/VE 166), and more generally still, to "what holds us firmly together, what links our origins to the emotions that constitute it" (OC 1: 404/VE 163). Such is the only way to remain true to the struggle against capitalism and the various closed systems its instability provokes—restoration, fascism, nazism, communism. In short, both the political failures and the structural limitations of the Left require a new understanding, one directed toward what Bataille calls the "ocean of men in revolt," which alone "can save the world from the nightmare of impotence and carnage in which it sinks!" (OC 1: 412/VE 168). The ontological direction of research undertaken by the College has palpable, practical motivations.

Walter Benjamin, who attended the College of Sociology regularly, reportedly worried that it, along with the program of Acéphale, lent itself all too readily to fascist and nazi appropriation.[7] Certainly the "ocean of revolt" that Bataille suggests might "save the world" is a disquieting response to threats immediately facing human life at the time, threats that clearly drew upon the very emotional bond that so interests the College. And Bataille himself identifies Mussolini and Hitler as heterogeneous elements initially recalcitrant to homogenous society. Certainly, heterogeneity does not guarantee desirable historical-political outcomes. But Bataille is also clear that the condensation of power in such figures of authority, "[t]he imperative presence of the leader[,] amounts to a negation of the fundamental effervescence that he taps; the revolution, affirmed as a foundation, is, at the same time, fundamentally negated from the moment that internal domination is militarily exerted on the militia" (OC 1: 362–63/VE 153). The dangers posed by affective emotion and its military constellation, far from requiring a retreat from the College's position, therefore, calls it forth. Even Benjamin's analysis of the aestheticization of politics—which he evidently began to level against the College—could not be proffered without this basis of attraction. This is no doubt the sense in which Bataille writes, what the College aims at, and what it must critique is "not merely the ground of an intellectual debate but rather . . . precisely the theatre where the political tragedy is playing" (CS 159/83).

The third crisis that marks the emergence of the College is, therefore, a crisis of the political itself, the fact that the most impending problems, in spite of their political shape, do not admit political solutions. Their imminence makes of the College an exigency. To address the unfathomable suffering wrought by the violence of limited political life and the established social order, it is necessary to develop a new, more comprehensive approach. Sacred sociology thus takes as its topos the "entire communifying movement of society" (CS 140/74), aiming at an understanding of the universal community affirmed in the "Programme (Relative to Acéphale)." The task, in other words, is "to apply intelligence less to so-called political situations and to the logical deductions that ensue, than to the immediate comprehension of life" (OC 1: 409–10/VE 166). This explicitly ontological task occupies Bataille for the rest of his life, finding mature theoretical expression in *The Accursed Share* and *Erotism*. During the period of the College, however, this task is developed in particular through the distinction between elective and traditional communities, and the interest of the College lay almost exclusively with the former. The College thus determines the ontological direction of its work in terms of an understanding of the relation of the individual and the social order, whose de facto ties are loosened in proportion to the formation of elective bonds.

During the inaugural session of the College, Bataille and Caillois cast the scope of elective communities in terms of religious orders and secret societies (and no doubt this is what bothers Benjamin, as though the College abandons the problems of the day and seeks solutions in secret brotherhoods!). Yet Bataille's development of the notion of elective community tends almost entirely in the direction of the break with de facto community, on the one hand, and the community of lovers, on the other. To the extent that secret societies exemplify the field of research undertaken by the College, Bataille is more interested in the secret than he is the societies and religious orders that would provide for that research a more accessible and determinate object. Obsessed by the "secret" at the heart of our contact with one another, Bataille's interest has little or nothing to do with that which could be held or shared or protected by a secret organization. In relation to the two determinations of community set forth by the College—traditional and elective—the tragic human being and the lover, respectively, therefore, bear more and more the burden of Bataille's revolution. The contestation of community becomes less and less programmatic and at the same time, more fateful, its possibility belonging to the ontology of social life at the very point where action, will, and understanding discover their limits, and where this discovery is devoid of transcendence and the possibility of recuperative accumulation.

Thematically explicit in the title of a lecture Caillois was unable to deliver—"Brotherhoods, Orders, Secret Societies, Churches"—it is therefore remarkable and telling that Bataille's introduction to the event focuses on concerns altogether different from those Caillois intended to address. Rather than speak about the character of clandestine organizations, Bataille describes instead three types of human being, three types of relation to de facto or traditional community, which at the same time successively correspond to the three crises described above. The first type, the "armed lout," aims at expelling everything foreign, forcing it to the outside, and he dominates the war, sustains it, as it were, and in doing so no doubt motivates the formation of the College. Like the "armed lout," the "man of law and discourse," the second type, is also motivated by the threat of impotence, but his action is itself impotent and inevitably serves the inertia of arms. Because he perpetuates that against which he fights, the "man of law and discourse" is for Bataille a comic figure, like the fool who impotently wipes the shit from his shoe on his own carpet, ineptly spreading what repulses him, like leftist revolutionaries carrying the value of production into the revolution, or carrying the revolution into the state-sponsored halls of negotiation. Bataille writes, "Deep down I think there is something wretched, something obnoxious, about opposing a reality, such as the one threatening human existence today, with discourses alone, assertions of law, a whole blaring discord and the armies belonging to this discourse and this discord. I do not believe it is possible to oppose the rule of arms with anything except some other rule: and, other than the rule of arms, only that of tragedy exists" (CS 271/147). The third type, tragedy, is thus born from the impotence of human life in the face of blind and indifferent forces of nature, politics, or history. Both the structure of an event and a comportment in relation to the event, tragedy opposes the world of work and production and will as the necessary exposure to a recalcitrant and unworkable chance, what Bataille calls the "sovereignty of existence laid bare." Tragedy exposes the impotence of action, the fact that action always serves ends other than its own, that even its accomplishments are impoverished. "The neophyte learns that [even] the will to efficacious action is one that limits itself to dismal dreams," says Bataille (OC 1: 528/VE 226).

The tragic figure not only suffers subjection to currents and forces he cannot contain, but through that suffering he becomes aware, albeit too late to be educated, if that requires contribution to the normative social order. He is the one who sees that which does not itself see, the one who, like Oedipus, is turned toward his own blindness and confronted with the impossibility of restoring its sight.[8] The tragic figure witnesses the impotence of action without that awareness itself acting or doing anything other than confirming its impotence in the world of action, thereby setting itself apart from that world, making of its subjection an inassimilable and accursed share. He therefore imposes a silence on what surrounds him, the only response to the crisis of the political itself—not a silence of withdrawal or escape from the domination and slaughter of life, but one that stands outside or under the structures and values that perpetuate it, as the silence of the witness whose presence is more disturbing than is his voice. Tragedy is for Bataille, therefore, a bearing toward the reality threatening human life, the reality that human life is always threatened, exposed before a death it neither knows nor can prevent, and that its own will to dominate and construct, explain and negotiate, are inseparable from that threat. "If the man of tragedy bears within him the reality of inmost human existence lost in the immensity of the universe, it is clear that the community—the only place this existence is realized—will have meaning in human terms only to the extent that it provides a place for tragedy, to the extent that it acknowledges the tragic spirit as its own reality" (CS 272/148). But there can be no such acknowledgment in the homogeneous security of de facto community, and that is what requires the tragic bearing in the first place.

Elective Communities: The Community of Lovers, Community with Nietzsche

It is the necessity of exposure to the blind forces of chance that solicits tragic comportment and separates the tragic person from the dominant homogeneous social order. But it is this very same chance that binds her to others in what Bataille calls "elective communities," that is, those "for whom the community is a value and not a fact," as Hollier so aptly puts it (CS 156/407). To speak of communities in terms of value rather than fact indicates a turn away from de facto traditional communities and their equally traditional sociological analysis, a turn toward another sort of contact altogether, one whose stability is as precarious as the luck that makes it possible. While heterogeneously imperative communities, such as those that take shape in fascism or nazism, undoubtedly rest on the organization of an affective basis, that is, the attraction of a value and not fact, their violence consists in the attempt to transform that value into a fact, to render it operative, to integrate or transform the heterogeneous force of attraction into a homogeneous order of production. Elective communities, by contrast, stand apart from the homogeneous order, bound by the silence sustained in tragic comportment, sharing that silence, communicating themselves in it. The turn away from de facto communities toward elective communities is thus for Bataille a turn toward the nonappropriable force of attraction, which withholds itself from every form of homogeneous integration.

In giving expression to the sense of elective communities, Bataille's exposition relies heavily on the figure lovers. Lovers are exemplary of elective community, finding one another by chance, attracted by one another with a momentum and intensity indifferent to the demands of work and social cohesion. The appearance of the beloved on the scene falls with the swiftness and decisiveness of an ax, tearing the lover away from all other interests, including that of self-preservation, bestowing on him the exhilaration of total risk. The beloved shines with a "precarious radiance" that exerts upon the lover a violence and suspension like that of falling dice, which arrange existence anew. "The lovers' world, like life," writes Bataille, "is built on a *set of accidents that give an avid, powerful will to be the response it desires*" (CS 51/20). In other words, the attraction configured by chance requires the lover to stake herself, putting her entire being in play, but it requires this as an obsession and not an obligation. As Bataille puts it in *On Nietzsche*, "the desire in us defines our luck," shapes the chance constellation of beings and events wherein it finds itself, and it does so by risking itself and by virtue of the risk it itself is (OC 6: 88/ON 73; tm). And that means the coincidence of wills in the face of chance—which is the contact of love itself—results from a gamble and not a calculation. "It 'risks' me and the one I love"; it plays us [*Il me 'met en jeu,' met en jeu l'être aimé*], says Bataille of carnal love. The lover's response to the radiance of the beloved is incomprehensible and outrageous! So much so that "[c]ompared to the person I love, the universe seems poor and empty" (OC 6: 84/ON 69).

The example of lovers is of particular importance because it articulates both the insufficiency and the innocence that dominate Bataille's ontological considerations. In a sense, the tenuousness and tenderness of lovers reflects a more generally constitutive condition of human life, that "[t]here exists at the basis of human life a principle of insufficiency" (OC 5: 97/IE 81). When that insufficiency is repressed and mythologized into the ontological primacy of the individual, making of sociality a contract added on for the sake of security, existence is rendered guilty. But guilty insufficiency is as restricted a sense of human being as Marxist economic analysis is of community; indeed, both subsist on the refusal of chance, the one staking its future on the calculated probability of survival, the other on dialectical necessity. The lovers who chance everything and are constituted in that risk (*hasard*), however, exhibit all the "magnificence" of an existence "created in the image of a universe untouched by the defilement of merit or intention" (CS 53/21). Their contact is so innocent that it excises itself altogether from the world of reward and punishment, justification and critique, their insufficiency excessive to the impoverished world of need. Thus, Bataille insists, "What characterizes man from the outset and what leads up to the completed rupture at the summit is not only the will for sufficiency, but the cunning, timid attraction on the side of insufficiency" (OC 5: 105/IE 88). And "what attracts isn't immediate being, but a wound" (OC 6: 45/ON 22). Excessive insufficiency is an ontological condition, since "[a] being that isn't cracked isn't possible," writes Bataille (OC 5: 259/G23). The cracked being, however, is at once, at the very point where its self-enclosure ends and it opens onto the world, exposed and naked, falling outside itself, a lucky being, a chance being. Insufficiency and the excess of suffering that characterizes it is the condition of play. With it and through it "we go from enduring the cracks (from decline) to glory (we seek out the cracks)" (OC 5: 259/G 23).

Community is not, therefore, an extant division or willed unity within the social order, but a configuration of luck and chance where one being opens onto another and is what it is only through this opening. The language of exposure and ex-position goes a long way in articulating the structural conditions of this occurrence, but it is nevertheless insufficient to characterize the contact here at issue. Bataille insists rather that this opening is a wound and elective community the affective attraction of one lacerated insufficiency by another. Community is constituted in the overlapping of wounds, the sharing not only of what cannot be shared, but the sharing of a suffering that is neither mine nor yours, a suffering that does not belong to us, but which gives us to one another, and in doing so both maintains and withdraws the beings so configured. In community, the other does not complete me but completes my insufficiency, shares the luck which is never only mine. Elective community is like a lovers' kiss—an exhilarating affirmation of chance, the will to be what befalls it but that its will could never produce.

With respect to the lover, we desire like a gambler wagers. "Like the winnings of a gambler," writes Bataille, "sexual possession prolongs desire—or extinguishes it" (OC 6: 106/ON 86). The sheer momentum of the movement requires that its strength be squandered. Desire is unsatisfied not because it fails, but because it exceeds the search for satisfaction, because it is also raw expenditure. For this reason, desire is misunderstood if it is represented as the infinite tragic movement toward an inaccessible object, as though desire not only is prohibited by its very structure from attaining its aim, but as though its structure is fundamentally teleological. The obsession with this logic is always mournful (psychoanalysis) or moral (transcendental philosophy) and in both cases remains theological insofar as the concern is governed by or measured against an imaginary sense of propriety or ownership or end. The desire that binds lovers is not so much directed toward an unattainable summit, however, as it is itself the summit, the point "where life is impossibly at the limit."[9] Desire and summit can no more be separated than lightning and its flash. In this respect Bataille is unequivocal: "*The summit isn't what we 'ought to reach'* " (OC 6: 57/ON 39; tm)). Rather, "It's *what is*. Never what should be" (OC 6: 111/ON 91). If desire is unsatisfied, that is because it exceeds the conservative search for satisfaction, because it is not teleological, because we are driven beyond the need of satisfaction without being driven to anything, because our unfinished character is in this very way excessive, not impoverished. If love is unsatisfied it is because it has perished, leaving us wasted and ruined.

The lovers' love is sacred. It does not belong to the profane order of work and its accumulated labor, the profane and banal order of capital. For Bataille, the sacred designates an object that is beyond all others in value, but the sacred character of our carnal love has nothing to do with divine love. The sacrifices brought about by the love of lovers require expenditure without recuperation; we give up our careers as dancers, we speak on the phone for hours on end, we waste the day in bed, and we give ourselves over entirely to that waste and identify ourselves with it. These sacrifices have nothing to do with the sacrifice of theology. As Bataille puts it, "in divine love, the limit is given in perfection," and this limit necessarily excludes play and its risk. Certainly, one risks nothing by loving God, whose infinite perfection is expressed through an infinite and undiscriminating love, just as one risks nothing by loving the flag. And that is as good as to say that in neither case does one really love, even if there remains operative a libidinal bind that does not fail to risk those others who refuse the religious-nationalistic sublimation of carnal desire, of the lovers touch or its absence. God and nation stand before us as the ugly symptoms of efficiency that guarantee that desire not only leaves the lover intact but also yields a profit. By contrast, carnal love and the love of lovers concerns the excess of suffering, and Bataille insists that "without this excess we could not play" (OC 6: 86/ON 71).That is, it is by way of the excesses of suffering carnal desire that we are ourselves put into play, thrown like dice. And finitude is unbounded just in the sense that dice in their inevitable free fall carry an unpredictable combination that proves exhilarating or devastating, and in any case leads to ruin, even as it leads to the affirmation of what we are in love.

The oscillation expressed above in terms of the acceleration leading to summit or decline, the ecstasy of insufficiency, is not only a thematically explicit object in Bataille's writings, privileged and important because of the manner in which it bears upon and articulates the ontological task. Rather, Bataille's work itself is characterized by the very movement it describes, constantly fluctuating between decline and glory in its expression. This is not to say Bataille's writing is motivated by the task of adequation between form and content, *Sache* and expression, but to insist that the ontological task is born from and gives expression to fundamental conditions of human life, conditions that enter into that expression and call it forth. Insufficiency is not, therefore, a category or concept to which the world must measure up, by which it would be rendered intelligible, but is rather the condition out of which Bataille writes. The work is ontological, then, not only because of its explicitly thematic ontological concerns, but because it exhibits in its very structure, expression, and aim, the ontological conditions it also diagnoses, the reciprocity of chance and insufficiency, isolation and contact. Thus, the same insufficiency thematized in the *Somme athéologique* at once tears that work apart, rendering it *désoeuvrée*—inoperative, unworking, fragmentary—and in this way it accounts for the alternately depressed and ecstatic articulations of naked existence exposed to chance, the violent and sometimes incoherent shifts of focus, mood, and intention. The work itself is an open wound communicating with those who read and those who are read, the elective community of Bataille's readership.

Perhaps no part of the *Somme* exhibits the elective communities involved in this work and its unworking (*désoeuvrement*) as clearly as does *On Nietzsche*, which denies its readers any systematic or historical or critical exposition of Nietzsche, which is not even *about* Nietzsche at all, contrary to the most basic initial assumptions elicited by the title, but which offers instead articulations that have more to do with coffee shops, toothaches, and pretty girls than the academically overburdened and overdetermined will to power. Throughout the violent and radically unstable terrain of the works comprising the *Somme*, Nietzsche is present neither as thematic object nor authoritative voice, but as part of an elective community, as participant in the bond of attraction and inclination to the community of chance and risk that requires of Bataille that he write. In *Inner Experience*, Bataille announces, thereby placing the production of his own work squarely within the ontological claims it makes: "It is from a feeling of community binding me to Nietzsche that the desire to communicate arises in me, not from an isolated originality" (OC 5: 39/IE 26–27). And similarly from *Guilty*: "My life with Nietzsche as a companion is a community. My book is this community" (OC 6: 33/ON 9). Not a dialogical community of interpretation (*Auslegung*), but an affective community bound by chance, attracted to one another and the luck that configures that attraction—"Chance, it turned out, corresponded to Nietzsche's intentions more accurately than power could" (OC 6: 17/ON xxv). Bataille's books and those that read them are bound like lovers or suspended like a crowd before a dead-heat horse race entering the chute, one momentum configuring another and holding it together while luck falls. "Thus *we* are nothing, neither you nor I, beside burning words which could pass from me to you, imprinted on a page: for I would only have lived in order to write them, and, *if* it is true that they are addressed to you, you will live from having had the strength to hear them" (OC 5: 111/IE 94; em). Not a community of like minds struggling to give shape to a *Sache*, but beings bound by the passion of chance, suffering their luck as their lot.

When Nietzsche proclaims in *On the Genealogy of Morals*, "atheism and a second innocence go together,"[10] he at once condemns the theological interpretation of the world as guilty. Nothing devalues *our* insufficiency like the attempt to lie meaning into the world, denying chance, personalizing luck, thus writing it off. But a being subject to chance is acéphalic, a headless being, a being not ordered theologically, and that is to say, not ordered at all, but shot through with desire and cast into the world as one particle among others. To the same extent that Acéphale is not and cannot become a program, atheism is not a belief or a position. It concerns rather, as Nietzsche puts it, "the meaning of the earth,"[11] that is, the sense of life without transcendence, the immanence of falling luck, the exposure to love and death, ecstatic and finite existence. Bataille's community with Nietzsche is the community of those attracted by that luck, bound to one another by the passion of chance, the lucky suffering that need not make of itself a meaning, the risk and play of ecstatic insufficiency that is effortless in its beauty and cruelty and momentum. The community with Nietzsche, the ecstasy of acéphalic atheism, is the affirmation of desire and its risk, the incomprehensibility of the chance that constitutes our being: "Only when *our* response to desire remains incomprehensible is that response true. . . . *We are to the degree that we risk ourselves*. If the risk ceases, if I withdraw some aspect to keep it from changing, the resulting regularity will be misleading: I'll pass from the tragic to the ridiculous" (OC 6: 87/ON 72; em). Nothing is more ridiculous, therefore, than theology and its guilt, nothing more absurd than the façade of our most serious understanding, which serves the social order and de facto community as its justification. Atheism is a matter of play, a matter of chance, a name for the way we are played by our luck. The community with Nietzsche, the community of lovers, the tragic community, elective community—never a matter of fact, but only value, the force of attraction that makes us crazy and feverish and delivers us over to one another in tears, laughter, and orgasm. Elective community is the point of acéphalic contact.

Notes

1. On the "secret society," see Georges Bataille, "Autobiographical Note," OC 7:459–62/BR 113–17, 461–62/115–16; Maurice Blanchot, *Unavowable Community*, trans. Pierre Joris (Barrytown, NY: Station Hill, 1988), 13–14.

2. Blanchot, *Unavowable Community*, 13.

3. Acéphale lasted from 1936 through 1939, the College of Sociology from March 1936 through September 1939, and the *Somme athéologique* comprised of texts written during the period from 1937 through 1944. In fact parts of the *Somme* were written as early as 1924 but revised in 1942; the letter to Kojève, dated December 1937, appearing in the Appendix to *Guilty*, seems to be the earliest unmodified piece included in the *Somme*.

4. See Jean-Luc Nancy, *The Inoperative Community*, trans. Peter Connor, Lisa Garbus, Michael Holland, and Simona Sawhney (Minneapolis: University of Minnesota

Press, 1991); Jean-Luc Nancy, *A Finite Thinking*, ed. Simon Sparks (Stanford: Stanford University Press, 2003), 51ff. ; Denis Hollier, "Forward: Collage," *The College of Sociology*, ed. Denis Hollier (Minneapolis: University of Minnesota Press, 1988), ix.

5. "6. Take upon oneself perversion and crime, not as exclusive values, but as integrated within the human totality" (OC 2: 275/BR 121).

6. "[W]e find here the stance with which French sociology confronts the Marxist trend. For Marxists society is defined by a conflict (class struggle). For French sociology, society is defined by what it calls "cohesions." See Mauss apropos Durkheim: He " 'strongly objected to any war of the classes or nations' " (CS 140–41/406).

7. As reported by Klossowski; see CS 586–87/389.

8. The tragic man is the one who "becomes aware of human existence. He sees the violent and contradictory forces that stir him; he knows he is prey to human absurdity, prey to the absurdity of nature, but he affirms this reality which has left him no outlet other than crime" (CS 272/147).

9. That limit is impossible because it is only in being undone. It cannot be thought of as an exterior boundary sustaining an in tact interior; its is rather the limit that transverses or radiates from finitude, rather than encompasses it. It is a living limit—with all its vicissitudes—not the limit of death.

10. Friedrich Nietzsche, *On the Genealogy of Morals*, trans. Walter Kaufmann and R. J. Hollingdale (New York: Vintage, 1989), 91.

11. Friedrich Nietzsche, *Thus Spoke Zarathustra*, trans. Walter Kaufmann (New York: Penguin, 1966), 13.

CHAPTER THREE

The Horror of Liberty

Stuart Kendall

The true passion of the twentieth century is servitude.

—Albert Camus, *The Rebel*

I am not speaking to those who cling to their servitude.

—Georges Bataille in a letter to Albert Camus, 1950

By 1947, the world had become sadistic and the Divine Marquis was back in print. In our world of hook-ups, internet porn, and cheap thrills, it is easy to forget that Sade was once unobtainable. His books were banned and burned even by the butchers of the revolution. His manuscripts were stolen from his cell at the Bastille or burned by his son (facing a terrible anxiety of influence). *The 120 Days of Sodom*—"the book which signified to its author, and was the first to signify, the full horror of liberty" (Bataille, OC 9: 243/LE 108)—lingered in legends, not libraries.

When Apollinaire wrote about Sade, Sade's books were the rarest of rarities. Maurice Heine and then Gilbert Lily brought Sade to light during the 1920s, but the works did not begin to enjoy even small circulation for another twenty years. The "greatest" generation, in short, was the first to read Sade. Critically, Klossowski, Blanchot, Paulhan, de Beauvoir, Adorno, and Bataille made the work public for the first time in the immediate aftermath of the greatest political and social disaster the world had yet seen.

Sade's thought went public just in time. Bataille: "We need a thought which does not fall apart in the face of horror" (OC 8: 10/AS 2: 14); "Could minds ready to draw back from horror possibly measure up to the problems put in front of them by the present times? Accursed times par excellence" (OC 8: 13/AS 2: 18). Not Sartre's *temps modernes*; Bataille's *temps maudits*. "The depth of the horror of things proposes itself to human beings as the truth to uncover" (OC 11: 264). For Bataille, Kurtz' breathless, stuttering end is the beginning of modern thought. The term "horror" deserves an explication that unfortunately exceeds our present concerns. Behind the word one sees the capitalist rape of colonialism, the absolute negation of the Dadaists, and Nietzsche's phrase, God is dead. For Bataille, "horror" signals a state of equivocal and ambiguous fascination commingling terror and delight: "If they horrify us, objects that otherwise would have no meaning take on the highest value in our eyes" (OC 8: 90/AS 2: 104).

In his postwar writings, Bataille formulates the challenge presented to thought by World War II—the challenge of the thought of horror—over and over again, and with urgency. "It's a matter of using up *without war* that unprecedented accumulation [of wealth], which has turned the whole world into a colossal powder keg" (OC 8: 454/AS 3: 428). "The necessity of giving economic, military, and demographic questions a correct solution, if we are not to give up the hope of maintaining the present civilization" (OC 8: 13/AS 2: 18). "How on the one hand do we sever the impulse of revolt from the contrary inclination to force others to our will? And how, on the other, do we avoid the dangers of verbal incitement, of an impotent multiplicity of opinions in which language can no longer measure up to the reality of action, gets carried away, becomes frustrated and finally exhausts itself?" (OC 12: 158).

The task set before Bataille's thinking by World War II is thus several fold: first, to regulate the expenditure of wealth—natural and human—*without war*; second, to balance individual passion—the impulse of revolt—and social responsibility; and third, to express ourselves without provoking others in a thoughtless manner and without exhausting the content of our own speech. The root of all of these problems may be traced to our ultimate freedom: our freedom to wantonly produce and to spend, our freedom of expression, and the freedom of our passions.

The horror of liberty is the paradox of autonomy and responsibility; it is the problem most violently stated and demonstrated by the life and writings of the Marquis de Sade: how can we live our life fully, as fully as our pleasures—unleashed, in all their mad delirium—will carry us, without fear of our final annihilation, of personal and collective suicide? What kind of life can we expect if our passions carry us beyond respect for the categorical imperative, beyond identification with the other, into the realm of absolute autonomy? Can life be at once autonomous and viable? Sade's thought goes furthest in thinking the horror of liberty, and it becomes an essential, though often secret, reference for Bataille.[1] The exploration and revelation of this secret will be the purpose of the pages that follow.

The volumes of *The Accursed Share* constitute Bataille's systematic response to the challenge of horror. They are books of broad scope and intricate design and boast a primarily ethical and political purpose (OC 7: 23/AS 1: 13). The fundamental principle is clearly stated at the beginning of the first volume: "It is not necessity, but it's opposite, 'luxury,' which presents living matter and human kind with their fundamental problems" (OC 7: 20/AS 1: 10). "The living organism, in a situation determined by the play of energy on the surface of the globe, ordinarily receives more energy than is necessary for maintaining life; the excess energy (wealth) can be used for the growth of the system (e.g. an organism); if the system can no longer grow, or if the excess cannot be completely absorbed in its growth, it must necessarily be lost without profit; it must be spent, willingly or not, gloriously or catastrophically" (OC 7: 29/AS 1: 21). Understanding expenditure in these terms requires one to measure *all* forms of expenditure, not simply those forms that traditionally fall under the heading of political economy. Eroticism and intoxication, the social spectacles of sporting events and organized religion, our arts and entertainments, our wars—each in its way fulfills the purposes of glorious or catastrophic expenditure. "A nun intoxicated by God, a coquette intoxicated with clothes come to seek in the same way for the meaning of that which is perhaps at bottom only a senseless passion" (OC 8: 352/AS 3: 313). Expenditure.

Despite decades of rumination and writing, the project remained (and remains) unfinished. In his preface, Bataille tells us he wrote and rewrote drafts of the first volume on and off for eighteen years before publishing it; his manuscripts reveal that he wrote and rewrote the second volume, *Eroticism*, for close to ten; he never published the third volume.[2]

The Accursed Share came together only after the war. The first volume, *Consumption*, can be traced from Bataille's notes on the pineal eye and the Aztecs in the late 1920s to articles of the 1930s such as "The Notion of Expenditure" and "Celestial Bodies," and finally through successive drafts written during the war and immediately thereafter.

The second, *Eroticism*, began in notes for an *Erotic Phenomenology* (1939) but was transformed in the late 1940s by Bataille's renewed interest in the Marquis de Sade. In 1947, he announced a book entitled *Sade and the Essence of Eroticism*, in 1949, *Sexual Anguish: From Sexual Anguish to the Misfortune of Hiroshima*. A year later, he wrote *The History of Eroticism* but abandoned it.

The *History* nevertheless provided an ur-text for *Eroticism*, published in 1957: a book that proposes the formula, "eroticism is assenting to life up to the point of death" (OC 10: 17), a thought worthy of and inspired by Sade.

The third volume of the series, *Sovereignty*, originated in the late 1940s, in outlines for a book titled *Albert Camus: Politics and Morality*. The project evolved from articles on Camus published in *Critique* and then in drafts and outlines under new titles: *Nietzsche and Communism*, *Sovereignty and Revolt*, and finally *Sovereignty*. In 1956, Bataille published sections of the *Sovereignty* draft in *Botteghe Oscure*: the manuscript carved up and effectively cast out, incomplete. *Albert Camus* had been effaced by the year its subject won the Nobel Prize. Nevertheless, while Bataille never published *Sovereignty*, other than in pieces, he did publish the essays and reviews from which the text draws its momentum. No final priority, however, can be established here: *Sovereignty* undoubtedly was intended to correct whatever real or imagined faults Bataille perceived in the ur-texts. A game of mirrors.

Bataille's *Sovereignty*, again, and this is the point to be developed and understood, originates in a series of essays and reviews on Albert Camus' novels, plays, and essays from the late 1940s and early 1950s.[3] The major concerns of the text, its major questions, and its primary orientation can be traced to these essays and reviews, which also help us understand the place of the text—the place in which Bataille was attempting to situate his thought—in the debates and dialogues of its time: which is to say primarily in the debate with, for, and against the place of communism in postwar-French society; and, too, in the debate as to whether and to what extent communism could be a humanism.[4]

By situating his thought in proximity to Camus, and Camus' Nietzscheanism, Bataille was also situating himself in proximity to and distinction from both André Breton and Jean-Paul Sartre. While Bataille found himself "more often in agreement with Breton than with Camus" (OC 12: 156)—and, of course, in constant and violent disagreement with Sartre—Camus' agenda and orientation, his questions, references, and methods, signal the basis of what Bataille characterized as a "true friendship."[5]

On March 5, 1949, Bataille wrote to Camus from Vézèley: "I'm thinking of collecting a series of studies on morality setting out from your position (which has much more sense in that it is actually what unites most people. I'm not talking to those who cling to their servitude)."[6] The outlined series of studies included several on Camus as well as essays on Sade, Simone Weil, Michelet, and Baudelaire. (Bataille later published several of these essays in *Literature and Evil*.)

Bataille locates himself "near" Camus' position, though with marked points of difference, of which both men were aware (OC 11: 410). In his letter of March 5, Bataille notes Camus' recent remarks about the Marquis de

Sade, remarks that favored Nietzsche's thought to Sade's, but Bataille places himself in closer proximity to Sade. In the remarks in question, in response to an interviewer's comparison of Camus' "Apollonian" Nietzscheanism and Bataille's "Dionysian" Nietzscheanism, Camus said: "I argue for happiness, not ecstasy, that's the difference [between Bataille and I]."[7] In his letter, Bataille nevertheless insisted on their proximity: "I think you imagine me agreeing with cruelty, while only the horror of all condemnation, punishment, and judgment, makes me search for a morality beyond justice."[8]

The proximity and difference between Camus and Bataille—the shared search for a morality beyond the law, whether Nietzschean happiness or Sadean ecstasy—has yet to be studied in any depth, and we can only signal it here. To situate Bataille in proximity to Camus in these years is to situate him on the side of Nietzsche against (Sartre's) communism and against surrealist artistic "inconsequentiality" (see OC 5: 171/IE 148).[9] This is the fundamental theme and approach of both Camus' *The Rebel* and Bataille's *Sovereignty*. To distinguish Bataille's Nietzscheanism from Camus' is to distinguish the influence of Sade from that of Nietzsche, and we will do so below.

In 1952, Bataille defended Camus against Jeanson and Sartre in the controversy over *The Rebel*, but Camus nevertheless receded as a direct referent in Bataille's writing. Notes and drafts for *Albert Camus: Politics and Morality* became *Nietzsche and Communism* and, eventually, *Sovereignty*, a book that Bataille, in the end, did not publish. Only the questions, the problems remained.

For Bataille, speaking of "today," in *Sovereignty*, there were "only two admissible positions remaining in the world. Communism, reducing each man to an *object* . . . and the attitude of Nietzsche, liberating the *subject* at the same time from the limits imposed by the past and by the objectivity of the present" (OC 8: 402/AS 3: 368).

Capitalist democracies, it should be remembered, had been ruled out of European politics between the wars: this by default of democratic rule by the mob and its attendant and inevitable lowering of standards; its politicians ultimately no better than carnival barkers. Fascism, socialism, and communism were perceived to be the only viable options. Fascism had shown its stripes in Ethiopia and Spain even before the invasion of Poland. (Bataille's analysis, notably in the pages of *La Critique sociale*, had been apt and even prescient.) Communism in the form of Stalinism reached a kind of pinnacle in its purges. The Soviet state had been bitterly denounced by André Gide in his *Return from the U.S.S.R.* (1936).

Yet the lure of communism remained in a way that that of fascism did—and could—not. It had been the political romance of a (naïve?) generation and, Marxist or not, its basic assertion was undeniably appealing.[10] For Bataille, again in *Sovereignty*, "communism claims, in the name of each human being, the right to live" (OC 8: 399/AS 3: 365). Colette Peignot and Simone Weil—to name only these two profound influences on Bataille's life and thought—were among those idealists of their generation who followed this dream to the Soviet Union during the 1920s. (Both returned in broken health.) Bataille's enthusiasm for the cause, however, never carried him away.

In fact, Bataille's early and ever-lasting conception of communism was as an administrative state run by bureaucratic functionaries, and as a Statist religion. Its image can be gleaned from a passage in his 1928 article "Extinct America." Bataille wrote of the Inca that they were "an entire people [who] obeyed the orders of functionaries the way one obeys the officers in a barracks. Work was distributed, marriages decided by the functionaries. The land and crops belonged to the State. Festivities were religious festivals of the State." He went on to say that "this organization should not be confused with that of present day communism: it differed essentially because it rested on heredity and the hierarchy of classes" (OC 1: 153). Heredity and hierarchy separate the Inca system from that of the classless society, but this distinction hardly favors either system.

If, in the early 1930s, Bataille participated in Boris Souvarine's Democratic Communist Circle and published in *La Critique sociale*—"Like the rest of my generation, I had to lean toward Marxism," he says—his essential view of Stalinist communism hardly wavered from "Extinct America" to the volumes of *The Accursed Share* (written twenty years later; OC 8: 404/AS 3: 370–71). If Bataille "lean[ed]" toward Marxism, he did not lean far. The Democratic Communist Circle was outspokenly unorthodox in its agitation for a non-Soviet communism. Boris Souvarine, its founder and head, was both an early and ambitious Marxist militant within the Soviet Union and an early and ambitious dissident from it.[11] Leaning to the side of Souvarine set Bataille in opposition to the pro-Stalin French Communist Party, an opposition from which he would never waiver.

But Bataille nevertheless leaned. He leaned, with the rest of his generation, because communism is a humanism, because it "claims, in the name of each human being, the right to live." It strives to abolish the oppression of man by man and to permit each man to live in conditions of equality with his fellows. Bataille advances this notion respectfully: this is why communism is "admissible." But his thought cannot sustain the thought of equality. In *Sovereignty*, Bataille radicalizes the notion of equality, pushing it to its breaking point: absolute equality must necessarily obliterate individualism.

It does so logically: conditions of absolute equality forbid the (Hegelian) process of recognition through which individual identities are internally established and externally differentiated. Absolute equality suspends subjectivity in a state of indistinction: the necessary indistinction of a classless society.

The idealized body of the communist state is, in the end, a kind of "undifferentiated humanity" (OC 8: 322, 341/AS 3: 281, 301–02). A classless society denies—offers no mechanism for—the humanity of its members. "Humanity" requires distinction; it requires man to distinguish himself not only from his fellows but from his own animal nature. "The principle of equivalence is contrary to the essence of a species constituted in the ceaseless exclusion, in the malediction, of that which it placed lower than the stage it reached" (OC 8: 373/AS 3: 337).

Racism arises from this morass: in search of our own identity, we condemn the *inhumanity* of the other (OC 8: 373/AS 3: 337). Man's desperation to distinguish himself from his animal nature fixates on the animality of the other, the trace of which is inescapable. Our will to degradation, to self-denigration or self-denial, takes the opposite tack: foregrounding our own animality, we let nameless others take us as nothing more than a body.

The struggle for recognition is essential to the maintenance of our identity, of our basic humanity. Communism and the will to equality, however, stands opposed to it. For Bataille, and "without qualification, the communist movement is essentially a machine for eliminating the difference between men: everything called 'distinction' must disappear forever, overwhelmed, crushed in the cogs of this machine" (OC 8: 385/AS 3: 350). Bataille's vision of a classless society is a vision of indistinction; the subjects of communism absent figures.

> If every man is destined for complete nondifferentiation, he abolishes all alienation in himself. He stops being a thing. Or rather, he attains thinghood so fully that he is no longer a thing. In becoming, by means of an *all*-around qualification, a fulfillment of the thing, a perfection of utility, hence of servility, he stops being reducible to a *particular* element, as things are. A thing is *alienated*, it always exists *in relation* to something else, but if it is connected with *all* that is possible, it is no longer determinate, nor alienated; it is not any more a thing than would be what I imagine in front of me, which I could not name, and which being neither a table nor a stream could be a stream, a table, or whatever one wanted. (OC 8: 341/AS 3: 302)

An utterly indifferent mass.

Bataille's critical gesture here resembles his "mimicry" of absolute knowledge in *Inner Experience*. In that case, Bataille pushed absolute knowledge to the point of absolute nonknowledge: here he pushes the absolute equality of individuals to the point of their absolute nondifferentiation, to the collapse of identity.[12]

The lure of equality remains the promise of freedom, the freedom of the autonomous subject. And the subject wagers himself on, and hence also postpones himself for, this "humanist" ideal. The subject of communism renounces his autonomous, or sovereign, subjectivity in favor of the sovereign *end* of a free humanity. Under feudal conditions, only the sovereign possessed sovereignty, only the sovereign was autonomous and free (and only the sovereign paid the price of that sovereignty). The bourgeois and liberal revolutions of Britain, France, the United States, and Russia (as well as the earlier Protestant revolution of Bavaria) evidenced the mass rejection of this organization in favor of a redistribution of wealth and responsibility. No longer would the sovereign in these states hold a monopoly on autonomous subjectivity. No longer would the sovereign hold a monopoly on the expenditure of superfluous wealth. Revolution, by this logic, is rejection: it is an expression of revulsion in regard to the sovereign's willingness to squander wealth.

Under feudal conditions man ideally identifies with the sovereign: the sovereign represents the autonomous freedom that the subject longs to possess but does not. Under communism, the sovereign is (theoretically) absent; the subjects of communism identify instead with the humanist ideal. The humanist ideal—the "equal" individual of the classless society—is the ideal product of the state; and communism, in its search for the ideal relation of man to man, zero to zero, subordinates all men equally to the needs of the state and subordinates the state to the demand for the production of its ideal. The demand for the production of the ideal must first however fulfill the ideal of production. Again, the subject wagers himself, renounces his sovereignty. "For the irreducible desire that man *passionately*, *capriciously* is, communism substituted those of our needs that can be reconciled with a life entirely taken up with producing" (OC 8: 353/AS 3: 315).

Bataille ultimately sees little difference between capitalism and communism (OC 8: 346/AS 3: 306). Both systems subordinate the lives of workers to the need for production, and both subordinate production not to the senseless expenditure that characterized the aristocratic sovereigns of the past but to the "responsible" accumulation of wealth. The life of the worker is subordinate to the production of wealth that is accumulated rather than spent. Both capitalism and communism, considered as political systems in actual fact rather than as theoretical constructs, evidence a mass rejection of aristocratic autonomy and aristocratic expenditure.

In Bataille's vision, communism fulfills the ideals of the bankrupt (Western) civilization: subjectification, productivity, utility. His communism, fundamentally, is an intensified state capitalism: it reduces man to a means, a tool for the production of an ideal humanity. His communism is an "improvement" upon capitalism. Communism is capitalism cleansed of the limiting force of individualism: individual caprice, individual inequality, individual waste (OC 8: 333/AS 3: 293). "The individuals' freedom in the bourgeois world is the freedom not to be reasonable. But in socialism only the collectivity is concerned, and by definition the great number is consistent with reason; in principle, socialist rigor alone is consistent with reason" (OC 8: 335/AS 3: 296). Communism, in other words, is rationalism; indeed it is the most rigorous form of political rationalism.

The revolutionary rejection of sovereign expenditure is also, and significantly, the rejection of sovereign autonomy, of sovereign subjectivity. Communist society, like capitalist society, is a society of things rather than a society of subjectivities. It is a society of subjects subordinate to the production and accumulation of the state, which is to say a society not of people but of tools for the state. And it is a society of subjects willingly subordinating themselves to objects which can be accumulated, which "last," rather than of sovereign subjectivities living in and for the moment. As long as subjectivity is "under the domination of the object, [it] does not yet exist for itself and rediscovers itself only in the dazzle of the moment" (OC 8: 381/AS 3: 345). Without the reciprocal recognition that is provided by a sovereign, self-discovery occurs *materially* in the system of objects.[13]

The communist denial of man is thus at least twofold: communist man is subordinate to the humanist ideal and communist man is subordinate to material objects, to the things he produces. If sovereignty—sovereign autonomy—is the "primordial condition of each human being" (OC 8: 323, 325/AS 3: 281, 284), and sovereignty reflects "the use of resources for non-productive ends" (OC 8: 322/AS 3: 280), then communism, for Bataille, is the "most active contradiction" to sovereignty (OC 8: 305/AS 3: 261). The phrase "active contradiction" here stands out in Hegelian splendor: communism negates sovereignty, recuperating the human freedom it represents for the "larger" humanist ideal. For Bataille, "being more or less truly a man depends on the degree of sovereign dignity that we attain" (OC 8: 381/AS 3: 345). Communism denies man access to sovereignty and therefore denies man access to his humanity.

Here again, horror. "Horror is the limit of the individual. What it proclaims is man's reduction to thinghood" (OC 8: 271/AS 3: 223). Communism reduces each man to the status of an object, to the status of an individual without identity, a means to the end of the state. Communism, in the end, is an activism, an activism of identification with objects and ideas, accompanied by an attendant and necessary disconnection between thought and life.

If, as the essential precept of *The Accursed Share* maintains, luxury rather than necessity presents mankind with its fundamental problems, and if communism is a system of sovereignty denied—and hence also a denial of the luxurious expenditure that sovereignty entails—communism cannot present contemporary man with a satisfying solution to his fundamental problem. In contrast to the communist world of sovereignty denied, Bataille proposes a Nietzschean vision of sovereignty affirmed.[14]

For Bataille, Nietzsche is "on the side of *those who give*, and his thought cannot be isolated from the movement that tried to promote, in opposition to the bourgeoisie, which accumulates, a resumption of life in the moment . . . Nietzsche's gift is the gift that nothing limits: it is the sovereign gift, that of subjectivity" (OC 8: 404/AS 3: 370). Nietzsche's gift is the gift of subjectivity. What does this mean?

Nietzsche's life's work might be summarized in two questions: Can life be lived in coincidence with thought? And: can thought be forged in such a way as to coincide with life? Everything else is analysis, elaboration, and experiment. If Nietzsche formulated a new morality, beyond the law, beyond good and evil, if he forged a new style of writing and interpretation, a style supple and subtle enough to suspend the weight of Hellenic metaphors and to render reading operatic dance, without recourse to the God of metaphysics, he did so to carry us beyond ourselves, to birth a new vision of humanity.

Nietzsche does not reject science so much as he rejects scientific reductionism; he refuses Descartes' first principle. A world so manifestly complicated as this one cannot be understood without recourse to complexity, yet the Cartesian reduction leaves scientists only simples without synthesis. Moreover, Nietzsche's thought on endeavors to be systematic without elaborating a reductive system: the reader must elaborate the system on his or her own, by working through the connections set forth in different parts of his text.[15]

Nietzsche's rejection of traditional morality, of Western religions, and of Christianity in particular, follows from the religious rejection of this world, of this life. Christianity, in his reading, is a religion of renunciation rather than of the gift. In Christianity, Christ alone possesses the sovereign power to give his life for another's. The peasants in the pews merely renounce their lives, and their savings, in hopes of something better later on. Earthly aspirations to Christlike self-sacrifice constitute the lives of saints.[16]

Inserting his thought between the gods of contemporary culture, science, and religion, Nietzsche appeals to a *complex* image of the world and of man. Bataille summarizes Nietzsche's "humanism":

> The human world is finally but a hybrid of transgression and prohibition, so that the word *human* always denotes a system of contradictory impulses, some depending on those that they neutral-

> ize but never entirely eliminate, and others delivering a violence mixed with the certainty of peacefulness that will follow. Hence the word *human* never denotes, as the naïve imagine, a stabilized position, but rather an apparently precarious equilibrium that distinguishes the human quality. The word man is always connected with an *impossible* combination of movements that destroy one another. (OC 8: 378/AS 3: 342)

In Bataille's summary, Nietzsche's vision of humanity entails the endless destruction of man.

Bataille does not simply agree with what Nietzsche says; he is not merely influenced by him. Of his relation to Nietzsche, he writes: "I am the only one who presents himself not as a commentator on Nietzsche, but as being the same as him . . . [My] thought places itself in the same conditions as Nietzsche placed his" (OC 8: 401/AS 3: 367). Bataille's language, here as always, is precise, even in its complexities. Bataille presents "himself" not his thought. Bataille, for whom "each thing is the parody of another, or the same thing in a deceptive form," presents himself as the same as Nietzsche. As if to clarify this statement, he tell us that his "thought places itself in the same conditions as Nietzsche placed his" (OC 1: 81/VE 5).For Bataille, thought is nothing if it is not situated (see OC 7: 285/TR 9). Thinking is in no way distinct from living. In *Beyond Good and Evil*, Nietzsche phrases the problem in these words: "To understand one another, it is not enough that one use the same words; one also has to use the same words for the same species of inner experience; in the end one has to have one's experience in *common*."[17]

Phantasm? Biologism? Naïve materialism? Bataille grafts this idea into the marrow of his existence.[18] "My life, in the company of Nietzsche, is a community, my book is this community" (OC 6: 33/ON 9). When Bataille writes *On Nietzsche* his writing dissolves into a tissue of quotations; his words indistinguishable from Nietzsche's. He claims to be conscious of the extent to which his thought diverges from Nietzsche's, a divergence he characterizes as "infidelity" (OC 8: 401/AS 3: 367), but he nevertheless speaks in Nietzsche's tongue, hides himself behind Nietzsche's words. An unfaithful other to Nietzsche, he is also, in his way, an other to himself.[19] Bataille's practice here should be understood as in keeping with the twin precepts of modern literature, Rimbaud's assertion that "I is an other" and Lautréamont's dictum that "plagiarism is necessary, progress implies it" (*Poésies*).

"With a few exceptions, my company on earth is that of Nietzsche . . . Nietzsche is only one in solidarity with me—saying *we*. If *community* does not exist, Nietzsche is a philosopher" (OC 6: 27/ON 3). If Nietzsche is a philosopher, his words are mere words, they designate concepts, thoughts about life, not *of* it. In Bataille's reading, "Nietzsche wrote 'with his blood': criticizing or better, *experiencing* him cannot be done without bleeding in one's turn" (OC 6: 15/ON xxii). "I could only write the book I planned about him *with my life*" (OC 6: 17/ON xxvi). Bataille's assertion, then, and his experience, returns: Nietzsche's gift is the gift of subjectivity.

Nietzsche writes with his blood so that we may live. His writings betray an energy, a pace, a multilayered complexity, that inhabits us with the powerful force of an unexpected contagion. His writings make demands on our attention, but the shape that this attention assumes is their offering. Reading Nietzsche means making him our own, animating his thought with our blood, our passion.

Communism proposes a rationalism, a humanism, an activism. Communism reduces man to a thing, a thing in pursuit of the humanist ideal, a thing in service to the production of the state. Between Nietzsche and communism, the primary comparison and point of contrast—in the two long quotes above—is between the final elimination of "equality" in the classless society and the tumultuous, ebullience of Nietzschean subjectivity. Both visions entail the destruction of man. In communism, man is eliminated in the servile and abstract whisper of the humanist ideal. In Bataille's Nietzschean vision, a sovereign subjectivity boils over: the self of self-sacrifice.

Bataille entitled his 1947 review of Albert Camus' novel *The Plague*, "The Morality of Unhappiness." It begins: "It is paradoxical in principle to link Sade and Albert Camus" (OC 11: 237). The rudiments of this linkage have been sketched above. The essay proposes the following formula in regard to World War II. "The evil is in the fact of the S.S. of the camps, who acquired power through murder, who increased the power of the regime they served through murder . . . The evil is in the fact that passion had been made servile, made to serve a legal power, which can only exert power coldly. Pure passion is naturally rebellious, and never wants legal power: in general, it even does not want power as an end, but ruins it, limitless expenditure rapidly destroying power" (OC 11: 248–49). The rebel, the man in revolt, expends power, which is to say, surrenders it. This is the gift of subjectivity. The gift of subjectivity is not subjectification; nor does it create subjects. The gift of subjectivity offers subjectivity to the world.

In these turns, Bataille's thought is Nietzsche's, but his argument, significantly and surprisingly, is Sade's.[20] And he uses this argument *against* Nietzsche: "Nietzsche's mistake, in my view, is essentially having poorly understood the opposition of sovereignty to power" (OC 8: 401/AS 3: 367). Nietzsche, in this reading, and in Bataille's perspective, insufficiently emphasizes the necessity of sacrifice. The will to power, in Nietzsche's terms, expresses itself against resistances; but, for Bataille, the will to power expends itself in this expression.

Sade—more so than anyone else—takes thought to the extreme limit, to *this* limit, of autonomy. His sovereigns sacrifice themselves to their passions and are prepared to make the ultimate sacrifice for the passions of another. Sade's sovereigns model, for Bataille, an ethics of autonomy, an ethics without identification, a thought beyond the categorical imperative. Sade's sovereigns are in this way his saints. The primary value in Sade's system is the value of nature, which is to say of energy in the raw.[21]

Bataille's contribution to the history of ideas is not simply a thought; it is a method of mingling thought and life, and it is the same as Nietzsche's, or it endeavors to be, with essential differences, essential betrayals. Bataille, after all, is not a philosopher. Idea men and women, philosophers create concepts. They strive to be useful, for their thought to boast coherence and application. They continue and contribute to a discussion that has been on-going since the dawn of Western civilization. Speaking to them, in *Method of Meditation*, to Heidegger in particular, Bataille proposes another alternative: "I am not a philosopher, but a saint, maybe a madman" (OC 5: 218/US 285). His ethics of autonomy proposes a self that dies.[22]

Notes

1. Marking something of the difference between the immediate postwar era and our own, we might observe that while the thought of the postwar era grappled with an all-too-visible range of horrors, ours is an era of compartmentalized depravity, of infinitely isolated degradation. Sade's Shilling is no longer a single geographical location; it is any place of sexual license in hiding, hidden not only from our friends and families but often from ourselves, our personal narrative of self-recognition and identity. Our lusts are lost to our sense of self. There are no tears to the Eros of *Sex in the City*. Ours is a culture of desire beyond representation.

2. The English language versions of these books tell none of this story. Their notes mark none of the origins, unfinished chapters, or omitted materials, the parts published elsewhere. Bataille's draft of *Sovereignty*, for example, ends with the essay on Kafka now in *Literature and Evil*.

3. Bataille referenced Camus frequently in his postwar writings and devoted several long essays and reviews to his work. They are: "La Morale du malheur: *La Peste*," *Critique* 13–14 (juin–juillet 1947); "Le Bonheur, le malheur et la morale d'Albert Camus," *Critique* 33 (février 1949); "Le Temps de la révolte," *Critique* 55 (décembre 1951)/AM 158–76; "L'Affaire de *L'Homme révolté*," *Critique* 67 (décembre 1952). The dialogue with Camus' work that motivates Bataille's *Sovereignty* can also be read between the lines of "Nonknowledge and Rebellion" (OC 8: 210–13/US 129–32) among other pieces.

4. Michel Surya, *La Révolution rêvée* (Paris: Fayard, 2005).

5. Georges Bataille, *Choix de lettres: 1917–1962,* ed. Michel Surya (Paris: Gallimard, 1997), 394.

6. Ibid.

7. Claudine Chonez, "Portrait d'Albert Camus," *Paru* (octobre 1948).

8. Bataille, *Choix de lettres,* 394.

9. On this point, it is unfortunate that Michael Richardson anthologized, in *The Absence of Myth* and in however disorganized a fashion, Bataille's writings on surrealism rather than assembling a collection including his writings on existentialism and on Camus, among many other significant postwar essays.

10. Just as fascism effectively removed itself from consideration as a political option during the generation following the First World War, communism removed itself in the generation following the Second. The word has come to mean something other than what it seems to mean; it carries a weight that it cannot bear and therefore fails to sustain itself as the emblem of either a politics or an ethics in anything other than theoretical discussions.

11. On Boris Souvarine, see in particular Anne Roche, *Boris Souvarine et 'La Critique sociale'* (Paris: La Découverte, 1990).

12. See also Bataille's poem "Undifferentiated Being Is Nothing" (OC 3: 367–76), originally published in *Botteghe Oscure* in 1954, the year he wrote *Sovereignty*.

13. Bataille's (unpublished) reflections along these lines directly anticipate Guy Debord, *The Society of the Spectacle* (see Bataille, OC 8: 384–85/AS 3: 349–51, in particular).

14. Bataille's relationship to Nietzsche has been picked over by scholars; we will only elaborate its essential features here. François Warin's *Nietzsche et Bataille: la parodie à l'infini* (Paris: Presses universitaires de France, 1994) provides the most complete and compelling account.

15. Here I am following Laurence Lampert, *Nietzsche's Task* (New Haven: Yale University Press, 2001).

16. For more on this idea see Edith Wyschogrod, *Saints and Postmodernism: Revisioning Moral Philosophy* (Chicago: University of Chicago Press, 1990).

17. Friedrich Nietzsche, *Beyond Good and Evil,* trans. Walter Kaufmann (New York: Vintage, 1966), sec. 268.

18. Pierre Klossowski has studied this aspect of Nietzsche's thought more insistently than anyone else in his book *Nietzsche and the Vicious Circle* (1969). Denis Hollier has elaborated this aspect of Bataille's proximity to and use of Nietzsche's thought in "De l'au-delà de Hegel à l'absence de Nietzsche" in *Bataille à Cerisy* (Paris: UGE, 1973), 75–97.

19. It is in this precise sense that we should understand the following statement of Blanchot's from *The Unavowable Community,* trans. Pierre Joris (Barrytown: Station Hill, 1988), 4: "Bataille's own infidelity, the necessary mutation which forced him to be unceasingly other while remaining himself and to develop other exigencies which resisted becoming united either because they responded to the changes of history or to experiences, which, not wanting to repeat themselves, had become exhausted."

20. It is also the *Tao te Ching*, trans. Stephen Mitchell (New York: Harper and Row, 1988). Compare: "When two great forces oppose each other, the victory

will go to the one who knows how to yield" (sec. 69); "The Master says: I let go of the law, and people become honest. I let go of economics and people become prosperous. I let go of religion, and people become serene. I let go of the desire for the common good, and the good becomes common as grass" (sec. 57).

21. This thought is of course a substantial betrayal of Sade. Sade's kingdom is one in which men and women struggle for domination (not recognition) until they are extinguished by a stronger, more cunning, individual. Here again Bataille betrays the thought by pushing it to its limit, to the point of life at the point of or against death.

22. The "self-that-dies" is, of course, the central figure of Bataille's oeuvre. It originates in "Sacrifices" (OC 1: 89–96/VE 130–36).

CHAPTER FOUR

Of Goods and Things: Reflections on an Ethics of Community

Chris Gemerchak

> That's the trouble, gentlemen, that there exists something which is dearer to almost every man than his greatest good . . . that there exists one most valuable good . . . which is greater and more desirable than all other goods, and for the sake of which a man, if need be, is ready to challenge all laws, that is to say, reason, honour, peace, prosperity—in short all those excellent and useful things, provided he can obtain that primary and most desirable good which is dearer to him than anything in the world.
>
> —Fyodor Dostoevsky, *Notes from the Underground*

"Does Bataille have an ethics?" This was the question posed to me some time ago. It was the last question to the final lecture of a weekend saturated with lectures. It was hot: Faulkner-hot. In view from the viscid lecture chamber was a shaded courtyard where chilled white wine and beer and fresh air for the smokers beckoned. So I did what under the circumstances I believe all present save one hoped I would do, which was to execute a quick and somewhat artful dodge—an attempt at a joke, a rather obvious reference to Nietzsche, a suggestion that we look again at Mauss, and thank you for your challenging questions. This approach may have expedited our exit from the room but was hardly satisfactory, not to mention that there were several legitimate answers available. For instance, I could have viably claimed that

Bataille assimilated the wisdom of the underground man who realized the inhumanity of subjecting oneself to reason and mathematics, calculation and prosperity, and who asserted the positive value of letting pure caprice and whimsical desire command one's actions, even if—no, precisely *because*—it goes against reason and common sense. Alternatively, I could have asserted that the foundation of Bataille's ethics rests on a refusal to submit to the homogeneous economy of goods insofar as that is to forfeit the fullness of our humanity, that one should not treat others as things insofar as that is to turn oneself into a thing among things, self-same, separate and isolated. Neither response would have been wrong, but neither do they get to the obscure heart of the matter—the very obscurity of which is why it was and remains a very challenging question, one that has stayed with me ever since that sweltry afternoon. For while it may be true that there are obvious answers, it is not necessarily the case that they do justice to the question, or even understand the question in a deep sense.

On the one hand then, it is possible to specify clearly Bataille's views concerning ethics or morality as those terms are commonly understood: namely, as concerning the deliberative choices of a subjective agent, an individual who autonomously determines the best course of action in the interest of the greatest good and according to existing norms. For it is precisely this style of normative, utilitarian ethics that Bataille will challenge on the grounds that it is inadequate to the breadth and ambiguity of life. And this is because every term involved in such an ethics—*deliberation* and *action*, but particularly *individual*, *interest*, *good,* and *should*—is representative of the very type of humanist ideology and representational thinking that Bataille sees not only as distorting but also as alienating with regard to the human province. This is not to suggest that Bataille advocates an unrealistic, anarchistic gesture of eliminating morality full stop. In fact the existence of traditional morality is rather convenient in terms of having something against which one can resist. What he contests rather is the hegemony of an ethics that adheres to the principle of reason, which, as he asserts frequently, comes down to the calculations of interest for the good of the individual or a community of individuals and is oriented toward survival in the future rather than life in the present. If he is to contest the ethical perspective that guarantees the sovereign rights of these terms—'individual' and 'community,' 'good' and 'interest'—then the first step is to undermine the stability of these terms themselves.

To approach the core of Bataille's thought with respect to being "ethical"—or *ethical being*—we will thus follow Bataille's methodology as he tries to unearth the component elements of traditional ethics from their sedimentation. This method involves a double gesture. The first move is a radical questioning—or better, putting at risk—of the ethical individual, the humanist subject (individual or group) as the paradigm of an ethical being.[1] That which undermines the individual perspective, and thus is at the core of his ethical thought, is a moment of communication, an "inner experience" (*l'expérience intérieure*) that reveals the existence of community. This will become clearer as we continue. For now let us say that his new ground and paradigm of ethical thought will be community. The second move then, as just suggested, will be to rethink this alternative "ground" of ethics and to rethink "the Good" which is at stake, a task that will engage us in an exploration of his thought concerning the transformation of communal being, the being of community.

No Interest in the Individual

Bataille was infamous for the lengths to which he would go to undermine our habitual perspectives, and the fundamental target at which his various excesses took aim is the one habit it seems hardest for us to unlearn—the individual perspective. As indicated above, the first step in any articulation of his morality is the calling into question of the subjective agent itself, the human subject understood in the traditional sense of an active, self-reflexive identity or ego (the "I" or the Cartesian subject) who autonomously determines a course of action based upon prior knowledge of its goals and in conformity with a doctrine of human goods and norms. In question is effectively any notion of a transcendental subject with good intentions.

The central problem to address when articulating Bataille's ethics of community is thus his critique of the ideology of the subject *qua* individual, which is the primary obstacle to overcome if community is to emerge. Yet Bataille knew how recalcitrant our mentality is when it comes to challenging this notion. He knew that the individual perspective is not to be swept away with a single gesture. Indeed, one of the cornerstones and constants of his thought is precisely the attempt to undermine the notion of a self-identical subject—the subject as a *thing*—or the notion of identity full stop. One might even go so far as to say that the entirety of his anthropological and religious thinking rests on the notion of the insignificance of the individual in isolation. This assertion, however, brings with it an entire shift of perspective concerning our activities and values, our capitalist economy and parliamentary democracy, and of course our ethical doctrines. For with this challenge to humanist ideology as a starting point, all those ways in which an individual affirms oneself and *pursues one's own interest*—right down to the very desire to persevere in being, to stay alive, to banish death from life—are viewed as betrayal of the truth of existence: the truth of "intimacy." *Intimacy*, to be sure, is a term which resists positive definition. It is not a state that can be *achieved*. It is simply there in anguishing and ecstatic moments of self-loss or *communication*: anguishing because of the violence enacted on the individual who has the impression of being torn, of dying to oneself *as an individual*; ecstatic in that the habitual perspective of being a separate individual—of having one's own existence apart from others and the things of the world—dissolves in communication with the outside, a brief moment of release that effectively extends one beyond (one's) being and out into nothingness. These terms will be clarified as we continue.

In short then, the challenge of intimacy or communication to the hegemony of individuality is the hidden foundation of Bataille's identifiable morality. The challenge is precisely this: intimacy and communication occur in moments where one puts one's existence into *play* by assuming the *risk* of death (*se mettre en jeu*),[2] such that failure to do so, to flee from death or fear for one's continued existence in the future is to forgo the truth of "sovereign" (free and useless) existence and accept a life of servitude: "Play . . . leads to the inoperable spirit (*à l'esprit désoeuvré*)" (OC 5: 234/US 208; tm); play has "as its end the indifference to every end, being only an occasion to show a soul beyond the concerns of utility" (OC 12: 106). To the "obvious" answers to the question of Bataille's ethics that I mentioned above, we could thus add something like this: to exist in the service of some interest, to subordinate present life to an end or future goal, to judge actions according to their usefulness, consider the greater good or even think of consequences beyond the present moment . . . in short, *to work* or *employ one's negativity* in any way is a betrayal of the humanity within us, is a "fragmentation" of existence and the time of existence.

Consequently, if Bataille privileges chance occurrences such as laughter, eroticism, or tears, it is because they are confined to the "present moment." They are not involved in the calculations of productive activity. *They simply happen*. Thus when he denigrates the "paradoxical time" of work, which is *"the putting off of existence to a later point"* (OC 5: 59/IE 46) and gets life caught in "the absurdity of an endless deferral" (OC 7: 298/TR 28), it is not to advocate some hackneyed notion of living for the moment or the disregard of commitment. Rather, it is an attempt to shift our focus, to get us to open our eyes (*donner à voir*) to seemingly insignificant moments that, when seen for what they are—sensual and senseless—can offer resistance to the bourgeois-capitalist system of goods and values, to the suffocating structure of modern society and political systems that reduce the human being to a homogeneous *function*.

His rethinking of ethics thus shifts from the expression of moral ideas about the best way to act in order to achieve the greatest good—or normative ethics—to a manner of relating to exceptional, ostensibly meaningless moments that happen quite independently of a subject's intentions. Furthermore, by being open and attentive to these moments—not for the gain they might bestow on us but for what they are in themselves—the possibility arises to generate a new type of relation to being itself, to the "truth" of being(s) in communication. His ethics is in effect an *ethos*, a manner of being in the world. It is not, however, merely passive, but involves a distinct method of "contestation": it *repudiates the economy of goods* insofar as it "really wants that each of us go as far as possible in the direction contrary to interest" (OC 12: 112). This was already suggested by the opening quotation from Dostoevsky—whose influence on Bataille has been underestimated—insofar as it indicates that something else is at stake in ethics than individual interests and desirable goods. And indeed, it is not difficult to find examples that expose the potential for incommensurability between the value something has for my well-being—by which it is judged as a good—and the value that thing has for me regardless of, and perhaps very much contrary to my 'interests.' Having briefly examined *what* it is that Bataille wants to contest, namely, the type of ethics grounded on the notion of individual interest, let us now deepen our investigation of *how* he sees this contestation occurring.[3]

The Obscure Heart of Community: Inner Experience

'Inner experience' was the first major concept to emerge in Bataille's writings after his dream of forming an actual, affective community effectively collapsed. Understanding what he means by inner experience is crucial not only for its assault on subjective identity and its primary supports (individual consciousness, language, action), but also for its relevance to other key concepts such as 'communication,' 'community' and 'intimacy.' Let us spend a few words then on these terms, but since defining inner experience is a bit like doing negative theology, I will focus primarily on its effects.

First and foremost, inner experience is not what it seems to be: internal (inner, interior) to an experiential subject. Rather, it serves to undermine the classic opposition between inside and outside, subject and object, as there is no interior place into which the subject can retreat: 'inner' experience is ex-centric experience. Indeed, the *only* sense in which it can be referred to as "inner" comes from the fact that it escapes assimilation by any external authority (language or knowledge) and does not refer to any goal or reality transcending the experience itself (God, state, salvation, or profit in any form). It is, as Bataille claims—following a suggestion by Blanchot—its own "authority," but one that must "expiate" itself, atone for any gain or knowledge it might bring to the 'subject' (OC 5: 19/IE 7).[4] And indeed, it is precisely the 'subject' of experience that is put in question by the experience itself. Yes, experience must be lived "from within," but this "within" is only such insofar as it cannot be broken up into intellectual or moral categories imposed from without. From the common discursive perspective of 'subject' and 'object,' this experience is elusive, ungraspable or 'impossible.' "Experience," Bataille asserts, "attains in the end the fusion of object and subject" (OC 5: 21/IE 9) a fusion he often refers to as *intimacy*. And while it may be the case that to locate inner experience one must "reenter oneself," withdrawing from those discursive operations that would diminish its significance by reducing it to another object of knowledge, this "oneself," as he claims, "is not the subject isolating itself from the world, *but a place of communication*" (OC 5: 21/IE 9;em).

While Bataille gets himself into some difficulties by retaining the language of 'subject' and 'object,' the salient point is that—in inner experience or communication—the notion of a subject as an isolated and intact individual is undermined as the subject becomes a vacant place, a wall-less opening to the outside, a 'flow' traversed by other flows.[5] In the inner experience of communication, the individual "as subject, is thrown outside of itself, beyond itself; it ruins itself in an undefined throng of possible existences" (OC 5: 76/IE 61), a throng we can now identify as "community." To be sure then, when he speaks of communication it is anything but the kind of linguistic or legal communication between separate individuals in negotiation over their needs and interests in search of a consensus, as found in a standard notion of ethics. Communication in Bataille's sense of the word is rather the volatile experience of being "outside" oneself, "beyond" oneself in relation to another human being. It only takes place between two beings "mutually penetrable each to the other," exposed to the other and at risk of losing one-*self*, "destroying the integrity of existence in myself and in others."[6] As for the notion of truth implied therein, Bataille claims that "there is no truth when people look at each other as if they're separate individuals. Truth . . . only happens *going from one person to another*" as in "shared laughter, friendship or sex" (OC 5: 282/G 44–45). Truth—the truth of *communication*—requires a *community* of beings.

But just like the 'subject' is set aflow in inner experience—its stable identity lost in communication—so is 'community' *not* to be understood as a fixed, stable, or transcendent referent.[7] It is crucial to keep this in mind moving forward: when reflecting on Bataille's ethics of community, it is imperative that we take care to distinguish the (inner) experience of community from *a* community: a point of reference *outside* the experience itself; something to which the experience can be subordinated. Rather we must treat ethics as a way of *relating to* an indefinite and elusive inner experience of community or, alternatively, intimacy. As we will see, however, things are not so simple when it comes to thinking the community according to these principles. It is difficult to maintain the distinction between the two senses of community precisely because of the difficulty of thinking community as a pure opening where one experiences the loss of self, rather than as some form of closed set or entity that is enriched by the subject's loss. Or to be more exact, the exigency is to conceptualize a notion of loss apart from its dialectical counterpart of gain; to conceive of loss outside of a dialectical economy—indeed, independent of economics altogether—which becomes increasingly difficult when we know that Bataille's central paradigm for loss is in fact expenditure. This is the next problem to address as we continue.

Situating the Question of Community: Self and Totality

It is possible to pinpoint almost exactly the crossroads where this difficulty first became explicit. We jump to July 4, 1939, the date of Bataille's final lecture to the loose association of influential intellectual figures known as the "College of Sociology." Political forces and technological rationality had combined to bring Europe to a state of critical mass. With the dying breath of the Collège, Bataille articulates what he claims to be the "final question of man, or, to take it further, the ultimate question of being,"[8] which hangs in the balance as the group disbands, and its members go their separate ways. Now during his lecture leading up to the formulation of this 'ultimate question,' Bataille refers to certain cardinal notions that had emerged in his most recent writings and that he would continue to reformulate and refine with an increasing sense of urgency in the years that immediately followed.[9] Foremost among these is one of his most influential concepts penned in the seminal article from 1933 ("The Notion of Expenditure," OC I: 302–20/VE 116–29) and pursued under different guises for the better part of thirty years, namely, the "principle of loss" or "nonproductive expenditure." With this he means violent, destructive, or "unreserved" expenditure that is blind to and in defiance of recompense and that generates sacred, symbolic, or nonutilitarian value.

In addition to, and perhaps in contradiction with, the active sense of loss as excessive expenditure that had often dominated his thought to this point, in this final lecture to the Collège he also emphasizes one of his other fundamental principles, the "insufficiency" of being(s),[10] which brings with it mutually implicative ontological and anthropological connotations. First, the principle of the insufficiency of being rejects the traditional notion that Being is something substantial and knowable (or even something at all), some higher identity or essence that serves as a foundation and goal of existence. Being, rather, is no-thing and nowhere, is movement and pure difference. Second, this principle also establishes the radically desirous, open, or social nature of the human being. According to the insufficiency of being, the human being is desire pure and simple: "revealed nothingness, an unreal emptiness, the presence of the absence of a reality,"[11] which seeks to recognize itself in another being of desire, another emptiness housed within an external form. If one is not to close one's eyes to an upsetting consciousness of the truth of existence, then one must be willing to acknowledge the fact that one is essentially nothing, an absence misguided by reflection into thinking it is a presence. It is just such a revelation that Bataille, in countless ways, attempts to bring to light. But as suggested earlier, the principle of individuation is always putting up its defenses to this abysmal truth.

Consequently, the insufficient or "incomplete" nature of the human being entails that the being in question is always and everywhere searching for something that will provide it some self-assurance and restore its sense of identity. If the subject is essentially insufficient or incomplete it will attempt to fulfill or complete itself outside itself, whether through production, acquisition, or merger. It would seem then that the human being is defined by a fundamental impasse: the desire to lose is coupled with desire as insufficiency, which quickly translates into the desire of the individual to "lose itself in some other ["vaster being"] that exceeds it" (OC 2: 369/VE 250), to gain being by losing it. Again, he declares a fundamental 'need' for loss as expenditure: "Men, assembling for a sacrifice and for a festival, satisfy their need to expend a vital excess." This "loss," however, is not exactly irrevocable: "The individual who participates in loss is obscurely aware that this loss engenders the community that supports him" And this brings us back to Bataille's "ultimate question," which reads as follows: "[I]t is difficult to know to what extent the community is but the favorable occasion for a festival and a sacrifice, or to what extent the festival and the sacrifice bear witness to the love individuals give to the community" (OC 2: 371/VE 251). This simple opposition, proving undecidable, would have a crippling effect on Bataille's attempt to identify a real community that would remain faithful to his inviolable principles.

The impasse boils down to this: Bataille invokes two different models as methods of achieving a singular form of experience. The experience is that of ecstatic self-loss in which one's very existence seems at risk—an (inner) experience in which anguish and felicity coincide. The models: on the one hand, we have an individual who *undergoes* a confrontation with something that is suddenly there, that overwhelms one's expectations to the extent that one's conscious sense of identity is momentarily dissolved; on the other hand, we are dealing with excesses of resources (energy, wealth, vitality), being spent without any aim, with a sovereign disregard for results or recompense.[12] The problem with the latter is that Bataille wants such a loss to be pure and uncompromised (as in his paradigm of solar expenditure, the sun expending energy continuously and in excess of what the earth needs), and yet there is always some context in which this expenditure takes place. And when it occurs in relation to a clearly defined *Sache*[13] such as an actual community or society, there is no way to prevent it from being dialectically recuperated in such a way that it *serves the interests* of that community in one way or another, thereby remaining within the confines of classical utility. The person, group, or society that apparently wastes to no end in fact "misuses the negation he makes of the utility of the resources he wastes, bringing into contradiction not only himself but man's entire existence" (OC 7: 75/AS 1: 73). At issue is the very existence of the human being as radical negativity caught in the webs of self-mediation and recognition from which, so long as history is still in motion, there is no escape.[14] Yet escape is precisely what Bataille has in mind.[15] If his early reflections on community actively promote the search for an alternative community as the site of unleashing heterogeneous forces creative of sacred values, he eventually recognizes the need for a withdrawal or escape from social life altogether because it first levels and then sublates expenditure and communication to an instrumental function. Whenever expenditure, the negation of *self*, occurs in relation to a *Sache* it gets caught in the dialectic of self-mediation: the negation of self is reintegrated into the totality.

It would seem then that a different approach is needed in order to articulate a communal ethics that avoids the trappings of the dialectic that restores expenditure to the economy of goods. Bataille is not unaware of the need for a different approach: "throughout history . . . there developed *reasons* to proceed to the summit and risk ourselves. The difficulty beyond this is to proceed to the summit without motivation and without pretext. . . . But what then will we do with the excess energies that fall to our lot? . . . In all honesty, I have to admit that, as it stands—on the level of economic calculation—the question loses in sharpness what it has gained in amplitude. *The reality is, the question has changed*" (OC 6: 59–60/ON 42–43; second emphasis added). The same dilemma is articulated somewhat more rigorously in the closing paragraph of the first volume of *The Accursed Share* where he brings into play the question of intimacy. The same impasse is at stake, namely, how to think of a 'good' that does not get caught in the economy of goods; how to think an ethical framework that does not betray the intimate truth of being: communication. "It is a question," he writes, "of arriving at the moment when consciousness will cease to be consciousness of *something* . . . that is, a consciousness that henceforth has *nothing as its object*" (OC 7: 178/AS 1: 190). If I may rephrase the question, it is an issue of conceiving of desire without an object, desire for a Good beyond the good, a Good that cannot be located, reduced to a thing, acquired and turned into another good. It is a matter of attaining clear consciousness of being outside oneself (in the double sense) without this consciousness being a consciousness of self. So we start our reformulation of the ethical question.

Ethics from Freud to Kant via Lacan

Bataille was certainly not without antecedents and contemporaries with regard to repositioning the question of ethics, and a few watershed conceptions require attention if we are to situate the problem correctly.[16] The first we will address is Freud's pleasure principle and Lacan's use of its 'beyond'; the second is the one that inadvertently set the others in motion, namely, Kant's transformation of morality into a science of mathematics, a mechanical apparatus to be applied indiscriminately so long as it is applied consistently and without contradiction. The perceived coldness and cruelty of the categorical imperative lay in its rigorous detachment from what Kant called the "pathological object," from any object of affection, anything capable of actually moving one's emotions or appealing to one's interests. This is in effect the hard core of Kant's correction of previous ethical systems: the *only* good is the good will that acts on its own law unconditionally, without regard to the consequences, without a care for empirical considerations such as pleasure or happiness.

The Good of the *gute Wille* that acts in accordance with the imperative has nothing to do with any particular, recognizable goods and is divorced from all considerations of beneficial action. The ethical will is called upon to simply follow the orders of its unyielding master, the Law that produces the formula: "Act only according to that maxim whereby you can at the same time will that it shall become a universal law."[17] Okay, thinks the moral subject in an internal dialogue with its own reason, so what does that mean I should do? "Act in such a way . . ." Yes, yes, I know, but what then should I actually *do*, in *reality*? "Act in such a way . . ." This is a slight distortion of course; nevertheless it points forward to the reason why *The Critique of Practical Reason* paved the way for that moral treatise known as *La philosophie dans le boudoir*. Kant isolated the good will of the moral agent precisely to safeguard against the possibility that the pursuit of pleasure, happiness, or our natural inclinations would result in evil actions, and yet its formal nature opened the door to precisely that possibility. One can be perfectly reasonable in one's evil. Lacan reflects extensively on this predicament in his *Ethics* seminar, particularly in reference to Antigone, but he characteristically adds another perspective to the issue, a rather different take on the relation of the good and the Good (*Gut*) that, to be sure, is only vaguely related to Kant's moral thought. What Lacan does is wed Freud to Kant in a way that will be very relevant for our consideration of Bataille. But first a few remarks on Freud.

In one form or another, the pleasure principle has been the stalwart of ethics from Aristotle and Epicurus to Mill, "for moral excellence is concerned with pleasures and pains."[18] Whether it is a matter of the eudaimonistic, utilitarian, or more general consequentialist tradition is not our primary concern. The issue for us here is how pleasure and pain serve as essential reference points for determining good and evil, such that when one makes an attempt to divorce good and evil from pleasure and pain entirely, as does Kant, the moral concepts threaten to become unintelligible. Now it would seem that pleasure functions nicely as a psychological framework for the good of utilitarian/consequentialist ethics in which value is directly attributable to beneficial or disadvantageous effects, this effect measured by avoiding pain or gaining pleasure. It seems obvious that the good would be the path of pleasure, yet this is precisely what Lacan—following Freud, Sacher-Masoch, and de Sade—called into doubt: at the heart of Lacan's *Ethics* exists a Good outside the realm of pleasure.

In other words, for Lacan the pleasure principle "naturally embodies a beyond, but . . . it is, in effect, calculated to keep us on this side of it [of pleasure] rather than beyond it."[19] In other words, pleasure is a way to avoid too much pleasure (*jouissance*). Does this mean that a good (pleasure) is a way to avoid a greater good (more pleasure, beyond pleasure)? Or, on the other hand, does it mean that an excess of pleasure goes beyond the good and over into something else entirely, something intolerable? The answer is yes on both counts. Stating matters simply if reductively, this distance between the signs of pleasure and the ultimate, intolerable pleasure is where Lacan tries to locate the space of ethics. He demonstrates it with reference to Freud but could equally be referring to Bataille, insofar as Lacan bases his reflections on the Freudian principle that the finding of an object is in fact the refinding of an ultimate object that, to be clear, can never be found.[20] Yet this "object" that is to be found again cannot be entirely lost insofar as its empirical representatives, the object-signs of desire, gravitate around that from which they maintain a distance. There is thus something toward which we gravitate, to which we are bound as subjects, something radically unknown that nevertheless functions as a sovereign good, something "which eludes us all, which nobody can seize: we cannot possess it like an object, but we are doomed to seek it" (OC 9: 305/LE 193–94). We have provisionally located Bataille's Good Thing, the intimacy at the very core of his thought. For the moment, however, we must pause over Kant.

Lacan's Kant is actually a curious amalgam of Freud and Lacan and is situated within the problematic of the extreme consequences made possible by the formal nature of Kantian ethics. Now, claiming to follow Kant's lead, Lacan describes the Good as *das Gut des Objekts*, the good object that is neither 'good,' nor strictly speaking an object, but is rather what Lacan calls "the Thing: *das Ding*," that 'beyond-of-the-signified' at the center of the subjective world, or rather: "*das Ding* is at the center only in the sense that it is excluded. That is to say, in reality *das Ding* has to be posited as exterior, as the prehistoric Other that it is impossible to forget . . . something strange to me, although it is at the heart of me."[21] In other Lacanian terms, one could identify *das Ding* with the primordial Real beyond the symbolic realm of signifiers, the seamy side of the world of things. In Bataille's terms, it would refer to that overwhelming plenitude lost with the onset of consciousness—that lost intimacy for which he is constantly searching. We will say that *das Ding* is the noumenal, inaccessible thing that is the object of desire, the transcendental and unreachable law of desire. Which is to say that while desire is structured around *das Ding,* it is only in direct contact with signifiers (mis)taken by the desiring subject to be the direct representatives of the ultimate object. Of interest to us here, however, is the strange dual function of this Thing: fascinating and forbidden; most desired and most inaccessible; the Sovereign Good. How does this work?

Lacan is trying to illustrate how moral life is oriented around this Thing, and to do so he takes his lead from Kant who, in Lacan's view, understood its function "better than anyone else."[22] First of all then, he claims that *das Ding* is a noumenal thing—noumenal not in the sense of being purely intelligible, but as an inaccessible *causa noumena.* It is there as a mute reality, "the reality that commands and regulates" without commanding anything in particular.[23] That is to say, in addition to being an abysmal, forbidden reality, *das Ding* is also said to function as a universal maxim, an ethical law one must obey even though it dictates no specific action: where Kant claims, "Act only according to that maxim," Lacan provides an equally indeterminate maxim, "Do not give up on your desire." This of course is a very opaque formula: first of all because desire is unconscious and therefore unknown; second of all, insofar as desire is oriented to *das Ding,* real satisfaction of desire would be devastating to the desiring subject. Thus the ambiguity of Lacan's interpretation of the moral law as situating desire in relation to *das Ding.* The moral law dictates that the subject cannot take aim directly at the Thing (let us be clear—we are talking about the mother and the law of incest); but in fact, the law actually brings the Thing into existence by forbidding it, after which this Thing functions as a sort of 'horizon' against which all other things are seen, and for which all other things are inadequate substitutes. The law thus has the dual function of bringing the Good into existence in the act of forbidding it and of organizing a world of things—of goods—such that they keep the subject at a distance from the Good. "[The subject] cannot stand the extreme good that *das Ding* may bring him."[24] The Good is evil inasmuch as it would entail the death of the subject.

Have we not stumbled upon the very structure and ambiguity of sacrifice and transgression that permeates Bataille's writing? The structure: a barrier of consciousness surrounds us and maintains life within the confines of the world of things; this barrier takes the form of the prohibition of death; in order to escape the world of things and be exposed to the intimate unknown or the sacred (the Thing), in order to commune with the core of being in a moment of communication in which the walls of individuality are undone, one needs to experience death in life; but the experience of death, of self-loss, of intimacy, is no experience at all, for when intimacy is there, the subject is not, having been momentarily dissolved. The ambiguity: in order to experience intimacy, to be conscious of the vanishing of one's subjectivity, a substitute is required lest one plunge headlong into death. If this is the case, however, if the intimate Thing (no-thing) is in fact the sacrificial law that obliges one to find substitute objects in order to protect the subject from falling into the abyss, to what extent does sacrifice—Bataille's privileged structure of intimate communal experience—fail to live up to Bataille's maxims? "The *law* by which we seek the greatest loss or the greatest danger" (OC 8: 91/AS 2: 105, em). "The *principle* according to which desire demands the greatest possible loss" (OC 8: 123/AS 2: 141; em), which demands that we go as far as possible in disservice to our interests? How are we to rhyme Bataille's sovereign disinterest in interest with the transition he makes, for instance, from actual sacrifice to the "trickery" of literature: literature "which helps us to bear what, if it were real, might exceed our strength and depress us. We do well to live vicariously what we don't dare live ourselves" (OC 8: 91/AS 2: 106); literature that assists us in becoming conscious of death, assists us in attaining self-consciousness, all without leaving our easy chair.[25] I am admittedly being a bit misleading, setting up the question to fail—which is not to say that there is not a real issue here and a real sense of "failure."[26]

An insidious structure is always at work in the background of Bataille's thought, one that undermines his attempt to articulate a disinterested ethics and a formless community of pure ecstasis. It is more or less the same structure that rendered unanswerable the "ultimate question" posed of community; that is illustrated by the unrelenting work of the dialectical economy, which makes every loss *work* in service of a larger community—of people, of knowledge, and so on; and it is the same structure that forced Bataille to turn his attention from the social community to the community of lovers—an isolated community of communication, communication that creates rips in one's perceived identity, opens one to the outside, and allows one to exceed one's limited being. This structure is in fact betrayed by the language of its terms: subject and community. For as much as Bataille intends for community to do away with interest in the subject, they ultimately serve each other's ends. Is there a way out? Is there an ethics of community that would undermine and subvert the identifiable, stable community without establishing a new one in its place? This is our rephrasing of Bataille's 'ultimate question.'

Dissatisfactory Concluding Remarks

"Does Bataille have an ethics?" That was the question. Are we any closer to an answer? That is another question well worth considering. It seems at times that we too have been circling around our community-Thing without being able to access it. Practicing some negative theology if you will, subtracting characteristic after characteristic that the ethics we are after does not possess, which might not be all wrong insofar as community seems more like a negative community than anything we can identify positively. That being said, I think it should be clear by now what an ethics of community is not, and we should as well have an idea of what it is: an ethos, a way of relating to a relation we have identified as communication. What to say then about this way of relating? We have suggested it involves chance, both in the sense of the subject being put at risk and in the sense of being a relation without intention. This is a relation that can neither be sought nor achieved. It happens. Community is, and it happens. It is, and it happens in the way intimacy is and happens: it is simply there as the hidden, intimate connection of the community of beings, is lost in the process of individuation and delineation of the world of things, and happens when the veil of things is rent apart, revealing, again, nothing. When it happens, subjectivity is opened to the outside in a way that must be different from the way that opening occurs in the dialectic of desire or self-consciousness, for in this fundamental dialectic the otherness encountered is one's own otherness in a temporarily alien form, and thus not really alien whatsoever.

This is where Lacan's 'Thing' or 'Real' becomes a fertile concept. I would argue that both Bataille and Lacan want to express a similar idea, but with Lacan one finds it more clearly (or less poetically) illustrated. The idea I have in mind is that the Thing is something to which one is riveted above all other things, something unknown and undefined that has seized the subject at the very core of its being, something to which one is bound, and that can arrive at any moment to drive the subject beyond the good in pursuit of this sovereign good. The subject is riveted to something that escapes its comprehension; the humanist subject is undermined, and the ethical subject is as if suspended in relation to this good-thing. The typical example is Antigone, who is bound by a tie that takes her beyond the law and sends her to her death. And indeed, Bataille motions to something like this in a rare mention of "loyalty [to a family, clan, city, nation or lover] that is to say, communication [which] in principle must be and remain prior to the association of interests" (OC 11: 544).[27] But in fact a simple facial expression or stupid feature, a vocal inflection or some other minutiae one is unaware of may suffice to rivet one to another person insofar as this sign indicates that the person is the bearer of *das Ding*.

To illustrate, I should mention that there is an understanding of *das Ding* that has not been addressed in this exposé, namely, the profoundly disturbing aspect of the fellow being or beloved. There is an impenetrable aspect of the other that is a residue of our first encounters with the (m)other. The child can comprehend the other by bringing fresh perceptions into association with those trusted perceptions of affection that constitute its world of subjective representations. Yet there are certain inert perceptions of the other that do not integrate seamlessly with the representational complex already formed: they simply remain fixed in place and mute. Not recognizing them, the child cannot comprehend them—so the strange penetrates the familiar. If the familiar is an experience of reassuring satisfaction coming from the other, then the strange is experienced as loss and dissatisfaction. This generates the feeling that the world does not in fact conform to one's expectations, that it is indifferent to me, and this is confusing. It is in this gap between desire and thwarted expectation that the Thing arises. The expectation of satisfaction is undermined by an inconsistent and unpredictable object, the other who gives mixed signals—sometimes loving, sometimes indifferent—and this leaves one exposed and vulnerable. One is exposed to the world because one does not know what one can do to be loved or even why one was loved to begin with. This scenario carries over into a more adult dialectic of recognition: one can see others and understand them, but one cannot know what is meaningful for them: one cannot know why someone cares for us or why someone is committed to something (a cause, an identity), for they too are bound to something they cannot articulate. Correlatively, the other may well be a mirror, but this mirror sees us from a vantage point we can never have. There is a dimension of us that is hidden to us, and we cannot but disclose it to others who, again, hold us in suspense. This confronts us with what is in us but is beyond our control, what is "in me more than me" as Bataille once claimed.[28]

It would be a stretch to suggest that this alienating dialectic is the hidden structure of community, but it does involve a few elements ubiquitous to Bataille's thought. First, the intimate relation—communication—is a relation with the unknown. It is hard to find a text of Bataille where this does not play a role. Certainly, the desiring subject is in relation to an object, but we already have an indication of how this object puts the subject in suspense. Second, we should note how the disturbing aspect of the object comes to light when the expectation of satisfaction is thwarted, the moment when "anticipation," which Bataille views as being at one with reason and action, "dissolves into NOTHING" (OC 8: 260/AS 3: 210). Indeed, one should note that Bataille is a sort of prophet of dissatisfaction, dissatisfaction that he sees as life's bottom line, its core truth. Why? Because in the relation of intimate desire—the only relation that counts—what one encounters is neither the other nor one*self*, neither this nor that desired object. The intimate relation is not self-mediation, but a community of beings together in a relation that sends each beyond their individual being—a relation that is in fact a non-relation, pure ecstasis. And if an ethics is somehow to genuinely relate to this (non-)relation, I would suggest that an ethics of community proscribes fetishism. When one encounters the lack in the other, it is an evasion of the truth of intimacy to cover that lack with an object, to hold to that object as the guardian of threatened identity. But this, in effect, is what we have been suggesting all along.

With this in mind, if I were to propose an ethical maxim for Bataille, it would certainly be this: "*Do not give up on your dissatisfaction!*" In fact, however, I think Alain Badiou has articulated well the ethical question Bataille's thought confronts us with: "[H]ow will I . . . *continue* to exceed my own being? How will I link the things I know . . . via the effects of being seized by the non-known?"[29] And indeed, the questions relevant to Bataille are similar to the one that Badiou suggests, namely, how to get along with the known once one has been confronted with the unknown, how to resist the temptation to reduce the unknown to the known; how to relate to that excess beyond oneself without appropriating that excess *for* oneself; how to persevere in that which exceeds your interests of self-preservation; how to accept the fact of being broken. We may do well to conclude by suggesting an ethics of communication is an ethics of risk: "*In risk* I now perceive a movement that, rather than relating the individual's present to his or her future, connects it to *a person who doesn't yet exist*. In this sense risk doesn't assign action to the serving of an agent but serves a still inexistent person. And in this regard it exceeds 'being's limits' " (OC 6: 167/ON 149). Perhaps the community is this being to come, its ethics a promise of loyalty to that Thing that has always existed beyond the limit and is always on the verge of coming into existence, a promise one is powerless to keep.

Notes

1. Jean-Luc Nancy rightly identifies this problematic in the opening pages of his text, *The Inoperative Community*: "[It] is *man*, taken absolutely . . . that constitutes the stumbling block to a thinking of community." Edited by Peter Connor, trans. Peter Connor, Lisa Garbus, Michael Holland, and Simona Sawhney (Minneapolis: University of Minnesota Press, 1991), 3.

2. Note that Bataille's *jeu* may be translated as "play," "risk," "game," or "gambling," as when one has to lay one's chips on the table: "*Messieurs, faites vos jeux.*" When Bataille uses either play or risk they usually imply the other, so "*se mettre en jeu*" (put oneself in play) and "*met sa vie en jeu*" (put one's life at risk) say the same thing.

3. It would be appropriate, particularly in an essay on morality, to mention here that the entirety of the previous section effectively deals with Bataille's problematic of "Evil," which—in a nutshell—concerns *living* life by entering those regions that the desire to *preserve* life would have us avoid. In Bataille's words (from *Literature and Evil*), Evil has a "sovereign value" and demands a "hypermorality" (OC 9: 171/LE ix) that goes against conventional morality, which "goes against our own interests and which is brought about by a passionate desire for liberty" (OC 9: 211/LE 65). Thus evil actions performed for material benefit or advantage are not actually evil (OC 9: 175/LE 17). He summarizes as such: "Though the being is not doomed to Evil, he must try to avoid becoming enclosed within the limitations of reason. He must first accept these limitations and acknowledge the necessity of calculated interest, but he also must know that an irreducible, sovereign part of himself is free from the limitations and the necessity which he acknowledges" (OC 9: 186/LE 29).

4. For Bataille's comments on his discussion with Blanchot concerning experience being its own authority, see OC 5: 67/IE 53.

5. For Bataille's discussion of life as 'flow' or 'flood,' see in particular the article "Communication" found in OC 5: 110–15/IE 93–98.

6. This sampler of descriptions for the phenomenon of communication is taken from Bataille's *On Nietzsche*, part 2: "Summit and Decline" (OC 6: 39–63/ON 13–48).

7. On this point I share the emphasis Benjamin Noys places on the unstable play between the 'flow of communication' and the subject (or community-subject) as a temporary stopping point of the flow in his *Georges Bataille: A Critical Reader* (London: Pluto, 2000), particularly ch. 2.

8. Georges Bataille, "The College of Sociology" (OC 2: 364–74/VE 246–53), 371/251; em. This article is also found in *The College of Sociology 1937–39*, trans. Betsy Wing, ed. Denis Hollier (Minneapolis: University of Minnesota Press), 333–41. I follow primarily Stoekl's translation, with some modification when Wing's seems more accurate, as here.

9. By his "most recent writings" I am referring to the texts written between 1936 and 1939 for the journal *Acéphale*, which anticipate the concerns that would occupy him in his *Somme Athéologique* (*L'Expérience intérieure, Le Coupable, Sur Nietzsche*) and thereafter.

10. "At the basis of human life there exists a *principle of insufficiency*." Cf. "The Labyrinth" (OC 1: 434/VE 172). Another version of this article, entitled "The Labyrinth (Or the Constitution of Beings)," is to be found in *Inner Experience* (OC 5: 97–110/IE 81–93).

11. Alexandre Kojève, *Introduction to the Reading of Hegel: Lectures on the Phenomenology of Spirit*, assembled by Raymond Queneau, ed. Allen Bloom, trans. James H. Nichols Jr. (Ithica: Cornell University Press, 1993), 5.

12. Bataille's privileged model for this type of expenditure is the *potlatch*, the principles behind which he assimilated from Marcel Mauss' text *The Gift: The Form and Reason for Exchange in Archaic Societies*, trans. W. D. Halls (New York: Norton, 2000).

13. I use the German *Sache* (thing, affair as in a disputed legal matter or clear object of human exchange) because of its fertile difference with the word *Ding* (thing),

particularly in the work of Lacan. Lacan draws upon the notion of the *Nebenmensch* (fellow being) in Freud's *Project for a Scientific Psychology* (*The Standard Edition of the Complete Works of Sigmund Freud*, vol. 1, ed. and trans. James Strachey [London: Hogarth, 1966], 283–397) to specify how the being closest to us (in childhood, i.e., the mother) splits apart into an inert, unnamable and incomprehensible *thing* and the identifiable *attributes* of this thing which become familiar representations through the association of perception and memory. The point is to articulate a Kantian-style schism in our experience of reality: there is that which is in conformity with our categories of experience, and there is the unknown core at which our perception aims but cannot access.

In fact there is little consistent usage of these two words in German philosophy. Kant uses *Ding (an sich)* in a negative way as a limiting concept of intuition and as the unknowable ground of appearances, an idea rejected by most of the major figures who came after him, i.e. Fichte, Schelling, Hegel, using *Sache* as more of a corporeal thing (*res*). Hegel uses them in many ways, but notably uses *Sache* rather than *Ding* for the essential matter, the 'real point' or 'main issue' (*die Sache selbst*).

14. This would normally be the place to introduce Bataille's notorious concept of 'unemployed negativity' or the problem of what one does with one's negativity once there is nothing left to accomplish in history, but I have written about this extensively, and it also gets caught in another impasse of recognition. I will therefore take a different approach in what follows.

15. On the notion of "escape" from the compromises of homogeneous society, see the recent translation of Bataille's "Critique of Heidegger" and the essay preceding it by Stefanos Geroulanos, "The Anthropology of Exit: Bataille on Heidegger and Fascism," *October* 117 (Summer 2006): 3–24, 25–34.

16. In what follows I will largely avail myself of the analysis provided by Jacques Lacan in his *Ethics of Psychoanalysis, 1959–1960: The Seminar of Jacques Lacan, Book VII*, trans. Dennis Porter (London: Routledge, 1992).

17. Immanuel Kant, *Grounding for the Metaphysics of Morals*, trans. James W. Ellington (Indianapolis: Hacket, 1993), 30.

18. Aristotle, *Nicomachean Ethics* in *Introduction to Aristotle*, ed. Richard McKeon (New York: Modern Library, 1947), bk. II, ch. 3, 1104b.

19. Lacan, *Ethics*, 185.

20. "It is, of course, clear that what is supposed to be found again cannot be found again. It is in its nature that the object as such is lost. It will never be found again. . . . It is to be found at the most as something missed. One doesn't find it, but only its pleasurable associations." Lacan, *Ethics* 52.

21. Lacan, *Ethics*, 71.

22. Ibid., 55.

23. Ibid.

24. Ibid., 73.

25. "One might say rather precisely that true joy would require a movement to the point of death, but death would put an end to it! We will never know authentic joy. . . . Moreover, death itself is not necessary. . . . [Not] only is trickery necessary in order not to die, we must avoid dying if we are to attain joy. Thus, only the ficti-

tious approach of death, through literature or sacrifice, points to the joy that would fully gratify us, if its object were real" (OC 8: 94/AS 2: 109).

26. I am thinking of the "immense failure" of Bataille's attempt to restore the glory of bygone days so glaringly absent from modern society. For a discussion of this failure, see Nancy, *Inoperative Community*, 7–19.

27. Cf. also the "Preface" to *Literature and Evil* where Bataille writes: "Literature is communication. Communication requires loyalty. A rigorous morality results from the complicity in the knowledge of Evil, which is the basis of intense communication" (OC 9: 171–72/LE ix).

28. This quotation is from memory. I believe it is from *Guilty*. Notice an almost identical phrase in Lacan's definition of *das Ding*: "something strange to me, although it is at the heart of me" (*Ethics*, 71).

29. Alain Badiou, *Ethics: An Essay on the Understanding of Evil*, trans. Peter Hallward (London: Verso, 2001), 50. I am not suggesting that an ethics in Bataille would be similar to Badiou's "ethic of truths," but Badiou does make some interesting remarks that have been helpful in my considerations of Bataille.

CHAPTER FIVE

Transgression and the Community of the Sacred

David B. Allison

In an early section of his book *Eroticism*, Georges Bataille gives what is perhaps his most succinct definition of transgression: "Erotic or religious images draw forth behaviour associated with prohibitions in some people, the reverse in others. The first type is traditional. The second is common at least in the guise of a so-called 'back to nature' attitude, the prohibition [in this case] being seen as unnatural. But a transgression is not the same as a back-to-nature movement; it suspends a taboo without suppressing it. Here lies the mainspring of eroticism and of religion too" (OC 10: 39/E 36).

This kind of language is quite Hegelian in nature, and Bataille readily admits it. Whether or not he is ultimately bound to the model of Hegelian dialectics is not entirely clear. Two commentators of Bataille—Foucault and Derrida—would argue convincingly that he is not.[1] But what is clear is that transgression, as defined by Bataille, is complicated, if not conceptually problematic. He says that transgressions "are connected with [or are bound to] the taboo [or the prohibition] on which they are based" (OC 10: 40/E 36). This involves a certain "duplicity" at least, since the account seems to reconcile—as Bataille himself admits—"what seems impossible to reconcile, [namely] respect for the law and violation of the law; the taboo and its transgression" (OC 10: 40/E 36).

At this seemingly opaque point of contradiction, however, Bataille notes that his analyses of transgression are predicated on a peculiar, a unique, domain of experience, what he calls "inner experience." Again, I quote from the first chapter of his work *Eroticism*:

> Eroticism as seen by the objective intelligence [i.e., from the outside] is something monstrous, just like religion. Eroticism and religion are closed books to us if we do not locate them firmly in the realm of inner experience. We put them on the same level as things known from the outside if we yield, albeit unwittingly, to the taboo. [For] unless the taboo is observed with fear, it lacks the counterpoise of desire which gives it its deepest significance. The worst of it is, that [those particular] sciences whose procedures demand an objective approach to taboos [e.g., anthropology or ethnology] owe their existence to them but at the same time disclaim them [precisely] because taboos are not rational. Inner experience alone can supply the overall view, from which they are finally justifiable. (OC 10: 40/E 37)

Let us simply note, then, some of the initial considerations for Bataille's discussion of transgression:

1. The account begins with the imposition of taboos, prohibitions. This is to say, that his whole account rests on the presence of codes, of codified, socialized, socially restricted activity. Thus, transgression is—at its most basic level—a distinctively human activity. The "return to nature" attitude he mentions is thus a simple regression to what he would term "animality as animality," i.e., to sexuality, but not to eroticism (OC 10:39/E 36).

2. The subject *feels* these taboos or prohibitions to be in effect: they are operative and serious. They inspire *fear*, for example, yet they need not themselves be rational. By and large they are not rational, which is precisely why they have such an affective or emotional claim on the subject.

3. As a response to this fear, desire itself is intensified.

4. It is desire, therefore, and the intensification of desire, that invests transgression with significance and yields pleasure.

5. The domain in question is, again, that of our inner experience. The indebtedness to Freud is obvious. A desire—its blockage—the intensification of desire—thus, pleasure and significance are produced as a result of the intensified desire's satisfaction,

> entailing the suspension of the taboo, at the very least. Now, this may involve a complete displacement of the initial object of desire—a displacement or shift from the originally prohibited act to the transgression itself. That is, the prohibition invoked may in turn be thematized, and its very suspension, its overcoming, may constitute the new satisfaction.[2]

The next move enables us, perhaps, to initially situate Bataille's entire reflection: if transgression is concerned with the suspension of taboos, then, clearly, the nature of the taboo or prohibition first needs to be examined. Two texts of Freud would provide background here, *Totem and Taboo* and *Beyond the Pleasure Principle*. And just as certainly, Nietzsche lurks behind the text of Bataille as well, especially his *On the Genealogy of Morals*, which is concerned, as Nietzsche says, to exhibit the mechanics of what he terms "the inverted will." By extension, this would be the primary or original place to examine the broader concepts of 'repression,' 'sublimation,' 'transference,' 'displacement,' and so on, as well as to examine the motivations for the entire project of de Sade. Clearly, the text of Bataille is literally furrowed by these three figures: Sade, Nietzsche, Freud.

A fourth figure effectively situates these three, however, and this is Durkheim. It is Durkheim's account, in his *Division of Labor in Society*, and especially, in his magisterial work of 1912, *The Elementary Forms of Religious Life,* that introduces the specific content of Bataille's initial reflection, namely, the thematics of labor. Why labor? Because society itself—wherein taboos and prohibitions occur, or rather, where law in the widest sense occurs—society itself is made possible through the coercive organization and division of labor. As Freud would remark in *The Future of an Illusion*,

> It seems . . . that every civilization must be built up on coercion and renunciation of instinct; it does not even seem certain that if coercion were to cease the majority of human beings would be prepared to undertake to perform the work necessary for acquiring new wealth. . . . For masses are lazy and unintelligent; they have no love for instinctual renunciation, and they are not to be convinced by argument of its inevitability. . . . To put it briefly, there are two widespread human characteristics which are responsible for the fact that the regulations of civilization can only be maintained by a certain degree of coercion—namely, that men are not spontaneously fond of work and that arguments are of no avail against their passions.[3]

It is this necessity to organize labor that gives rise to the distinctively human creature.[4] At once society arises, and with it there emerge two new worlds: a work world in distinction to the earlier, natural world. But also, there is posed an antidote to the work world, namely, a supplementary or complementary world of festival, intensified delight, joy, and abandonment: not merely a world of leisure, but the intensified, compensating world of what Bataille, following Durkheim, calls "the sacred."[5] And only on the condition of a divided world does there arise a divided subject—and, within that, the distinctively human world of inner experience.

Now, Bataille wants to argue—in a way fully consistent with the tradition he invokes—that the inner world answers to the sacred, to a world that is basically opposed to the work world, opposed to what is conventionally termed the "profane" world of productive labor and its governing laws, laws that ultimately govern the social-political organization itself. The emotional intensities arising within the inner experience, those intensities that interest Bataille, at least, are specifically erotic and religious in nature. The terms he will use to describe these emotional or affective intensities are *orgy, frenzy, anguish, ecstasy, loss, fusion, plethora*or, as he also terms it, affective "continuity" or "immanence" with that in which we invest our deepest emotions.

Note that these are the most general and historically widespread terms of an extreme emotional, or affective, intensity. It is a history that runs through Nietzsche's account of Dionysian dispossession, the Maenadic fury evoked by Euripides in his tragedy, the *Bacchae*, and the erotic transports of de Sade, Gilles de Rais, and Don Juan. It also traverses the religious ecstasy of mystical union, as pronounced by St. Catherine, St. Theresa, Meister Eckhart, Jacob Boehm, and Nicholas of Cusa. And we should also note that these are terms that generally escape the traditional discourse of philosophy. These terms, quite simply, testify to the extremes of human activity, to the indeterminate limit cases. They are transcendent limits, so to speak. Such states are not within the compass of philosophical language and discourse. Rather, they lie elsewhere; they are "trips," trips in intensity. Hence they are relatively uncharted, untrammeled by the rationality and objectivity—Bataille would say, the "utility" and "purposiveness"—of philosophical discourse.

Bataille discusses the fundamental agency of labor or work, in the section of chapter 10 entitled "The Orgy as an Agrarian Ritual."

> Work and material utility have certainly determined, or at any rate conditioned, the behaviour, religious as well as profane, of semi-civilized peoples. . . . Work set up the distinction between the sacred and the profane. It is the origin of the taboos which made man deny nature. On the other hand, the limits of the working world supported and maintained in the struggle against nature by those taboos also delineated the sacred world. In one way the sacred world is nothing but the natural world persisting

> in so far as it cannot be entirely reduced to the order laid down by work, profane order, that is. But the sacred world is only the natural world in one sense. In another, it transcends the earlier world made up of work and taboos. In this sense the sacred world is a denial of the profane, yet it also owes its character to the profane world it denies. The sacred world is also the result of work in that its origin and significance are to be sought not in the immediate existence of nature's creation but in the birth of a new order of things, brought about in turn by the opposition to nature, of the world of purposeful activity. The sacred world is separated from nature by work; it would be unintelligible for us if we did not see how far work determines its nature and existence. (OC 10: 115–16/E 114–15)

The initial groundwork is clear: nature is at best indifferent to man. At worst, nature is a kind of destructive chaos, which, unless ordered by man through the organized activity of labor and civil society, would prove to be his downfall. In this sense, nature would be the death of the individual through want and insufficiency, precisely by the absence of society and social organization. Nature announces a kind of death in both cases—by indifference or by destructive chaos.

Labor or organized work permits the emergence of society. Within society, the division and progressive organization of labor thereby permit society and the individual to flourish. Taboo or prohibition functions only within this horizon. Quite simply, they mark injunctions for the individual to act in such a way so as to preserve himself as a unit and to preserve society as a whole, through the effective regulation of the society's activities. Specifically, taboos are enjoined by the society against the individual; they prohibit what are felt to be the divisive and sometimes violent expenditures of energy, labor, and time. The most common taboos concern the injunction against murder (i.e., "death"), which acts would deprive society of its labor and weaken its necessary organization. Also, taboos are inveighed against sexuality (or, more specifically, against "sensuality"), since this is an expenditure of time and energy, which if left unchecked, would distract society from its necessary purposes of efficiently organizing productive labor, would render it enervated, and would generate particular interests at the expense of the whole, at the expense of collective interests. Relations of authority, power, and productivity would fall prey to the individual pursuit of pleasurable excess, bankrupting the political economy, the effective management of the state.

This is a threat indeed, and hence, taboos, prohibitions.

While taboos or prohibitions are in a sense, laws—in that they bind[6]—they belong generally to the body of unwritten laws, the laws and public opinion that bind the sentiments, customs, and habits of a people and constitute its *ethos*, its *mores*. Thus, as Bataille can remark, taboos may not be terribly explicit or concretely specified (and as a result, they often appear vague). At the same time, these taboos are most often *felt*, or at least, initially so. Consequently, they are in many respects *irrational*—and their rational justification may well appear somewhat specious, beside the point, perhaps overcritical, or, as Freud would have it, their justification might seem to be on the order of "secondary rationalizations," secondary "explanations."[7]

The positive function of the taboo is to enjoin us to work, which so determined is always work for the purpose of social stability, for material, cultural, social, and intellectual gain; taboos work for profit in the broadest sense. Taboos are the irrational elements that permit the edifice of a rational society—indeed, perhaps of reason itself. The institution of philosophy, for example, is inconceivable in the absence of highly developed institutions and institutional life *per se.* One knows full well who lives outside the polis, outside the city walls, outside the imperial capitol: barbarians, nomadic forces of dissolution, seething with despotic violence and rapacity.

Yet, it is the beast within that, in a sense, enjoins our compliance with the taboo. This is a continually fearful beast, one afraid of its own powers and its own weaknesses—a beast, Nietzsche would argue, that perpetually bathes in the luxury of exercising its own violence. In Cartesian terms, it is the passion that demands a counterpassion merely to persist. It is the irksome Id that often enough welcomes the ministrations of its counterpart. For Bataille, the importance of the irrational taboo structure is heightened since it has basically a broader social or collective dimension to it, and this exceeds the immediate sensibility of the individual's own psychic resources. Bataille points to this continually subjacent stratum of irrationality, which is to be found at the very heart of social coherency and political order:

> The taboos on which the world of reason is founded are not [themselves] rational for all that. To begin with, a calm opposite to violence would not suffice to draw a clear line between the two worlds. If the opposition did not itself draw upon violence in some way, if some violent negative emotion did not make violence horrible for everyone, reason alone could not define these shifting limits authoritatively enough. Only unreasoning dread and terror could survive in the teeth of the forces let loose. This is the nature of the taboo which makes a world of calm reason possible but is itself basically a shudder appealing not to reason but to feeling, just as violence is. Human violence is the result not of a cold calculation but of emotional states: anger, fear, or desire. We have to take into consideration the irrational nature of

> taboos if we want to understand the indifference to logic they continually display. (OC 10: 66–67/E 63–64)

From this it follows that it is plausible in certain cases that the taboos will themselves be violated, precisely due to the affective intensities within the subject, intensities that the taboos are meant to contain in the first place. Given that the taboo is itself grounded in the irrational, grounded in the primally ungoverned emotional drives—at least insofar as this testifies to our anger, shock, fear, or surprise at even recognizing our own reservoir of intensities—it beckons instability. Given that the taboo is acted upon in an affective state, and that the taboo itself may appear less than rational, it beckons transgression.

Now, Bataille goes on to argue that society, to a certain extent, expects and tolerates, indeed, encourages the violation of many, if not all taboos—but this is only under certain conditions, and subject to specific stipulations. Two elements of the argument are particularly interesting:

First of all, it is the case that the subject knowingly violates these taboos or prohibitions. This is one of the basic structures of transgression for Bataille, and it distinguishes transgression from what he calls "animal violence." The subject is, in a sense, subjected to an unhappy or divided consciousness: he knows the prohibition, yet he nonetheless transgresses it, much as the young St. Augustine did, when he stole the green pears. Knowing it was evil to do so, he did so anyway, saying he did so for the sheer joy of committing evil. We remember another instance of this violation of civil taboos in Nietzsche's account of the debtor-creditor relation, in book 2 of his *Genealogy of Morals.* When the debtor fails to repay the creditor a stipulated compensation, the creditor suspends all prohibitions against violence and seeks recompense, no longer in any equivalently valued commodity, but in the pleasure of violation itself: "Let us be clear as to the logic of this form of compensation: it is strange enough. An equivalence is provided by the creditor's receiving, in place of a literal compensation . . . (thus, in place of money, land, possessions of any kind), a recompense in the form of a kind of pleasure—the pleasure of being allowed to vent his power freely upon one who is powerless, the voluptuous pleasure of doing evil for the pleasure of doing it, the enjoyment of violation itself."[8]

Bataille's analysis is appealing for any number of reasons, but principally because it exhibits one of the most dramatic philosophical operations at work in the transformation and valorization of the nonphilosophical basis of philosophy itself. The subject draws upon a hierarchical or organizing set of categories—the philosophical operation par excellence—in order to valorize his primary processes, his unstructured, affective, emotional, or libidinal reservoir of intensities. Of course, when these drives do become governed, ordered, and rendered hierarchical, they become secondary processes, encoded energies, and thus they conform to social institutions. As socially bound and culturally encoded, they serve to sustain the very institution of exhaustive codes themselves, indeed ultimately, of reason itself. This is precisely why Nietzsche could say in *The Birth of Tragedy* that it was the Dionysian impulse, ultimately coupled with the Apollonian ordering drives, that preserved the great culture of classical Greece for so long—consolidating the political and social dimension of individual existence, and giving the feeling that the individual belongs to a greater whole, a community of enraptured celebrants. Effectively, this is the acknowledgment that the great expenditure of the "witches' brew" of Dionysian affect could be redirected to the then fading mythological beliefs in the gods of Homer and Hesiod, the "tragic union" of Dionysus and Apollo.

Bataille's principal example is the taboo against murder. Yet, by invoking a philosophical metacode, a more fundamental qualifying code, the individual freely participates in warfare, which is to say, she actively participates in murder—murder incorporated, legitimated.

The second element of Bataille's argument is continuous with the first. Society as a whole effectively organizes itself—again, in the case of war—to systematically transgress the taboo against murder. And again, at this more complete or extensive level, what is thereby sustained is society—its reasons, its codes, its division and organization of labor. Here, the discharge of the primary processes tells us that the taboos themselves were fragile indeed. Since it is the product of irrationality, the taboo cannot with good reason be expected to contain irrationality, unless it is subject to a continually shifting, ever operative scheme of a more encompassing rationality, which rationality never loses sight of the general purpose of taboos themselves, namely, to protect and preserve society itself, the agency that generates taboos.[9]

The example reminds us of Nietzsche's famous proclamation in his *On the Genealogy of Morals:* "It is not suffering in itself that is intolerable; rather, what is intolerable is that suffering should have no meaning."[10] The state, like the priestly mind, as recounted in *The Genealogy*, gives this suffering meaning in the very process of transgression itself: we must protect and defend the state. We must kill others, or even be killed, by our own act of self-sacrifice in order that others may live. And in doing this, the violence of the primary processes—controlled by the taboos that make organized labor possible in the first place—is surprisingly, but understandably, unleashed. Now, let war bring forth the most extreme violence, but in this instance, let us denominate it as valor, courage, bravery, national purpose, national sovereignty, and moral righteousness.

Here is where we sense the presence of Hegel and the movement of the dialectic: the reservoir of libidinal intensities is, of itself, capable of destroying the very possibility of individual and social being. Hence, its affirmation, its violent enactment or discharge, must be negated, and this is precisely the necessity for imposing taboos, for instituting prohibitions. At this stage, the intensities are negated as intensities. That is, they must no longer be unregulated, uncodified, so as to constitute random violence. They are now discharged, but basically transformed. No longer are they violent intensities as such, but, rather, they become labor. Their character has been altered by the imposition of taboos.[11]

But, with the instance of transgression, we have a new step, a dialectical sublation, that is, a synthesis combining both the affirmative intensities and the negative operation of the taboo—moreover, a synthesis that retains the violent intensity as intensity and that also retains the taboo structure even as it redirects both into a higher, more rational, organizational unity. This is a unity that is no less violent and intense, but what differs here is that this new unity is not simply self-canceling; rather, it retains itself as a unity by directing its synthesized elements elsewhere, otherwise. In this case, it emerges as warfare. Violent murder and the taboo against murder get combined to enable the transgression of the murder taboo: war. In other words, kill them, do not kill us, and we will prevail!

Effectively, suspend the murder taboo by appealing to the higher category of social and political interest: again, kill them, not us. Therefore, the prohibition is in fact retained in that what takes place is now regulated murder, murder that takes sides and stands for a higher purpose, not general, unrestrained, ungoverned murder.

This is what Bataille calls "limited transgression." One could, following a somewhat different vocabulary, call it "sublimated transgression," "sublated" or "recuperated transgression." For one reason or another, for strategic, tactical, or provisional purposes, transgression is in fact welcomed. This is because it serves the stability of the whole and is, in the end, governed by at least a *prima facie* hierarchy of values and goals (i.e., of categorical valorizations), each with its taboos and its permissible occasions of—and places for—transgression. It is a limited transgression since it is limited by the collective interests, the economy of the whole, of society at large. In an extended passage, Bataille remarks:

> Animals, recognizing no taboos, have never progressed from the fights they take part in to the organized undertaking of war. War in a way boils down to the collective organization of aggressive urges. Like work, it is organized by the community; like work, it has a purpose, it is the answer to the considered intention of those who wage it. We cannot [simply] say therefore that war and violence are in conflict. But [rather, that] war is organised

> violence. The transgression of the taboo is not animal violence. It is violence still, used by a creature capable of reason (putting his knowledge to the service of violence for the time being). At the very least the taboo is the threshold beyond which murder is possible; and for the community, war comes about when the threshold is crossed.
>
> If transgression proper, as opposed to ignorance of the taboo, did not have this limited character it would be a return to violence, to animal violence. But nothing of the kind is so. Organized transgression together with the taboo makes social life what it is. (OC 10: 67–68/E 64–65)

It is limited transgression, then. As warfare stands to murder—and let us extend this—so does sacrilege stand to the sacred; so does blasphemy stand to respect; so does marriage stand to sexuality; so does ritual orgy stand to marriage. Each, in one way or another—from one culture to another—"makes society what it is." Simply stated, and contrary to all appearances, perhaps, transgression serves to *constitute* society as such.

In this sense, we need our tricksters, devils, whores, and generals. Or as Nietzsche—once again—frequently remarked, perhaps we can gauge the strength of a culture by the number of criminals it can endure (cf. *Genealogy of Morals*, bk. 2, sec. 10). This is what Bataille means when he claims that "the taboo is there in order to be violated." In the end, limited transgression is simply that, limited. Summing this up briefly, Bataille remarks, "Often the transgression of a taboo is no less subject to rules than the taboo itself. No liberty here. 'At such and such a time and up to a certain point this is permissible'—that is what the transgression concedes" (OC 10: 68/E 65).

Limited transgression, therefore, is limited by the whole or by a final limit, a *terminus ad quem*. Thus, by the Hegelian model, it is limited by the absolute, the set of systematic sets, that constitutes absolute knowledge. Or it is limited by some "unsurpassable" place at which an interminable series of displacements is finally arrested, finally ended, thwarted: whether this be the status quo, the hangman, or God, it is the same thing.

But Bataille is far from satisfied with this. He suggests an entirely different economy, namely, an unlimited transgression, and he says that "in exceptional cases, unlimited transgression is conceivable. . . . In these cases, disorder knows no bounds" (OC 10: 68–69/E 65–66). The example he gives to illustrate this comes from the French ethnologist, Roger Caillois. Let us examine this example of what purports to be "unlimited transgression." But first—and this is a considerable but—exception may be taken to his example: the king dies, and license prevails. But it prevails only until the flesh of the dead king rots, exposing his bones. It seems, then, as if there are bounds; the finite period in which decomposition occurs seems to govern the expenditure of violence. Thus, the whole scene might appear as but one more ritual, one more among countless others, each subservient to the stability of the state and to its imperious demands, as surely as contracts are enforced after a tolerated or stipulated period of indebtedness and as long as there are banks, lawyers, and "enforcers." Bataille cites the example from Caillois:

> "When social and natural life" he says, "are summed up in the sacred person of a king, the hour of his death determines the critical instant and looses ritual license. This license corresponds closely with the importance of the catastrophe. The sacrilege has a social nature. It is committed at the expense of the kingship, the hierarchy and the established powers. No hint of resistance is ever offered to the frenzy of the people. This is considered as necessary as obedience to the dead man was. In the Sandwich Islands the people, on learning of the king's death, commit all the acts looked on as criminal in ordinary times: they set buildings on fire, they loot and they murder, while women are expected to prostitute themselves publically . . . In the Fiji Islands the consequences are even more clearly defined. The death of the chief gives the signal for pillage, subject tribes invade the capital and indulge in every form of brigandage and depredation.
>
> "Yet these transgressions still constitute a sacrilege. They break the rules that were in force yesterday and which will be restored tomorrow, sacred and inviolable. They appear in fact as major acts of sacrilege."
>
> It is noteworthy that the disorder takes place during " 'the critical period of decay and degradation represented by death," during "the time when its active and contagious virulence is in full swing." It "ends when all the rotting flesh has finally disappeared from the royal corpse, when nothing is left of the remains but a hard, clean, incorruptible skeleton." (OC 10: 69–70/E 66–67)[12]

Now, is this example subject to the caveat we suspected? It is, if and only if we examine this "period of disorder" from the outside—that is, as a determined and fixed period in objective world history—in which case it would merely appear as a brief, and perhaps curious, hiatus, which occurs in certain rather exotic oceanic cultures.

But this is the very attitude Bataille sought to exclude from the start. I will never simply see or observe sacrilege, anguish, frenzy, awe, delight, or ecstasy as they are; they are accessible only to my inner experience, to that domain that affectively undergoes and confirms what from the outside is but an anthropological, sociological, or psychological abstraction: taboo, transgression, eroticism, the sacred. Ultimately, there is nothing, really, to see. The sacred binds the community with a set of shared beliefs, and these beliefs, derived from communal opinion and sustained through communal ritual, are basically idealizations that invest their objects—their totems, or themselves as a clan or tribe—with a sacred intensity and irrational awe that seeks to rejoin the divine feeling of lost continuity, bliss, immanence. But as sacred, such idealizations exist only in the mind, in one's own inner experience.

More closely examined, what Durkheim had earlier described as collective "effervescence"[13]—a psychical excitation to the point of delirium, brought about by the intensely religious experience of the sacred—and what Bataille terms the "inner experience" of the religious or erotic, is precisely the transfiguration of individual subjectivity into a state of disindividuation.[14] In ordinary experience, one lives straightforwardly as an individual, defined by purposive activity, temporally projecting oneself into the future, concerned with tasks and daily obligations. All our experience in this sense is object related in a clearly defined space-time continuum, and our feelings and sensations are bound with specific object relations: I desire some thing; I love someone; something is blue and is hard to the touch. Such is the state of individuated, conscious existence or as Bataille would say, of "discontinuous" existence, where one is defined by clear and distinct relations between oneself, tools, objects, other beings.[15] One feels oneself to be a distinct individual with clear, spatiotemporal boundaries and simple—direct, or intentional—object relations. However, when a state of heightened excitation is brought about by the sacred object or totem—or by the eroticized object of a sexual prohibition—further intensified by ritual practices, chants, wailings, ululations, music and dance, one's feeling states become progressively dissociated or detached from specific object relations; the more intense states of emotional affect begin to emerge, and the dislocation from specific object relations increases dramatically. The excitement provoked in these situations is experienced as a fluidity of affect, in that intense emotional states lose their conventional associations and tend toward reinvesting their objects of awe and pleasure with more immediate, hallucinatory cathexes. Such states involve an extreme intensification of psychic discharge, resulting in a heightened increase of satisfaction. And to the degree that further intensification of psychic discharge occurs, so do the states of emotion or affect become progressively freed from object associations altogether, until the point of frenzy is reached, and the underlying drives become completely free flowing, anarchic, and unbound.

When this frenzied state is attained the celebrant becomes literally ecstatic, the experience of a coherent spatial-temporal continuum is completely foreclosed, causality becomes magical, one undergoes the feeling of ego loss, and with this, the sense of individuation is transcended in a dizzying state of immediacy and a totalizing continuity—of intimacy—with the entire sensory field. This is the state of disindividuation, where clarity and distinctness of experience explode, where articulation of one's own frenzied state dissolves into babble, froth, and drool.

Inner experience is not something viewed at a distance. Such a state is conceivable and is in fact experienceable.[16] That it may well terminate at a later date—in measurable clock time—is beside the point. At that point, lived experience, inner experience, may once again revert to the tedium and daily drudgery of labor it is most often condemned to, but in the meantime, in the between, it has soared to an infinity, in intensity. I suffer anguish, and you see, perhaps, or observe from without, what appears to be but a distracted or petulant individual, a somewhat furrowed brow, or the quaking figure of a delusional visionary.

Here, we finally come to what Bataille has to say about transgression.

Transgression produces a new world, that of the sacred—sacred as opposed to profane: bliss, joy, delight, terror, sanctity, fusion, and effusion—as opposed to the workaday, the quotidian necessity of laboring, the rule-governed tedium of the human condition. That conditionis the one into which one is born, without asking to be, throughout which one is condemned to labor, and in which one is bound to die, by all that is natural, by means of every petty misfortune.

But if the social order is constituted by the taboo structure, it nonetheless admits a supplement, a complement: the sacred. In the extreme case, transgression "opens the door into what lies beyond the limits usually observed" (OC 10: 70/E 67). And the sacred world—that world invested by the reservoir of libidinal intensities—"the sacred world depends on . . . transgression. It is the world of celebrations, sovereign rulers, and God" (OC 10: 70/E 68). Lest we be mistaken at all about this, for Bataille, the sovereign ruler is also the transgressor, the general transgressor. But what machine is at work here? What spring, what drive?

> This approach is a difficult one, in that the sacred simultaneously has two contradictory meanings. Whatever is the subject of a prohibition is basically sacred. The taboo gives a negative definition of the sacred object and inspires us with awe on the religious plane. Carried to extremes, that feeling becomes one of devotion and adoration. The gods who incarnate this sacred essence put fear into the hearts of those who reverence them, yet men do reverence them none the less. Men are swayed by two simultaneous emotions: they are driven away by terror and drawn by an awed fascination. Taboo and transgression reflect these two

> contradictory urges. The taboo would forbid the transgression but the fascination compels it. Taboos and the divine are opposed to each other in one sense only, for the sacred aspect of the taboo is what draws men towards it and transfigures the original interdiction. The often intertwined themes of mythology spring from these factors. (OC 10: 70–71/E 68)

In the simplest terms, the taboo renders sacred, and the transgression reinvokes the taboo. And the taboo must be regularly reinvoked so as to keep the sacred in the collective consciousness of the community; elsewise the sacred would be forgotten and replaced with the secular, with the inevitable death of the gods. The taboo renders the proscribed object awesome, magnificent, admirable, and desirable in the extreme. It thereby becomes the object of greatest satisfaction and value to the extent that it is removed, taken out of circulation, and worshipped precisely for its rarity, its speculative and surplus value, its invested absence. Its use, its circulation, would be the invaluable satisfaction, the primary object of fixation, of libidinal cathexis—a value maintained by scarcity and confirmed by the very paucity and tedium of the inescapable human condition.

Notes

1. Michel Foucault, "A Preface to Transgression," in *Language, Counter-Memory, Practice*, trans. D. Bouchard (Ithaca: Cornell University Press, 1981), pt. 1, ch. 1, 29–52, and Jacques Derrida, "From a Restricted to a General Economy: A Hegelianism without Reserve," in *Writing and Difference*, trans. Alan Bass (Chicago: University of Chicago Press, 1978), ch. 9, 251–77.

2. Interestingly, this notion is borrowed wholesale by Michel Foucault in his own later account, in *The History of Sexuality*, of what he calls the "deployment" and the "production" of ever-new sexualities.

3. The Standard Edition of the Complete Psychological Works of Sigmund Freud, vol. 21, trans. James Strachey (London: Hogarth, 1961), 7–8.

4. Durkheim's own approach places somewhat less stress on the coercive character of labor than does that of Freud or Bataille. Durkheim accounts for social organization, and hence the division between the world of work—the profane world—and what he terms the "sacred," through primitive ritual gatherings of the clan or tribe, which produces a moral and spiritual community. Such a community is effectively a "church," which imposes its collective power of opinion, and thereby, moral obligation over the individual.

5. Emile Durkheim, *The Elementary Forms of the Religious Life*, trans. Joseph Ward Swain (New York: Free, 1965), 52ff.

6. The etymology is classic: as St. Thomas long ago noted, "Law is a rule and the measure of acts, whereby man is induced to act or is restrained from acting; for law [*lex*] is derived from the term 'to bind' [*ligare*], because it binds one to act or

not to act." St. Thomas Aquinas, *Summa Theologiae*, vol. 28: *Law and Political Theory*, ed. and trans. Thomas Gilby O.P. (New York: McGraw Hill, 1966), Prima Secundae, question 90, article 1, 7.

7. At a wedding I attended not long ago, the officiating Rabbi explained the significance of brutally smashing a fragile glass, sheathed in a pure white linen napkin, under the heel of the bridegroom: "This is," he told the assembled guests, "to commemorate those dreadful events—events we must never forget—of Kristallnacht." Now, in itself, this was a transparent embellishment of a more primordial signification: open, no doubt, to just such an embellishment—the purpose of which would be to graft one taboo system onto another, thereby consolidating and intensifying the taboo. And this, too, is understandable; when (given the unsettled and confused nature of our times) there are ever fewer hymens and symbolic hymens to smash.

8. Friedrich Nietzsche, *On the Genealogy of Morals*, trans. Walter Kaufmann (New York: Vintage, 1967), II: 5, 64–65.

9. This is also Sade's monumental joke: enlightened reason serves him as an instrument to destroy the set of social codes, which codes would of course inhibit his own surpassing of rationality itself. On the "logic" of Sade's transgression, cf. David Allison, "Transgression and Its Itinerary," in *Must We Burn Sade?* ed. Deepak Narang Sawhney (Amherst: Humanity Books, 1999), 201–27.

10. Friedrich Nietzsche, *On the Genealogy of Morals*, trans. Walter Kaufmann (New York: Vintage, 1967), II: 7, 68; tm.

11. Or as Nietzsche would say, this is a perfect example of transforming aggression, aggressive drives, into work, and deeming the latter to be "virtuous."

12. Pp. 66–67. Bataille quotes from Roger Caillois' *L'Homme et le sacré,* ch. 4, "Le Sacré de transgression: théorie de la fête" (Paris: Gallimard, 1950). *Man and the Sacred*, trans. Meyer Barash (Urbana: University of Illinois Press, 2001), ch. 4, "The Sacred as Transgression: Theory of the Festival," 97–127.

13. Durkheim, *Elementary Forms*, bk. 2, ch. 7, 235–72.

14. At the very end of his work of the same name, Bataille remarks, "I should have said, all along, what 'inner experience' is and answer the questions which one asks about it. That was more difficult than one might believe. To begin with, I fail with the definition. I must content myself with empiricism. By 'inner experience' I mean what one normally designates by the name 'mystical experience'—the experience of states of ecstasy, of rapture, or at least of mediated emotion. But I envisage less 'confessional experience'—to which one in general refers—than experience in itself, free of ties, be they vague, to any confession whatsoever. This is what justifies the abandonment of the word 'mystical,' to which I could not adhere without having confusion" (OC 5: 427/IE 174).

15. On continuity and discontinuity, see especially Bataille, *Theory of Religion*, part 1, chs. 1 and 2 (OC 7: 291–306/TR 17–42).

16. Schopenhauer and the young Nietzsche went so far as to claim that those extreme states of disindividuation literally opened onto the World Will, the metaphysical realm of the noumenon—beyond the categories of space, time, and causality. By the end of his *Birth of Tragedy*, Nietzsche came to disavow any specifically metaphysical reality to these states and rather came to understand their remarkable, transfigurative nature as the effect of "musical dissonance."

CHAPTER SIX

Elements of Experience: Bataille's Drama

Kalliopi Nikolopoulou

> The practical difficulty of inner experience [*crossed out*: of method (dramatization)] stems from the faithfulness of a dog which man shows to discourse.
>
> —Georges Bataille, "Principles of a Method and a Community"

Wind: Bataille in Socrates' Theater

In a note to *Sovereignty*, Georges Bataille wrote: "My answer to anyone is first of all a question. I hope to ask, from one man to another, whether he has ever suspected some hoax. On the surface, everything is in order, foreseen and defined, but none of this is certain."[1] This posture is anything but new within the philosophical tradition of Socratic questioning, and in this particular formulation it recalls much of Socrates' own justification of his philosophical practice in the *Apology*.[2] But how exactly does the question become the site of such an unlikely *rendez-vous* between Socrates, the origin of reason, and Bataille, the thinker who brings the concept to its ruin? For Socrates, on the one hand, at least at the outset, the question motivates his pursuit of positive knowledge, even though positive answers are hardly to be found in the Platonic dialogues or in the *Apology* for that matter. Insofar as the question is a test, or a proof *ex negativo*, Socrates nonetheless expects to derive from it the knowledge of who is the wisest, in the sense of who knows best. For Bataille, on the other hand, the question implies both a suspicion and a suspension of knowledge; it exposes that at the bottom of it all there lies a hoax, and when the rug is pulled out from under our feet there remains only the gaping abyss, a penetrating but ultimately impenetrable terror he calls "inner experience."

Yet the link is not so fortuitous, for both figures share more than first meets the eye. To be sure, Socrates (particularly as he emerges from the pages of Nietzsche, who most of all philosophers haunts Bataille's thought) is all but the stodgy, self-composed academician. Socrates is a man with a demon inside him, Nietzsche's Silenus, whose infernal laughter in the forest[3] appeals to Bataille, while Bataille's understanding of the necessity of reason in the destruction of its own edifice recalls Socrates' own mad conclusion that "one thing I know is that I know nothing" (*hen oida oti ouden oida*). In two consecutive fragments in *Inner Experience*, Bataille writes of this necessary participation of reason in its own undoing: "Principle of inner experience: to emerge through project from the realm of project," followed by "Reason alone has the power to undo its work, to hurl down what it has built up. . . . Without the support of reason, we don't reach 'dark incandescence' " (OC 5: 60/IE 46–47). We must be very clear not to relegate to Bataille a thoughtless celebration of madness; thinking beyond the concept is still thinking, and actually, a more rigorous and difficult thinking—not madness.

However, before discussing in greater detail the difference between a concept and an experience of community, which Bataille's work foregrounds, and which hinges on the primacy of nonknowledge over discourse, I would like first to elaborate on the nature of the question, less as a foundation and more as a challenge to philosophy. I would suggest that the moment in which the question passes from foundation to challenge is the moment it begs nonknowledge as its only legitimate answer, a moment linked to the question's capacity for what Bataille calls "dramatization." The legend goes that tragic drama was born when Thespis first posed a question to the chorus. Still, we must be careful to distinguish the meaning Bataille attributes to dramatization from its narrow theatrical applications. Dramatization is rather the movement by which a happening (a *dromenon*, an event) draws us in, in a way that we abandon our solitary selves to undergo the event in common, to experience compassion. Dramatization is the movement of sweeping away.

In suspending the border between objectivity and subjectivity then, dramatization for Bataille not only articulates the difference between philosophy and inner experience but itself coincides with the experience of this difference. At the same time, as this difference, dramatization is somewhat cryptically inscribed in philosophy's beginning, that is, in the Socratic ordeal and its Platonic stagings. When one thinks of Socrates, for instance, one often speaks of the coincidence—thus also implying the difference—between philosophy and life, concept and experience. If Socrates dramatizes for the West this commensurability between life and self-knowledge, Bataille stands at the other end, speaking with Nietzsche "*after a catastrophe of the intelligence*" (OC 5: 40/IE 27). This means that dramatization for Bataille is first and foremost that of the experience of the untenability of discourse to lead the human to where it is destined to go—namely, to exceed itself. It is the reason why he proposes dramatization as the only way, indeed as the method, of experiencing community.[4]

Bataille thinks of dramatization mostly visually, but in a way that opposes any such banality as the image or scenery. He writes of the photographs of the Chinese torture he had at home as dramatizations of an "object-point," namely, a visual center whose intensity of presentation draws us outside ourselves as if toward a black hole, while the picture itself loses any stability as an outside object. Object points as the loci of this double effacement of subject and object have the capacity to turn the mind into an eye (OC 5: 138/IE 118), in effect, to lead us away from the concept and toward an impossible kind of sensuousness, the kind felt at the throes of death. Similarly, the scene of the *Apology* as a court drama and Socrates' own excessive dramatizations within it serve to make manifest the supreme and undramatizable moment of the ordeal, the pronouncement of the death penalty, which in some versions of the text is only implied in Socrates' response, while in this version is contained in brackets as some strange kind of scene guideline. If there were a photograph of philosophy's "first" torment, it would probably join the one of the Chinese torture above Bataille's desk.

We will return to the notion of dramatization, but for now let us step back to trace this relationship of nonknowledge to discourse as it is articulated in the figure of the question, the structuring figure of the Socratic theater. In the *Apology*, Socrates presents his questioning of people as a means to ascertain the truth of the Delphic oracle, which had pronounced him to be the wisest of men. Like Bataille, Socrates too goes from one man to another, assessing their wisdom and not limiting himself to the politicians, philosophers, and poets, to whom higher knowledge is attributed.[5] Seeing that these have failed to understand what he means by knowledge, he turns to the artisans, the everyday men of project and production, who purport to know not only their craft but matters of this higher knowledge as well. They too fail, for they conflate the knowledge of facts and the possession of information for that other type of knowledge Socrates is seeking, the knowledge of oneself—in other words, the limits of one's knowledge. From one man to another, a kind of community is then established that is challenged by and called to respond to this question but is defined to a great extent by its inability to listen to the gravity and, ultimately, the unanswerability of this question. Socrates as challenger of the human limits remains alone within the community his questions precipitate, ending up as the sacrificial victim of it, making of his solitude the typical posture of the philosopher. Likewise, Bataille exclaims, "Thus I speak—everything in me gives itself to others" (OC 5: 151/IE 130), along with "I am alone, bitter . . ." (OC 5: 150/IE 129) in the solitude of the desert, but we will revisit this desert at the end of the chapter.

The paradox of undertaking a logical route to (dis)prove a divine omen aside, Socrates' ironic conclusion to his own quest barely hides the dark conundrum underlying his philosophical project: if he has proven the omen correct, that is, if he is indeed the wisest of men, it is only insofar as wisdom is not defined as positive knowledge, but as the limit of knowledge, the place where knowledge founders. From his first doubt concerning the oracle—"Whatever does the god mean? What is his riddle? I am very conscious that I am not wise at all"—to the moment of his defense, he asserts repeatedly: "I do not know, neither do I think I know."[6] He assigns to others unwisdom insofar as they pretend to know something that cannot be known.

Wisdom for Socrates comes to signify nonknowledge, yet in his practice nonknowledge is always the dialectical other of knowledge, not the radical departure from the concept. After all, the *en oida oti ouden oida* signifies both that I have no knowledge whatsoever, as well as that I have the knowledge of nothingness in the sense that I know what nothing is. To know oneself is to know how pitifully ignorant one is of oneself, but it is still to know something in discursive terms. Socrates would have never ventured in his theoretical interrogation of others, had he not thought that nonknowledge could be discursively represented. This may be the reason why his mode of communication was so tenuous, based as it was on an effort to theorize experience. Still, in an example he offers to the court from one of his conversations, Socrates suggests exactly this: the knowledge of human and political virtue (and we could paraphrase: the knowledge of what makes of the human a human in that it makes of him or her a communal being) is not a property of the human and cannot be professed as an expertise:

> "Callias," I said, "if your sons were colts or calves, we could find and engage a supervisor for them who would make them excel in their proper qualities, some horse breeder or farmer. Now since they are men [*anthropo eston*], whom do you have in mind to supervise them? Who is an expert [*epistemon esti*] in this kind of excellence [*aretes*], the human [*anthropines*] and social [*politikes*]

> kind? I think you must have given thought to this since you have sons. Is there such a person," I asked, or "is there not?" "Certainly there is," he said. "Who is he?" I asked, "What is his name, where is he from? And what is his fee?" "His name, Socrates, is Evenus, he comes from Paros, and his fee is five minas." I thought Evenus a happy man, if he really possesses this art [*technen*], and teaches for so moderate a fee. Certainly I would pride and preen myself if I had this knowledge, but I do not have it, gentlemen.[7]

It seems that there is a great difference between what are deemed the qualities proper to the human and their theoretical appropriation by the human. No one possesses this "art," because it is neither an art, nor an episteme, in the sense of *techne* or discursive knowledge, which could be owned, taught, or improved upon. In this sense, the irony of the Socratic quest consists in asking for something unanswerable within the discourse already set forth. Put differently, to the question "What do you know, or think, of such and such?"—where both the "what" and the "such and such" refer to positively identifiable, discursive signifiers no matter how impossible their definition—one is seldom insightful or capable to answer otherwise than, "I know, or think, this or that." Even a negative answer, the kind Socrates favors, would sound rehearsed and sophistic (as he often sounds), since it would come out of intellectual self-consciousness, not out of the loss of self-composure—a loss, however, far from foreign to Socrates.

This is where Bataille reformulates the question. Bataille asks Hegel (and we can presumably think he would have asked the same to Socrates): "why must there be *what I know*?" (OC 5: 128/IE 109). This question also asks, why must there be *that* I know at all, including the fact that I may not know. Why am I even capable of thinking this thought and yet have no way out through thought to answer it? The "why" begs an aetiology that exceeds the limits of epistemological inquiry. To put it bluntly, it asks, like a child does, for the reason things exist and for the necessity of one's knowledge of them; understandingly, it partakes in the childish unsatisfaction of the "so what?"[8] So what if I know all this, when I do not know what I know it *for*, when I do not know why I know, and when I cannot think the wherefrom of my thought? Academic philosophy, having privileged questions concerning the "what" as it now privileges the "how," grows often weary of this "why." The why ends up abandoned with childhood, or handed over to theology for better or for worse, dismissed for being naïve and irrelevant because it challenges the discursive *modus operandi*. Bataille's insistence on "why" brings about the *désoeuvrement* of the question itself as a mark of skepticism, a means toward a proof, or a rhetorical figure of philosophical authority. The question is no more the foundation behind a project of research; it is always posed in the beginning but from the end of research and the exhaustion of what cannot be answered. Hence, as if speaking for the first time, as if not returning to the primal scene of the Socratic trial, Bataille, using unattributed quotations, constantly responds to this question of knowledge, with the "I know nothing" with which philosophy began (OC 5: 49, 62, 67, 73, 125/IE 37, 48, 53, 58, 106).

However, all this would still be the mere comparison of a figure, if it did not reveal something about the movement of thought itself, namely, that the question for both Socrates and Bataille, being fundamentally the question of death, takes its authority not from philosophy, even if for Socrates philosophy forms its outer limit. The question takes its urgency from the unknown, and if the Socratic project conceals this impetus in the process, it also reveals it as the inception and the end (that is also, the limit, the horizon) of philosophical practice, lest we forget that the question of mortality prompted Socrates to doubt the oracle and become a philosopher in the first place, as it also sealed his last public speech in the *Apology*. What is most important, however, is how this question of the impossible is made possible, how the philosopher is drawn to it, and how he finds himself in the grip of it, lucid and broken at once amidst his accusers; all this is a matter of dramatization.

Socrates began philosophizing from the excess of finitude he felt, of which the Delphic oracle was a dramatization. What the oracle presented to Socrates (much like it did to Oedipus) was nothing but the enigma of human finitude formulated in terms of the totality of knowledge: how dare the god pronounce him the wisest of men? How does this superlative make sense in view of time? Is he wisest just for now, a kind of contradiction in terms, or will he remain as such after his death? And how can he, a mortal, know this—that he will be the wisest even after his death, except by taking the god at his word? But is this knowledge, to take the god at his word? If not, can there be knowledge of death, or after death? What does death do to knowledge? Socrates returns to this initial anguish near the end of his life.

This anguish sets much of the tone of the *Apology*, which puts Socrates in that terrifying line of those who know and wait for the exact hour of the inevitable. Here Socrates makes the question of death explicitly the last question he attempts to answer in front of the court. His answer prefigures Hamlet's famous line, "The undiscovered country, from whose bourn/No traveller returns,"[9] but with a rather more optimistic, and in that sense, mad spin—the kind of optimism that coexists in reason with an unavowed madness: since we do not know what death is, since no one has returned from its realm to give us a report, we cannot judge or assume anything—even better, we cannot assume the worst. Perhaps his old age claims the best of him and, wishing to escape the fate that awaits him, he dreams salvific dreams of meeting the shades of great heroes. Perhaps, though, his Silenic wisdom has not abandoned him, as he exposes himself to finitude, embracing it with joy:

> To fear death, gentlemen, is no other than to think oneself wise when one is not, to think one knows what one does not know. No one knows whether death may not be the greatest of all blessings for a man, yet men fear it as if they knew that it is the greatest of evils. And surely it is the most blameworthy ignorance to believe that one knows what one does not know. It is perhaps on this point and in this respect, gentlemen, that I differ from the majority of men, and if I were to claim that I am wiser than anyone in anything, it would be in this, that, as I have no adequate knowledge of things in the underworld, so I do not think I have.[10]

The *en oida oti ouden oida* takes on its proper content: I do not know what I cannot know; and yet, is it not precisely this—the unknown, my finitude—the most inviting and most primordial question behind all my attempts at knowing? Death makes a conceit of knowledge, but ironically Socrates' insistence on nonknowledge also shares a part in the conceit: Socrates implies that had he known more about death—as if this is not the very impossibility that causes our denials and our fear of death—he would be more in a position to pass a legitimate judgment on it. As if death could even hypothetically be put on the same register with other notions the philosopher can assess according to his degree of familiarity. Though Socrates speaks of nonknowledge, the conceit lies in the theoretical distance he is able to take. What if nonknowledge, however, stems not from philosophical distance, but from the proximity to the abyss?

The latter is where Bataille begins. He probes the same question, maintaining first that the experience of finitude marks the collapse of discourse, and second, that dramatization as the blurring of boundaries—not philosophy as distance—is the mode of finitude's disclosure: "It is through an 'intimate cessation of all intellectual operations' that the mind is laid bare. If not, *discourse* maintains it in its little complacency. Discourse, if it wishes to, can blow like a gale wind—whatever effort I make, the wind cannot chill by the fireside. The difference between inner experience and philosophy resides principally in this: that in experience, what is stated is nothing, if not a means and even, as much as a means, an obstacle; what counts is no longer the statement of wind, but the wind" (OC 5: 25/IE 13). Discourse can blow like a hurricane, but it will not freeze the mind from its busywork of tricks aimed at diverting it from its mortal anxiety. Experience interrupts discourse. In experience nothing is stated, whereby nothing (the *ouden*) is to be understood as the extreme limit.

This is a difficult formulation, which exhausts the attempt at meaning. Bataille may mean that there is no other experience but the experience of nothing, of nonbeing, an experience that cannot be as such; hence, he refers to the most spectral of the elements, the chilling and invisible wind. Consequently, we might also say that the only thing experience can state and still be experience—not discourse—is nothing. But how can nothingness as the extreme limit be expressed? Bataille gives contradictory answers throughout *Inner Experience*, at times allowing and even demanding for its expressibility, but more often emphasizing its unattainability particularly within discourse. As his further qualification in this passage itself suggests, experience ought to say nothing; but if it does say something, and because it is impossible to express nothingness, experience recognizes that this statement marks an obstacle to reaching the extreme limit. To a certain degree experience marks and mourns this diminution (the difference, the remainder) from affect to concept—or more radically, it testifies to the annihilation, the rendering nothing of affect.

This much is clear, that linguistic expression is not the attainment of inner experience, since it presupposes subject/object distinctions and reduces experience to an object of expression. For Bataille, language participates in the mind's evasions of mortality, and for this reason it too needs to be contested: "If we live under the law of language without contesting it, these states [the states of inner experience] are passing within us as if they didn't exist" (OC 5: 27/IE 14). Even literature, insofar as it is a statement *about* experience, remains a means, stopping short of the extreme limit: "When the extreme limit is there, the means which serve to attain it are no longer there" (OC 5: 64/IE 50). When the means disappear, communication takes place, which is not a means but the medium, *the element*, of experience. This is why eventually the only thing that matters is the wind. Philosophy differs from inner experience in that the former is a discourse that talks of the wind, while the latter is a state of being that listens to the wind and that lets the wind strike it. The wind is not a metaphor or image of communication; it is the element of communication. If the wind carries some words, they come and go indistinct, maybe even nonsensical; what remains is the force of the wind felt between us, the element that sweeps us away, that draws us toward each other and throws us apart from each other.

Immediately following this distinction between philosophy and experience, Bataille offers another definition of dramatization, for once again, this is the key term that makes the distinction possible by making us aware of those states of experience that would go unnoticed had we stayed permanently within discourse: "At this point we see the second meaning of the word dramatize: it is the will, adding itself to discourse, not to be content with what is stated, to oblige one to feel the chill of the wind, to be laid bare" (OC 5: 26/IE 13). Whereas before I mentioned dramatization in conjunction with visuality, here Bataille draws on its acoustic and tactile aspects. The wind howls in our ears and strikes our bare skin. Visual, acoustic, or tactile, dramatization is the contestation of language in the domain of affect and sentience; it puts the body in the posture of supplication, and here Bataille cites the example of dramatic art making "a character tremble on stage" and "using non-discursive sensation, making every effort to strike, for that reason imitating the sound of the wind and attempting to chill" (OC 5: 26/IE 13).

Dramatization is to experience what language is to philosophy, namely, the mode of its exposition. Lou Andreas Salomé once described Nietzsche with a phrase that is illuminating in this context: "In Nietzsche the most abstract thoughts habitually could reverse themselves into the power of moods."[11] What she describes is Nietzsche's proneness to dramatization, the capacity of the mood to usurp thought, certainly the most crucial feature of Nietzsche's appeal to Bataille. For Bataille, too, the philosophical question would not be a real question unless it came out of anguish, which is the reason why it needs dramatization. Dramatization infuses the question with torment [*supplice*], driving it to aporia, and transforming philosophy into supplication (OC 5: 48/IE 36). Only dramatization leads to an *ouden oida* that cannot be recuperated into knowledge by dialectical or theological maneuverings. Socrates himself, who, shunning tragedy, wore the tragic mask in the theater of death, and Bataille, who glimpsed inner experience by plunging into his "object-points" of suffering, meet at the juncture of dramatization. A peculiar kind of communication happens, a sharing of experience as the sharing of nonknowledge. "I do not know," they whisper to each other, or rather they let the wind whisper it. Why else would the legend have it that Socrates, the avowed enemy of tragedy, devoted his last days to learning the most Dionysian of instruments—the flute[12] or, should we say, the wind?

Ocean: Bataille off Limits

I have elaborated on the ancient links among philosophy, dramatization, and nonknowledge, because it will be also important for my discussion of Bataille's relationship to contemporary thought, where this uneasy triangulation is once again foregrounded and contested. In *The Inoperative Community*, Jean-Luc Nancy's reception of Bataille combines the commitment to a philosophy of experience, by which I mean a thinking not centered on conceptuality, with the sidelining of dramatization, which Nancy views as Bataille's participation in the false pathos of the metaphysics of the subject.[13] While Nancy does not use the term *dramatization* for much of what he disclaims in Bataille, his critique of communion as the fusional, oceanic moment of community is an instance of distancing himself from such dramatizations. In fact, fusion is not simply an instance, but a defining aspect of dramatization: if we recall Bataille's definition of object points, which for him are synonymous with dramatization, they incite the fusion of "subject" and "representation." Nancy critiques the notion of fusion variously, but the main charge remains that it supplies the human with a false infinity in a higher plane (resurrection in Christianity and sublation in Hegel, for instance), thus denying death and, at the extreme limit of fascism, making light of annihilation.[14]

Let me take this opportune moment to interject an overall impression of my experience of reading Nancy next to Bataille, an impression that I will try to think through in the remaining portion of this chapter. While I am conceptually convinced by Nancy's deconstruction of communion, particularly given some of its dangerous ethico-political ramifications, I cannot overlook the descriptive force this term has for Bataille in relating the experience of anguish. I think that this tearing that I experience in reading them reflects their difference as readers of the human, the difference between two modes of thinking and writing, and the (im)possibility of their communication.[15] Even though Nancy thinks of his work as a communication with Bataille rather than a critique, learning as he says from Bataille's experience rather than his theses,[16] I think that Nancy is closest to Bataille when he radicalizes the latter conceptually (an incisive and original closeness, since Bataille is virtually unapproachable through concepts), while he is the farthest when he describes, or narrates—that is, when he dramatizes experience. In fact, Nancy does not dramatize experience. Nancy achieves a conceptually consistent framework of thinking community in a nonsubjective way, but in doing so he unwittingly attenuates the specificity—I will not go as far as to say, the singularity—of Bataille's experience. He attenuates it not only in terms of his own soberer style but also in his choice of philosophical categories. I do not intend this as a criticism of Nancy, any more than I am in the least doubting Nancy's own candor about his willingness to communicate with rather than critique Bataille. Rather, I am suggesting that, in wishing to speak from the experience of Bataille (to "repeat" Bataille as Bataille repeated Nietzsche perhaps), Nancy is also bound to sacrifice Bataille much as he problematizes the notion of sacrifice itself.[17]

To return to the choice of philosophical categories: the shift, for instance, from Bataille's psychological aspects of subjectivity to the ethico-ontological ones of singularity admittedly does a lot to prioritize community and relationality over the individual subject, even though as Nancy himself acknowledges, "Bataille had no *concept* of the subject" in the sense of a consistently fixed category, and more often than not, his use of the term is analogous to singularity.[18] At any rate, though this shift affords a more rigorous thinking of community as a relation among singularities rather than an aggregate of individuals, it also equalizes the anguish that marks each singular being, an anguish experienced similarly but then also differently. The difference between similarity and identity (equality is a form of identity) is addressed by Nancy in the context of the dialectic of recognition: "The like is not the same," writes Nancy, pointing out the error of the Hegelian recognition, in which one sees in the other the mirror image of oneself, instead of seeing only resemblance.[19] We can carry this insight into the sharing of anguish, where I would emphasize the similarity and unpredictability, rather than identity, involved.

We are in relation to what gives us our being and our death, which for Nancy, following Heidegger, is Being. Our singularity then unfolds in the manner of this relation, as the part we contribute to this relation to Being, in effect, as the way we relate to relation. Hence, even though death is given impartially, that is, equally to all, its anguish is felt similarly, not identically, through this unique manner each singularity configures its relation to Being. If I may be allowed the monstrous expression, some get "more of" death than others. I see Bataille as being drawn to this mode of impartial share, which, however, appears always unbearably partial for the one who is under its grip: "In the abandon in which I am lost, the empirical knowledge of my similarity with others is irrelevant, for the essence of my self arises from this—that nothing will be able to replace it: the feeling of my fundamental improbability situates me in the world where I remain as though foreign to it, absolutely foreign" (OC 5: 84/IE 69). Even though Nancy would say that this is what is shared in common, the uniqueness of every singularity, I am interested not in the conceptual framework that guarantees a priori this statement's truth but in the moment of solitude and despair in which this truth is often revealed. This moment ruptures the with-ness to which being nonetheless is exposed, but which it experiences as a painful withdrawal.

Nancy, however, is interested more in the equality that the sharing assumes. To be clear, Nancy repeats that there is nothing that we "have" in common, thus equality is not to be understood vulgarly as in the distribution of goods. Instead, *we are in common*, in the sense that we partake in finite Being. We share in death, which means that we are equal in the sharing of Being and in its sharing of us into divided, limited, singular beings. This is what Nancy means when he defines singularity as a passion: "The singular being, because it is singular, is in the passion—the passivity, the suffering, and the excess—of sharing its singularity. The presence of the other does not constitute a boundary that would limit the unleashing of 'my' passions: on the contrary, only exposition to the other unleashes my passions."[20] It should be possible to say with Nancy that, if sharing is singularity's passion, it is passion because what it shares is also unshareable. Yet, despite Nancy's allowances for the excessive and plural nature of singularity, this passage also indicates his will to resolve Bataille's tension between the solitary and communal determinations of being on the side of the latter. Nancy's formulation suggests that whatever the particular nature of one's suffering, it becomes bearable in the knowledge that it is shared. There is no question of experiencing otherwise what indeed remains a fact, namely, that this anguish is in common. Nonknowledge shared equally and abstractly, without the anguish of dramatization, is no more nonknowledge; it is conceptual thought. There is no question of refusing the solace of this knowledge, for it is a kind of solace. It becomes both terrible and laughable (all the better probably for Bataille) to claim that, at some moments, the sharing of singularity does not make dying any more bearable, that the sharing of singularity is also impossible at the very moment singularity is "most" singular, the moment of dying. This is why the knowledge that finitude shares us is not enough for Bataille to reach the extreme limit. This is a knowledge we have in existing, not in the experience of dying: "No matter what I say, I *know* myself [*je me sais*] to be the member of a species and I remain in harmony, roughly speaking, with a *common* reality [finitude.] . . . The self-that-dies abandons this harmony" (OC 5: 85/IE 71; em).

Interestingly, boundaries, which are otherwise clearly drawn in Nancy's text,[21] since they are necessary for marking the exteriority of singular beings, momentarily disappear here. "[T]he other does not constitute a boundary" (an obstacle, a limit) to my passion. Could this mean that my passion flows into the other with no resistance? This would be Bataille's fusion, the ocean in whose waves flows "everything which is great and sublime in man,"[22] and clearly Nancy wishes not to have such boundaries blurred. The question involves the nature of the boundary in Nancy, which is thought of at once positively, as in delineating the singular and thus preserving its alterity (from what, one could ask—intrusion? Infusion? Invasion? Contagion? Flood?), and negatively, as in this case, implying that a boundary could be an obstacle to the unleashing of the other's passion. Nancy tries to keep a precarious balance between limits as places of interconnection and limits as dams against excessive outpouring. He gives us some sense of his notion of boundaries in his discussion of articulation, where boundaries function as junctures.[23] My extremity touches the extremity of the other. Our passions meet at certain junctures, where they "fold or stiffen, flex or tense" around the pivot, but they do not flow and fuse through it.[24] A striking image comes to mind: what if in resisting flow through them junctures become hardened, ossified, and brittle knots, confusions instead of fusions? Would not brittle joints break community as quickly as Bataille's fusional meltdown? At this point, I can only suggest that perhaps on the issue of fusion, the difference between Bataille and Nancy is that the latter thinks of touch as exclusive of permeability. Whereas in Bataille being feels its limits to be so despairingly limiting that it yearns for a thorough permeability, bringing on the flood, in Nancy the limits delimit themselves as intersections but also separations.

We can better understand this tension between the two philosophers in view of a larger context that involves Nancy's interest in conferring ontological precedence to community above all else. Indeed, *The Inoperative Community* aims at unveiling community as the central, albeit often repressed term of Bataille's thought. However, to show the underivability of community, Nancy relies on Bataille's explicit and passionate engagement with mortality, a "subjective" passion—Bataille's own, for that matter—which is the very hurdle Nancy must overcome in order to think community. Despite Nancy's understanding of singularity as passion, his reading repeats Heidegger's hierarchization of the existential analytic of death in *Being and Time* as superordinate over all other theorizations of death (BT sec. 49)—superordinate, in the sense that it analyzes death before it becomes a passion for the human being. This is exactly the assumption behind Nancy's own articulation of his difference from Bataille: "I am trying to indicate, at its limit, an experience—not, perhaps, an experience that we have, *but an experience that makes us be.*"[25] Implying that Bataille's understanding of experience is Kantian in nature—necessarily a posteriori—Nancy gives ontological priority to his own instead.

Indeed, that Nancy's nonanthropological thinking of community through finitude is the most original and rigorous of its kind is a humble understatement for a work that among its other merits has exhausted, that is, brought to the limit, our reading of Bataille. However, as it would not be in Nancy's spirit to think of this exhaustion as the completion of community, or the "last word" in the conversation, I would venture to pose some questions: Is there a proper way of thinking death, a question Derrida already posed to Heidegger throughout his *Aporias*?[26] In other words, can we prioritize one death narrative over another, to the point of proposing a foundational analysis of death? Is Bataille not proper to death's excess when he commits the philosophical error of speaking of death *after* it has become a passion for the human being yet insisting on this after as if it is always *prior*? Could we not say that death's excess resists accommodation into an a priori analytic, that death "makes sense" only as passion, as drama, namely, as something also nonsensical?

Regarding this issue of priority of being over having, a further argument can be made on Bataille's behalf, one that returns us to the notion of dramatization. In one of his descriptions of dramatization, Bataille writes that the dramatic "is simply to be" (OC 5: 24/IE 12), and to be in the sense that being opposes itself to acting: "In the will to suppress pain, we are led to action, instead of limiting ourselves to dramatization" (OC 5: 23/IE 11). Action, the world of having projects and goals, means flight from anguish and thus flight from being. Dramatization, as the contestation of the human itself, is the contestation of the subject of action. To exceed "being merely a man" (OC 5: 47/IE 35) means to exceed the human-all-too-human avoidance of the limit through work. What else lies at the heart of the most classic of the tragedies but the *désoeuvrement* of Oedipus as a man of knowledge and action? Tragedy, in a certain sense, is always the dramatization of such *désoeuvrement*.

Now the key difference between Bataille and Nancy is that Bataille links this *désoeuvrement* to the loss of self in fusion. Bataille turns to fusion because the opening beyond the merely human reveals paradoxically the inconsequentiality of the individual being. Exceeding oneself is the yearning of a finite being who is annulled less by its death and more by its death's meaninglessness in the cosmic order of things: "the complex, the gentle, the violent movement of worlds will make of your death a splashing foam" (OC 5: 112/IE 95). Faced with this inconsequentiality, the human being is besieged by a wish, both false and destructive, to efface its nothingness by fusing with others in the hope of preserving its meaningfulness through the whole. This is at least Nancy's reading. Or in another reading more appropriate to the sovereign, and closer to what Nancy calls "transcendence," this inconsequentiality reveals to the human being that to exceed itself means to give up on the delusion of effacing its limitations, which is also a delusion of mastery and self-preservation. Then being sinks again into the ocean of undifferentiation, but this time fusion is not a project: it is no more a means to salvation. It is an act of affirmative despair. This reading of fusion is ultimately bound up with Bataille's understanding of solitude, a notion that preserves the presence of boundaries at the very moment they are effaced in the self's effacement. At the extreme limit of this unworking notion of fusion, being gives itself over to solitude, whereby solitude means the refusal of recognition, namely, the refusal of individuality and of sublation (OC 5: 179/IE 155). Through this refusal, a disjointed being joins not only human others but the "nature" that it suppressed in making itself the measure of things. Fusion then turns out to be not simply the erasure of the limit but an encounter with the limit: it is nothing more than a glorious affirmation of the inconsequentiality of subjectivity *qua* human limit and a renunciation of anthropocentrism.

Desert: Lamma Sabachtani

If the human must exceed itself from being merely human, and if the truly human is inextricable from the communal, ought not the exceeding also signify the undoing (not only as unworking, but also as shattering, effacing, rendering absent) of community as the very possibility of experience? To rephrase: exceeding its humanity is what is most human about the human. But does this not also imply that a radical excess would involve not following the destiny of the human—namely, the communal—but turning away from this destiny all the while from within it? This is the impossibility that lies at the heart of Bataille's simultaneous yearning for community and the immense solitude behind his yearning.

This impossibility belongs to the order of tragedy, the art that for Bataille represents our mortal predicament, namely, the death we suffer because of death's knowledge: "Man dying *poorly*, distances himself from nature, engenders an illusory, human world fashioned for *art*: we live in the tragic world, in the false atmosphere of which 'tragedy' is the completed [form]. Nothing is tragic for the animal, which doesn't fall into the trap of the *self* [*moi*]" (OC 5: 88/IE 73). The human suffers from this awareness of finitude, an awareness that occurs, as Nancy shows, in the community. Whether the trap is the self or a singularity, it does not matter; after all, singularity is marked even more profoundly than the self by its knowledge of finitude. The difference lies in how this knowledge itself is to be viewed. For Bataille, being a trap, it is a curse, a knowledge of anguish, a tragic knowledge. On the contrary, taking it as such (but this is the question: do we know what it is as such, or that it is, or that we can accept it?), Nancy, not unlike Socrates, shuns such negative judgments in favor of demystifying death: "It is death—but if one is permitted to say so, *it is not a tragic death*, or else, it is more accurate to say it this way, *it is not mythic death*, or death followed by a resurrection, or the death that plunges into a pure abyss: it is death as sharing and as exposure."[27] Philosophy demystifies death, while the drama of the debate between philosophy and tragedy Socrates dreamed of resolving in the afterlife continues. To the matter-of-factness of philosophy, Bataille's tragic view allows for the impossible despair of not wanting to be human, not wanting to be at all, and not wanting to know—all negations that can only be human. Thus, the equally impossible thought of community's conflagration is the expression of a flight from death, but a flight which for Bataille is more sovereign than all the others since it rests not on death's denial, but on its all-consuming affirmation. In thinking this, Bataille thinks not simply excess, but the excess of excess. We could say that his thought of *dépense* is actually the expenditure of thought, a *pensée*, which is *dérobée* insofar as it is also *dé-pensée*, an antithought, an unthinkable thought inadmissible to philosophical optimism, calmness, and rigor. This is the thought of the desert.

Nietzsche's ocean morphs in Bataille into an ocean of sand. Bataille writes: "I know how to respond to the desire of Nietzsche speaking of a community having no object other than that of experience (but designating this community, I speak of 'desert')" (OC 5: 40/IE 27). When we speak of the desert, or rather when we think of the desert speaking, we think of "the voice in the wilderness," its failure to get across, to be heard, to communicate; we think of the Baptist's warnings uttered in vain, like Socrates', offending the public and claiming both their lives. Yet "desert" designates for Bataille the community that has as its sole object its own experience, that is, its communication. It may well be that the scare quotes around the term testify to this paradoxical aspect or suggest that we read the term figuratively, but most probably as marks of distancing, they enhance the distance that according to Bataille separates modern man from this community of the desert (OC 5: 40–41/IE 28).

But why use the desert and not the ocean? Much like the ocean, the vastness of the desert promises both fusion and inconsequentiality, where entire caravans vanish in its monotony, reduced as it were to a grain of sand. Why then does Bataille change Nietzsche on this point? I suggest that this transformation encapsulates the basic difference between Nietzsche's and Bataille's response to the problem of experience as Lionel Abel has also outlined it: whereas Nietzsche insists on the affirmation of life, Bataille takes the side of death.[28] It is neither fusion as resurrection nor fusion as the "good" transcendence via the refusal of recognition that the desert most of all beckons; it is rather obliteration, the undoing of everything that does not belong to the desert—the undoing of everything that is not undoing itself. In the desert, unlike the depths of the ocean, no fusion can add up to any totality, no organism will grow. Fusion turns instantly into diffusion and dispersal, into the infinitely finite grains of sand.

The desert refuses to be worked on. There, nature sovereignly sterile yields no products; it is inert, inoperable. Yet there is in the desert another kind of abundance, the continual laying bare of space and time in a standstill that disorients pointing only toward oblivion. The surface of the desert exposes relentlessly: it exposes everything to death, to vanishing under complete visibility. Then one caravan's remains become the warning signs for the next. Is this communication between two communities? Can there be communication between the living and the dead? Nancy would be strictly opposed to this spectral logic, and for good reasons, too, not the least of which is that, actually, there are no ghosts in the desert either. Nothing can withstand this level of exposure without turning exactly into that—nothing—and it is this nothingness that the "desert" communicates. However, it communicates this nothingness always in its distance from us, for if we ever made it there, we would not survive to hear the message. This is why despite Bataille's privileging of the ancient man's proximity to this "desert" (OC 5: 40–41/IE 28), we can see that this "desert"—always distant inside its quotations—marks the precinct of what has been and will remain unattainable in experience so that experience can be experience instead of becoming knowledge.

But the desert is also something else. It is the theater of what for Bataille might be the greatest dramatization in the history of modern man: the death of God. The scene is important because it shows "inaccessible death," the side of death that counters its being the "common inevitable" [*vulgaire inévitable*] (OC 5: 86/IE 71). Commonality compromises death's inaccessibility—in fact, vulgarizes it, to use the stronger sense of the French choice of word for "common." One cannot bypass this by saying that what is in common is this inaccessibility, for inaccessibility here means what cannot be shared, cannot be heard and responded to, and cannot enter into relation, although it cannot stop supplicating: *lamma sabachtani*. In the desertlike landscape of Golgotha, a place of skulls and bones where the "dark wind" of exhaustion blows (OC 5: 121/IE 103), Christ dies abandoned by his father: "There is no longer a God in 'inaccessible death,' no longer a God in closed night; one no longer hears anything but *lamma sabachtani*, the little sentence, which of all sentences, men have charged with a sacred horror" (OC 5: 86/IE 72). If death is inoperable and inoperative it is due to this inaccessibility, which is not in common and which interrupts community. Thus, the inoperative community whose sole "object" is its own experience—the experience of Being as Nothing—is the community that grants death's inaccessibility to be a radical, nondialectizable opposite to its commonality.

The significant repetition of this *lamma sabachtani* in *Inner Experience* (OC 5: 61, 86, 121/IE 47, 72, 103) runs parallel to the Socratic "I know nothing," both being formulations of the anguish of nonknowledge. If, as Bataille urges us to do, we read him from the vantage point of nonknowledge, we should also hearken to this cry he himself must have uttered or heard in those abyssal encounters that shaped his fiction and philosophy—the white of his syphilitic father's blind eyes, the gory death of Manuel Granero by the bull he witnessed as a young man, his weeping over Nietzsche's tears. To this *lamma sabachtani* there is no possible answer; community cannot answer to its horror, and though it seeks community in its supplication, its loneliness marks the limits of compearance.[29]

Nonetheless, since it is just as necessary to think and talk about the wind as it is to let it chill us, let us conclude with community—the thinking community—rather than loneliness. Despite my resistance to what I view as Nancy's systematization of Bataille, it was his keen eye for the latent Heidegger in Bataille's text combined with his wish to communicate on the level of experience that gave the impetus to my reading: trying to understand Bataille along with Nancy's Bataille, and the ways in which the former may have responded to his transformation by the latter, I became involved with the thought of the limit—the limits underpinning Bataille's and Nancy's thoughts on mortality, and the limits and delimitations involved in taking Bataille to his limit. Concluding his remarks on limits and mortality in Heidegger, and in taking Heidegger to the limit, Derrida's *Aporias* offers us a provocative model for reading, a reading in time, a finite reading:

> *On the one hand*, . . . [Heidegger's] existential analysis exceeds and therefore includes beforehand the work of the historian, not to mention the biologist, the psychologist, and the theologian of death. . . . However, *on the other hand*, conversely but just as legitimately, one can also be tempted to read *Being and Time* as a small, late document, among many others *within* the huge archive where the memory of death in Christian Europe is being accumulated. Each of these two discourses on death is much more comprehensive than the other, bigger and smaller than what it tends to include or exclude, more and less originary, more and less ancient, young or old.[30]

Hopefully, this discussion shows that Bataille's philosophical and experiential involvement with finitude can be read from this third site, the site of contamination between intellect and passion, priority and posteriority, superordination and subordination: the site of dramatization.

Notes

1. Quoted in Robert Sasso, "Georges Bataille and the Challenge to Think," *On Bataille: Critical Essays*, ed. Leslie Anne Boldt-Irons (Albany: State University of New York Press, 1995), 42.

2. Robert Sasso makes a quick reference to Socrates in relation to Bataille and the issue of the question but does not develop it (42–43). For the Greek original of the *Apology* I consulted James Riddell's edition of Plato, *The Apology of Plato* (Oxford: Oxford University Press, 1877; New York: Arno, 1973).

3. Friedrich Nietzsche, *The Birth of Tragedy,* trans. Walter Kaufmann (New York: Vintage Books, 1967), 42.

4. In *Inner Experience* dramatization is introduced under the chapter title "Principles of a Method and a Community." Bataille writes that "one reaches the states of ecstasy or of rapture only by *dramatizing* existence in general" (OC 5: 22/IE 10) and, "If we didn't know how to dramatize, we wouldn't be able to leave ourselves" (OC 5: 23/IE 11). For Bataille the experience of exposure is ultimately tied up with this process of dramatization, a process inherited from religious ritual and, via this ceremonial route, from the ancient art of theater. This, however, does not mean that dramatization must necessarily remain enclosed within the religious. Denis Hollier, for instance, offers a reading of the textual communication between

Nietzsche and Bataille—Nietzsche's presence as absence in Bataille—as an instance of dramatization that escapes the mythological demand of divine presence in his "From Beyond Hegel to Nietzsche's Absence," *On Bataille: Critical Essays*, ed. Leslie Anne Boldt-Irons (Albany: State University of New York Press, 1995), 61–78, 73.

5. Plato, *Apology,* 21e.

6. Ibid., 21b–e.

7. Ibid., 20b–c.

8. Bataille's literary community in *Literature and Evil* shares in this childish unsatisfaction.

9. William Shakespeare, *Hamlet*, ed. Cyrus Hoy, 2nd Critical Edition (New York: Norton, 1992), act 3, scene 1, 79–80.

10. Plato, *Apology,* 29a–b.

11. Lou Salomé, *Nietzsche*, ed. and trans. Siegfried Mandel (Urbana: University of Illinois Press, 2001), 43.

12. The story of Socrates turning to music and poetry while waiting for death is told in Plato's *Phaedo,* 60c–61d, in *Five Dialogues*, ed. and trans. G.M.A. Grube (Indianapolis: Hackett, 1981). In *Crito*, Socrates compares the inner voice that compels him to stay for his execution to the music of a flute (*Five Dialogues*, 54d). Section 14 of *The Birth of Tragedy* concludes with this image of the music-making Socrates.

13. The category most at stake in Nancy's thinking of finitude is that of the subject. For Nancy community cannot be thought through a philosophy of the subject, because the latter is caught up in what he calls "immanentism"—that is, the subject's dream of producing its own essence and of thinking freedom as self-sufficiency, which suggest the infinitude rather than the finitude of the human. Thus, Bataille's inability to escape from the philosophical confines of the subject—no matter how vulnerable and fragmented his subject is portrayed—always risks falling back into a discourse of capability and infinitude. Such discourse does not let death happen; it appropriates and sublates mortality, thus making out of the irreducible moment of death an operation, a work. Narratives of heroism and sacrifice, in which someone's death is collectively appropriated to serve "higher purposes," and then transcended—that is, annulled as a singular discontinuity—into the future achievement of nationhood or the realization of a certain ideal, are examples of such death works. Against this capitalized and capitalizing Transcendence of sublation, which is co-implicated in immanence, Nancy offers 'transcendence' in quotation marks, the horizontal relation among beings that exceed themselves by reaching to others (Jean-Luc Nancy, *The Inoperative Community*, ed. and trans. Peter Connor [Minneapolis: University of Minnesota Press, 1991], 24). This 'transcendence' is, according to Nancy, the single alternative to immanence.

14. Nancy, *Inoperative Community,* 17.

15. By (im)possibility I wish to emphasize the fact that the urgency behind their philosophical encounter, an urgency that is grounded on the need for communication, counterbalances their theoretical divergences. I would like at this point to thank my colleagues Krzyzstof Ziarek and Ewa Plonowska Ziarek for the many invaluable conversations concerning the dialogue between Heidegger and Bataille that Nancy sets forth, as well as the theoretical and ethical nuances that may bridge singularity to certain understandings of subjectivity.

16. Nancy, *Inoperative Community*, 25.

17. Lionel Abel writes on the unrepeatability of Nietzsche's repetition in Bataille. To read Nietzsche authentically is to become Nietzsche, but the only way this could happen is by not being Nietzsche, since Nietzsche's particularities and contradictions remain unrepeatable; Lionel Abel, "Georges Bataille and the Repetition of Nietzsche," *On Bataille: Critical Essays*, ed. Leslie Anne Boldt-Irons (Albany: State University of New York Press, 1995), 59. Nancy's communication with Bataille can be thought along similar lines.

18. Nancy, *Inoperative Community*, 24.

19. Ibid., 33.

20. Ibid., 32–33.

21. In his foreword to *The Inoperative Community*, Christopher Fynsk remarks that Nancy is closer to Heidegger in his preference for sharply demarcated limits. Fynsk opposes this to Blanchot's indeterminate limits, who is certainly more in the company of Bataille. Christopher Fynsk, foreword, *The Inoperative Community,* by Jean-Luc Nancy, vii-xxxv, xix.

22. Nietzsche as quoted by Bataille at IE 27 at OC 5:40/IE 27.

23. Nancy, *Inoperative Community*, 76.

24. Ibid.

25. Ibid., 26.

26. Derrida shows that 1. the delimitation of the field of the existential analytic relies on the classical philosophical argument of "presupposition," which implies a foundationalist logic; Jacques Derrida, *Aporias*, trans. Thomas Dutoit (Stanford: Stanford University Press, 1993), 28, 45; and 2. Heidegger's sharp limit between his formally empty existential analytic and the metaphysical contents of anthropological or theological analyses of death is problematic (54–55).

27. Nancy, *Inoperative Community* 66–67; em.

28. Abel, "Repetition," 55.

29. Nancy's neologism for the appearing-together of finitude (*Inoperative Community,* 28).

30. Derrida, *Aporias*, 81.

CHAPTER SEVEN

Contact and Communication

Alphonso Lingis

Fish, insects, mammals, and birds have evolved distinctive colors, patterns, ostentatious decorative fins, tails, antlers, plumage, and distinctive voices as diverse as there are species, by which they recognize their own kind. For these animal species, recognition is also attraction; for them to recognize members of their own species is to be drawn to them. Even solitary predatory species do not prey on their own kind (though they may well establish and defend their own territory from others of their kind with violent and even deadly attacks).

With humans it may seem that physical shape and voice help us to recognize members of our own species. But the approach of other humans is a territorial encroachment. Instead of being drawn to them, humans have, from time immemorial, formed themselves into particular groups and regard outside groups with anxiety, distrust, and fear. Culture is the means for us to acquire a particular identity: we identify with one another and against other groups by cultivating distinctive garb; a particular language; distinctive group-affirming performances such as games, dances, and feasts; and a distinctive religion.

What breaks us out of this group identity and identifies us to outsiders as of our own kind is for Georges Bataille not rational thought, but laughter and sexual excitement. In a foreign place, those with whom we have no language or commitment to ancestors, leaders, or gods in common, with whom we are not engaged in any common practical project, are remote and alien to us. Then something happens—the abrupt breakdown of practical operations, a planned and foreseen outcome that turns out to be unworkable—that releases an outbreak of laughter. The laughter rebounds among us and renders us transparent to one another: I see in the one who laughs with me someone of my kind.

Distinctive to human mammals is the propensity to become sexually aroused outside of any breeding season and outside of reproductive intent and even possibility. While most humans engage in sexual bonds and commitments with members of their own community and culture, they find themselves erotically aroused by foreigners and outcasts. In witnessing the erotic exhibitionism of courtesans and temple prostitutes, Hollywood celebrities, and idle adolescents in any foreign land, we are aroused and recognize in those aroused about us people like ourselves.

This sphere of communication in laughter—and in tears—and in erotic excitement precedes and makes possible, and is not superseded by, communication in rational thought and in practical projects conceived and regulated by rational language. Here communication is recognition of others as of our kind and attraction to them. Laughter and tears give rise to blessings and cursings—the primary form of speech. We gather together to speak of what amuses and what torments us, what we bless and curse.

We commonly say that language is a means of communication; through a common language individuals exchange their experiences and insights and build a knowledge that is common. But language continually breaks into diverse tongues and dialects and multiplies technical languages and jargons. And language, Voltaire remarked, could almost be said to have been invented in order that men dissimulate their thoughts.

Before the Second World War, in his book *The Crisis of European Sciences and Transcendental Phenomenology,*[1] Edmund Husserl argued that with rational language and the practical projects they regulate, humans, despite their cultural particularisms, achieve community. Rational thought captures the patterns and events that are observed in the field of perception of individuals in universal concepts and formulates the relations between things and events in laws and theories open to verification and contestation by anyone, anywhere. The rational individual submits his observations and reasons to the judgment of anyone endowed with the power of insight and understanding. The practice of rational thought projects, beyond particular communities bound together by common practical projects for defense and productive work, the idea, idea-limit, or ideal of universal humanity. Today the electronic communication technology invented after the Second World War and distributed across the planet is taken to assume and promote this ideal of universal rational humanity.

But the integral rational agent, as Immanuel Kant depicts him, in fact does not communicate: instead in her words and her actions she makes herself an exemplar for everyone. For the rational agent to respect the other is to respect the law that rules in her and that binds her also.

Humans communicate, we commonly say, in order to build, and by building, a common work—a productive enterprise, civil society, and a state apparatus. Each then makes himself or herself a means and not an end. What are left are the roads, the high-rise buildings, corporations, and the states that absorb the builders into their anonymous material subsistence or subsistence as an anonymous regional or global order.

Georges Bataille separates the notion of communication from that of commonality or communion; for him "communication" designates the contact of an individual with what is and remains beyond him. Communication requires sovereign moments in individuals.

This sovereignty is neither autonomy nor domination over others; it is a state individuals find in themselves. It is opposed to servility, which for Bataille is not only subjection to another's will but also subjection to the system of tools that are aligned toward utilitarian ends fixed by our needs and wants. The sense of a void inside, a lack felt as a need—hunger, thirst, vulnerability before cold or heat or predators—produces the search for outside objects to sustain us and motivates us to collaborate with one another in work and reason. But every healthy organism generates energies in excess of those it needs to maintain itself. Sovereignty is affirmed not in the use of these energies but in their intensity. These energies are discharged, imprudently, without calculation, without recompense. Sovereign moments are not achieved through work and reason; they are without expectation or hope. "We can in no way fabricate a sovereign moment from a servile state" (OC 5: 222/US 97).

Sovereignty does not reign and is and has to be unrecognized, hides itself, having nothing that is not ridiculous and unavowable. The craving and anxiety that compose it are speechless and appear in common language as dangers. "Sexual pleasure (which conceals itself and is laughable) comes closest to the essence of *majesty*. Likewise despair. But the despairing one and the sensualist do not *know* this majesty they have. To know it would be to lose it" (OC 6: 119/ON 99; tm). "This sovereignty cannot even be defined as a good. I am attached to it, but would I be if I were not certain that I could just as well laugh at it?" (OC 5: 222/US 97; tm).

In sovereign individuals Bataille finds a desire for communication. Here "communication" does not merely mean having access to other beings so as to be able to obtain from them the resources we need or the recognition we crave. That kind of "communication" is only the action that pursues and ensures self-sufficiency, the isolation of our own—or reciprocal—integrity, independence, or egoism. The deep urge for communication is for contact with beings unlike ourselves.

The desire for communication breaks open the self-sufficiency of a sovereign being, her autonomy, her integrity, and opens her upon something beyond her. This *beyond* is from the first empty; it is the void, nothingness. She is afflicted with anxiety; anxiety is the sense of nothing to hold on to, nothing supporting her. But this anxiety is ecstatic, felt in the release of superabundant energies, and confirms the sovereign intensity of the person who opens herself to the inappropriable. Out of her own excess energies the integration and integrity of the sovereign one is shattered.

The morality of good and evil subordinates every exaltation to respect for beings, to concern for the morrow, and for the endurance of states of being. In communication the discharge of excess energies does not respect the separation of beings. If the notion of good designates respect for the space and the integrity, the nature of others and the insurance of enduring integrity through action, the sovereign moment is closer to evil than to good.

To communicate with another is to break through his integrity, his independence, his autonomy, his nature—to intrude upon him, unsettle him, wound him. Communication takes place when beings put themselves at risk, each putting himself and the other in the region of death and nothingness. Communication is suicidal and criminal.

It is striking that the longing to communicate with those most unlike ourselves—with sacred and demonic beings—so dominates ancient humanity. The outer zone where the sphere of work and reason comes to an end is the sacred—*sacrum,* "separated."

Sacrifice—of goods, other animals, even of our firstborn children—is the most significant of all human acts (OC 2: 13/VE 73). It is as fundamental as the satisfaction of needs. The word *sacrifice—sacrum-ficio—*etymologically means "to make sacred." In a sacrifice something supremely precious—our finest harvest and livestock, our firstborn son—is set aside from all use, separated absolutely from the profane sphere. What is set apart from all profane use is separated absolutely, definitively, in being destroyed.

The knife that tears open the body of the sacrificial victim, tears apart his protective hide or skin that kept him functioning, releasing blood and the writhing turmoil of spilt organs, reveals the violence of a stag or boar taken from the wilderness, the inner violence of its life, reveals anonymous untamed forces in the child. The shaman, the priest, Abraham penetrates into the sacred zone, and there, in the violence of the knife and consuming fire, sacrifice reveals the sacred.

The sacrificial priest leaves the profane sphere to perform the sacrifice and act in the name of the people who identify with his act. Bringing to him of their harvest and livestock, the beast of the wilderness, or their firstborn child, they participate in his deed.

Those who perform sacrifice identify themselves with the victim. The

Aztec priests covered themselves with the blood of the sacrificial victims, excoriated them, and pulled the skin of the victims over their own naked bodies. And we who consign to the sacred sphere our resources, the game from our hunt, our own children, identify with them, identify with the victims. The stag or wild boar sacrificed would have sustained and nourished us. How could we not identify with our own firstborn child, sacrificed to the mountain god Jahweh? At the moment of the blood sacrifice, the participants find their own identity plunged into the void. When the fire blazes upon a sacred victim, it blazes too on us.

We slash open, crucify, or burn in holocaust the divine force that has been revealed in the sacrificial victim. The slashings and fire we inflict on what is precious to us—our finest livestock and harvest, our firstborn son—wounds us irremediably. We communicate with wounds inflicted and self-inflicted. The communication takes place between humans and sacred beings, each rent, wounded, exposed to one another by their wounds. God and humans communicate in the violation of the integrity of their natures, in crime.

The communication continues in feasts where immense resources are consumed and in saturnalia where we abandon our sense of ourselves and controlling will and find ourselves possessed with the forces of music, dance, the forces unleashed in the forests and rivers by night.

"In every accessible reality, in every being, we have to look for the place of sacrifice, the wound. A being is touched only at the point where it succumbs—a woman under her dress, a god at the throat of the sacrificial animal" (OC 5: 261/G 26; tm). The temple maiden, the prostitute, the woman or man who garbs himself or herself in seductive garb and gestures, clad in filmy dress or jacket and boots weighted with ornamentation and with languid or statuesque poses, sets himself or herself apart from the world of work and reason. The apparition arouses in the lustful gaze urges to break through this ethereal presence and expose the naked body and orifices beneath.

The denuding of the body exposes its integrity, its youth and health, and its vulnerability. It excites a craving to violate that integrity. The kisses and caresses render her or his body disarmed, denuded, silenced save for gasps, sobs, and laughter—dysfunctional, posture in a state of collapse, exposing orifices discharging excrementally mucous fluids, sweat, pantings, energies.[2]

The unmarked, unsullied silent nudity of another's body draws our eyes to the grain of skin and glow of down and draws the touch exploring the forms and contours, and the exposed orifices and pores releasing semen and blood, mucous and bile, sweat and spasms, lures and excites our own orifices and glands. "Your nudity, beautiful and offered to me—in silence and in the sense of a bottomless sky—is like the horror of the night" (OC 5: 408/G 156; tm).

The sense of obscenity is mixed with shame for the unsightliness of the genital organs. "The act of coition and the members employed are so ugly," Leonardo da Vinci wrote, "that but for the beauty of the faces, the adornments of their partners and the frantic urge, Nature would lose the human race."[3] The genital organs are also the excremental organs, expelling the dead, the cadaverous part of the body, which repels and disgusts. The disgust and fear are maintained by the fascination with nudity, with the grain of the denuded skin and the down floating on it, with the forms and contours of the body.

In a vertiginous attraction for the obscene orifices, we expose our own obscene orifices and defile another and ourselves. The communication in sexual grapplings and gropings draws us into an exuberance into which all our psychic and physical energies are poured, without any concern for the time to come. Carnal pleasure drives on into a dissolute forgetting of self, a consented extinction of self. "He who hates egoist solitude requires the loss of himself and ecstasy and seizes the expanse of the heavens by the throat, for it must bleed and cry out. A woman denuded abruptly opens a garden of delights (whereas decently dressed, she troubles us no more than a wall or a piece of furniture); as the body in its nudity gives itself to him the indefinite extension is rent and made open to the ravished mind that loses itself in it" (OC 6: 295/F 6; tm).

The vertigo that characterizes carnal communication transgresses the good—the integrity and endurance in their natures—of the partners and itself does not endure or produce anything enduring, is not itself a good. Nothing is produced; nothing is learned in the carnal abandon, which only repeats itself anew each time.

It is true that there may be engendered, by chance, an offspring, whose individual life is his own and not the effect of our deliberation and labor. He lives with our life but our life separated from us, irrecoverable by us. "Love is so great a negation of the isolated being that we find natural and even somehow ideal that an insect [the preying mantis] dies from the embrace that it desired. (The female is no less crushed than the male, for bringing into the world a new being or new beings is perhaps no less contrary to the law of individual isolation, which presides over life, than is death)" (OC 6: 305/F 14; tm).

Sovereign moments do not declare and affirm but hide themselves. The anxiety that intensifies them affirms nothing; the craving that ravages them dissimulates itself; for the reason that seeks to maintain self-sufficiency and identity they are dangers. Sacrifice appears as an obsolete and ridiculous means to make contact with the sacred. Sexual voluptuousness hides itself in the night and is unavowable and laughable. "Veritable sovereignty is a so conscientious putting to death of itself that it can at no moment put to itself the question of this putting to death" (OC 6: 119/ON 99; tm). Were it to affirm itself it would subordinate itself to the good, the endurance of beings, or to servile life.

The breach in the psychophysical integrity of another and of oneself is not a means for a higher good, which would be communication. Communication through these breaches in our and the other's psychophysical integrity turns in a vertigo, a solar explosion, independent of the consequences. Communication excludes concern for our interests, excludes concern for the time to come. Communication is not the good that we ensure or acquire through an action, which therefore requires us to coordinate, discipline, focus and narrow down, and subordinate our forces. It is itself not a future with which we are concerned: "the debauchee has a chance to reach the summit only if he has no intention to do so. The ultimate moment of the senses requires real innocence and the absence of moral pretensions and consequently even of the consciousness of evil" (OC 6: 57/ON 38; tm). Communication is not an enduring state; exhaustion comes quickly. It is not a good which requires conservation and preservation.

When our strength begins to fail, when we feel ourselves declining, we become preoccupied with acquiring and accumulating goods of all sorts, with enriching ourselves in view of the difficulties to come. We act.

Communication is disconnected from the concern for the future, but the relation between the summit and decline can be reversed in an effort to establish a relationship of utility between them. When sovereignty declines, communication is viewed and recuperated from the point of view of servile existence, of utility. Sacrifice and orgy will be viewed as actions achieving some good. They were seen to be expenditures useful for achieving victory in war. The victorious survivors knew the benefits of victory, acquired the women, booty, and territory. Sacrifice, which involves sacrifice of oneself with the victim, will be interpreted as a means to achieve personal salvation in another life. Sacrificing oneself was also seen as a means to achieve equality and justice for the community on earth. Throughout history, reasons were developed for one to head for the summit, releasing and risking all one's forces. Indeed, these reasons produced history.

Today these reasons have fallen away. Deprived of faith in another life, stripped of hope, even for an egalitarian and just community worth dying for, we have no motive for heading for exalted and sacrificial states. We find ourselves in sovereign moments without reason and exult in them without pretexts. We live at the mercy of laughter that breaks forth from us and shatters us and of sexual excitements that fill us with anxiety. "Ecstatic raptures and the burns inflicted by Eros are so many questions—without answers—that we put to nature and to our nature" (OC 6: 63/ON 47; tm).

Illegitimate sex and losing our heads over sexual outlaws survives among us as the orgiastic fragment of feasts; crime survives among us as the sacrificial fragment of feasts. "It is that not only the worst of the young are sent to prison," Norman Mailer wrote, "but the best—that is, the proudest, the bravest, the most daring, the most enterprising, and the most undefeated of the poor.... [They] are drawn to crime as a positive experience—because it is more exciting, more meaningful, more mysterious, more transcendental, more religious than any other experience they have known."[4]

Perhaps every felon who takes that first step outside the bounds of law already senses something of the intoxication of invading, violating the private space of another, and also degrading, dehumanizing herself. She senses something of a new kind of identification with her victim, as well as something sacrificial in her act.

Whenever a war is launched, for whatever declared cause, whether the evidence for the diabolical nature of the adversary and his weapons is reliable or not, men and women rush to join the war, and the populations support them, identify with them. "Without a profound complicity with natural forces such as violent death, gushing blood, sudden catastrophes and the horrible cries of pain that accompany them, terrifying ruptures of what had seemed to be immutable, the fall into stinking filth of what had been elevated—without a sadistic understanding of an incontestably thundering and torrential nature, there could be no revolutionaries, there could only be a revolting utopian sentimentality" (OC 2: 67/VE 101). In the war what motivates the soldiers is not the declared cause but the fraternity in combat, in risking one another's lives and in avenging their deaths. Most will never again know such a communication in civilian life; some will seek only to relive it in meetings with army buddies or in reenlisting. And in risking their lives they come to know the intelligence, wiles, bravery, savagery, impassioned commitment of their adversaries, whose intelligence, bravery, and savagery invade and occupy the void of their own ignorance and anxiety.

Immemorially, wars are followed by jousts, contests, and violent games and by plastic and now cinematic representations. In martial arts each seeks to throw the other with the strength of her own blow.

Tragedies, whether the real tragedies of individuals or those represented in tragic theater, hold us in anxiety and in fascination. Our energies are expended in contact with terrifying cataclysms of nature and with individuals torn asunder, whose agonies rend our self-sufficiency. Tears and grieving disconnect the future and recognize that the force and meaning of the past have come to an end. The forces of life hold on with strength and will to the present with all its irrevocable loss, inconsolable with words and projects. Tragic art holds humans in thrall to losses that they themselves have not known.

Communication occurs when doctors, nurses, and truck drivers go to the 50 million people today displaced by wars and famine, to perform surgeries in dusty tents, distribute sacks of food, nurse children dying of AIDS.

"What seems 'faultless' and stable—a whole that has a look of completion (house, person, street, landscape or sky). The 'fault,' or defect can appear though" (OC 5: 266/G 30). They too are incomplete. They are not crystallizations in the intersections of the universal laws of the universe. "On the same level you find—*the ridiculous universe, a naked woman,* and *torment"* (OC 5: 267/G 31).

In current language, communication strongly denotes communication among humans; but Walter Benjamin found biologists wondering whether in fact all animate organisms communicate, whether communication belongs to the nature of animate organisms. However, communication there meant the transmission of information. In *Being and Time*, Heidegger, replacing the substantive account of things with the relational account of implements, reduces things to the force that informs the user. The term *communication*, as Bataille uses it, to denote the contact of a sovereign being with what is other, is first the communication with the sacred and demonic; it is also communication with other species, inanimate things, the material universe. It is with our incompleteness, our orifices gaping open, and our unanswerable questions that we communicate with a world out of joint, spread about us disconnected, a concatenation of riddles, fragments, and dreadful accidents.[5] Indeed, communication with the sacred and with natural things is prior to communication with other humans.

Communication with things is not wresting of information out of them, but finding oneself invaded and ravaged by them. The pineal eye Bataille imagined opening on top of our heads opened directly to the incomprehensible vastness of the sky, opened to the sun that dazzles and blinds.

In early spring, it was raining; the car was going slow. In the fog Bataille found himself looking at each tree as it emerged, quite absorbed in it, and then leaving it regretfully as it passed, looking then at the next tree emerging, slowly approaching. As the tree emerged from the fog it absorbed his attention completely, as he felt a kind of pleasure and felicity in its approach and form. This pleasure was edged with a poignant and exquisite melancholy as each tree passed and was lost again in the fog (OC 5: 131/IE 112). We are all aware of how language inhibits communication. When the sacrificial knife strikes, in the intensity of sacrifice, before the photographs of Abu Ghraib we are speechless. Our sensibility retains only the traces the passage of things left in us; the things themselves have passed on, mutated or metamorphosed, disintegrated. Discourse retains not the force of things encountered but their meanings. In discourse the sense, force, and function of the opening word depends on the words to come. The present is subjugated to the absent, the future. Language is a labyrinth that leads ever to more words, more verbal distinctions, more statements. Linguistic reality is a laborious construction over a period of time. Its categories abstract and universalize, dedramatize.

However completely a building or a person has been described to us, the moment we face that building or are face to face with that person, there is always shock, astonishment, and discovery.

The word that designates an entity or event continues to do so when that event has passed or that entity is transformed or destroyed. In the movement of discourse the verb retains the noun already uttered, the sentence retains the prior sentence that it explains or justifies. Meantime the willow tree has shed many leaves and sprouted new ones, the lichens and vines and the rain have crumbled more of the ancient temple, the patina of grime has imperceptibly thickened on the painting. Through discourse we seek to compensate for losses, to appropriate them. The words that are retained await the recurrence of the things and situations they designate. The mind can mobilize our powers to recognize them, appropriate them, and reorganize them. The mind extends into action its ambition to approach, retain, possess, and manage everything.

Discourse integrates two bodies of experience and experimentation, reducing an original multiplicity. Anthropology reduces the myths and performances of cultures to the coherence and consistency of its rational discourse. Discourse integrates what is said by two interlocutors, making it common. "Each word exchanged, each line printed, establish a communication between two interlocutors, leveling what until then was a divergence in information," Claude Lévi-Strauss notes.[6] In each of us the streaming of tones, the patterns, the sounds, the density, resistance, and resilience of things are folded in with expectations and fears, thoughts, fantasies, and feelings; each of us is an organism and locus of a process of integration. Formulating the pieces or segments of our experience in words is a reduction to inertia, entropy.

> I resolved long ago not to seek knowledge, as others do, but to seek its contrary, which is unknowing. I no longer anticipated the moment when I would be rewarded for my effort, *when I would know at last,* but rather the moment when *I would no longer know, when my initial anticipation would dissolve into* NOTHING. . . . [T]his way of going in the wrong direction on the paths of knowledge—to get off them, not to derive a result that others anticipate—leads to the principle of *sovereignty* of being and of thought, which from the standpoint where I am placed at the moment has this meaning: that thought, subordinated to some anticipated result, completely enslaved, ceases to be in being *sovereign*, that only unknowing is *sovereign*. (OC 8: 258/AS 3: 208)

The thought that comes to a halt in the face of what is sovereign rightfully pursues its operation to the point where its object dis-

> solves into NOTHING, because, ceasing to be useful, or subordinate, it becomes *sovereign* in ceasing to be. (OC 8: 254–55/AS 3: 204)

Language itself can lead us to the frontiers and the depths where its words no longer take hold, where our mind finds itself empty, open upon nothing words can grasp. Thoughts thought too much no longer think anything, Maurice Merleau-Ponty wrote.[7] In moments of austere lucidity the thought that discovers ignorance in itself assents to this ignorance, plunges into it, sacrifices itself. No longer subordinated to some anticipated result, its ecstasy is the ecstasy of an utterly self-propelled and sovereign movement.

> I reflected on unknowing, and I saw that human life was full of moments—which I assign to knowledge—when the ceaseless operation of cognition is dissolved. I referred to those moments in speaking of sobs, of laughter that makes one gasp . . . saying that in them the train of thought was broken off. . . . The object of tears or of laughter—and of other effects such as ecstasy, eroticism or poetry—seemed to me to correspond to the very point at which the object of thought vanishes. Up to that point, that object might be an object of knowledge, but only up to that point, so that the effect of knowledge would regularly fail. (OC 8: 258–59/AS 3: 208)

But these passages veer off from a sovereignty that must seek, with all its excessive energies, contact with the other to a thought that in the extreme intensity of anxiety and fascination plunges into the unknowable, and has the sovereignty of a subject that exists in the apex of intensity without objects.

Bataille's notes on communication correct this vertigo: in making contact with what is inappropriable in the other, we make contact with him in his own being and with things in their own being. At the far end of the practice of understanding through discursive representation we discover a sacrificial ecstasy of the mind, austere and intoxicating. "There is an element in it which one cannot reduce, which remains 'beyond expression,' but ecstasy, in this respect, does not differ from other forms: I can have, can communicate the precise knowledge of it as much as—or more than—that of laughter, of physical love—or *of things*" (OC 5: 143/IE 123). "In these states of ungraspable transparency, the mind is inert, intensely lucid, and free. The universe easily passes through it. The object imposes itself on it in an 'intimate and ungraspable impression of déja vu.' . . . Only this state takes comedy to an extreme limit; it is infinite volatilization, effortless freedom, reducing all things to the movement into which they fall" (OC 6: 79–80/ON 64–65; tm).

But Bataille also recognizes forms of language that are noninstrumental, not efficacious factors in projects and work, not themselves forms of work, and not instruments for the transmission of information and that realize communication. There is, there has been from the beginning, poetry. Poetry is allusive and elliptical; its most subtle and precise phrasings put us in the presence of reality in its material singularity by making us feel not how much there is still to be said about the most familiar things, events, and mental states, but how all that has already been said and what is here being said reveals the presence of the most familiar things, events, and mental states as abysses of the unappropriated and unrepresentable.

There is an unavowed kinship between poetry and profanity, where words have lost their intelligible meaning and convey outbursts of savage forces. The word *shit* designates the expulsion of the unusable; *fuck* when used as an expletive designates not the reproductive and pleasurable sexual act but a nonreproductive release of energies that humiliate the one who is penetrated and violate his or her integrity. We use these words to reject explanations and justifications. These words are not only aggressions against the machinery of the working world and against the self-determination of persons but verbal aggressions against language. Poets recognize the poetic character of inner city street talk.

Communication through writing is not the transfer of a stock of messages from someone who has them and who continues to possess them, to augment the stock possessed by another. To be sure, writers write meaningful words and do so with a meticulous care and rigor that spoken conversation never has. But writers write of things unknown and unseen by their readers, things their readers will never encounter. The words only point to things and events in their irremediable absence.

The writer is not indulging in "self-expression"; it is the reader who speaks in the writer, who maintains in the writer the course of the discourse intended for her. Without the reader awaiting the words of the writer—the reader who thus loves the written text and will forget the author—without the presence and insistence of the reader the writer could write nothing.

Though the writer is the sole concrete reality upon which the text and the reading are suspended, the writer himself disappears in his writing. He forgets himself, even loses sight of his intention in starting to write; he becomes attentive only to the way the explanation has to be developed, the description has to be completed, the story has to be told. Kafka said he became a writer when he no longer wrote "I." There is a specific sober euphoria in the writer who thus divests himself of his identity. As the writer writes, he exists as the source of these words that leave him and which he can never recuperate, not even in reading them himself. When the book is published, the writer cannot really read it for its sense.

One writes not for a distinct person, but for anyone. For a reader, the writer is just someone she has not met and most likely never will. The writer's name, identity, and personal history do not change anything of what the reader reads. As the reader reads, she loses sight of her room, her wants and practicable projects, her own emotional and vocational history. She lets the words invade her and take possession of her. The writer and the reader are but two voices in the dark, the writer's voice reaching her reader perhaps after years, what the reader has to say, how she responds to the writer's voice never reaching her. They are like two waves emerging briefly on the surface of the dark sea.

Communication can come to pass in conversation, "just talk," where nothing useful, nothing that can be integrated in my discourse, is learned; nothing is appropriated. Jean-Jacques Rousseau speaks of "the babble of conversation": "Its progress, more rapid than my ideas, forcing me almost always to speak before thinking, has often suggested to me stupidities and ineptitudes that my reason disapproved and my heart disavowed at the moment they escaped from my mouth, but which, preceding my own judgment, could not be reformed by its censure."[8] Launched into conversation, the words, sequences, anecdotes, repartees, and the civilized, witty but polite, and entertaining rhetoric that governs them scuttle on; the listener does not catch up; he finds himself saying things whose meaning escapes him. (Even in lecturing before a class we find ourselves continuing with phrases whose meaning eludes our grasp.) At these moments we are bereft of any real thoughts we may have had and reduced to the uneasiness, attractions, desires, lusts, anxiety, mounting pleasure of our bodies making contact with those of others and with the world.

We find ourselves in anxiety and fascination with others who refuse to be known and interpreted by us and expose us to the disconnection between all the information we have accumulated and reality and between all words and reality. The world we know ceases to be there, and there opens fleeting domains of unappropriated beings and forces that are encountered in encountering others. Sovereign existence is lived in conversations, shared laughter, friendship, eroticism, and the world is what passes from one to another when we break out laughing together or when we love one another. Then the immensity of these worlds opens to me, and I identify with their flight (see OC 5: 282/G 44–45).

If all our discourse does not exist in order to serve production of ever greater comfort and security, the world also does not exist in order to be transposed into a universal system of words, and we do not exist in order to exist in conversation. Sovereign life is not a state but moments—moments of conversation, laughter at and with someone bungling and dysfunctional, orgies, perversions, childbearing, feasting, combat, contests, dance, compulsions to divest ourselves of all we have accumulated, traveling in strange lands, prisons, refugee camps, the killing fields of malaria, tuberculosis, AIDS, moments of diffuse impersonal joy without object, of wrenching ravishments, the void of the night.

Notes

1. Trans. David Carr (Evanston: Northwestern University Press, 1970).

2. "Your sex organs are the darkest and bloodiest part of you. Stuck in the underwear and tousled hair, they are a sort of half-being or half-animal, foreign to your surface habits. They are in extreme discord with what you show of yourself. However real is your violence, you present to others a civilized and polished appearance. You seek daily to communicate with them, avoiding shocks and reducing each thing to its poor common measure, so that everything can coincide and be put in order. The only part of you that does not enter into composition is your sex organs. That is why for once you have to enter into solitude, into the darkest night of your being, and listen to the cracked and barbarous voice that comes from the depths of your entrails. You will finally hear the lesson of your slimy root and your swamp of blood. The shamed, comical, avid genitals teach the most subterranean truth: we do not communicate by avoiding running into one another; we reach our fellow-human by shocks that frighten, lacerate, and overwhelm" (OC 2: 390).

3. As cited by Georges Bataille, OC 10: 144/E 144–45. Leonardo Da Vinci, *The Notebooks of Leonardo Da Vinci*, ed. and trans. Edward MacCurdy (New York: Braziller, 1958), 97.

4. Norman Mailer, introduction to Jack Henry Abbott, *In the Belly of the Beast* (New York: Random House, 1981), xii–xiii.

5. "I want never to lose sight of the immediate reality: an electric train is entering the Saint-Lazare station, and I am seated against the window in this train. I push away the weakness that wishes to see there something insignificant in the immensity of the universe, which would be alone charged with meaning. That is possible only if one ascribes to the universe the value of a completed totality, but if there is simply the uncompleted universe, each part, however small it be, is no less significant than the so-called whole" (OC 6: 297/F 7; tm).

6. Claude Lévi-Strauss, *Tristes tropiques* (Paris: Plon, 1955), 478. *Tristes Tropiques*, trans. John and Doreen Weightman (New York: Atheneum, 1978), 413–14.

7. "Ideas that are too much possessed are no longer ideas; I no longer think anything when I speak of them." Maurice Merleau Ponty, *The Visible and the Invisible*, trans. Alphonso Lingis (Evanston: Northwestern University Press, 1968), 119.

8. Jean-Jacques Rousseau, *Oeuvres comp lètes* (Paris: Pléiade, 1959), p. 1033. English translation in Marshall Blonsky, *On Signs* (Baltimore: Johns Hopkins University Press, 1985), xiv.

CHAPTER EIGHT

Sharing God's Wounds: Laceration, Communication, and Stigmata

Karmen MacKendrick

The crucifixion, Georges Bataille declares, "is a wound by which believers communicate with God" (OC 5: 267/G 31). Perhaps, I would like to suggest here, the stigmata, in which a small subset of believers manifests the wounds Christ received at or just prior to the crucifixion, can likewise be read as a mode of divine-human communication. Stigmata are relatively rare but incredibly popular and attention-gripping phenomena, perpetually re- and dis-appearing wounds with a unique religious resonance. Usually interpreted (depending upon the one doing the interpretation) as signs of madness, deviousness, or sanctity, for those who embody them they are, I would argue, literalizations of two of Bataille's favorite and related themes: laceration and communication (the laceration of flesh, the communication of sacred and profane). They are places of communication and of community and thus of the formation of identity in a curiously corporeal relation—not by identification but by a mutual, in this case exceptionally literal, cutting across. Thus, they also tell us something of the theological value or importance of the focus on woundedness and the mortal moment.

In communication, the stigmatic body necessarily reminds us also of community, in which mortality and finitude play such a vital role; and thus it reminds us too of identity as it is constructed by the placement and displacement of the self. This construction is not one of resemblance. The stigmatic wounds do, with more or often less accuracy, resemble Christ's, but this is consequent upon, rather than causative of, community: stigmatic wounds almost invariably appear in the sites of wounds on crucifixes familiar to those who bear them; stigmata in the wrists rather than the palms, for instance, are very rare, and the side wound varies from left to right and in its shape. The construction of stigmatic identity is rather one of communication, of bleeding-with, being opened-to—by the very focus on pain and death that makes the stigmata so deeply objectionable to many both within and outside the various traditions of Christianity.

Most work on stigmata since the twentieth century has been focused on the dual questions of etiology and "truth." That is: what causes stigmata, and is this cause (ever) the divine source claimed by stigmatics? Much attention, of course, has been focused on debunking stigmata, demonstrating that those who claim to have them have created the wounds surreptitiously, as an intentional deception or as a manifestation of mental illness.[1] Theories about possible mental sources abound; stigmata are said to manifest hysteria, self-hypnosis, dermographia, "florid sadomasochistic neuro[sis]," and even multiple personality.[2]

General skepticism about religious explanations is not the only source of doubt. Many worry more generally about the focus on the crucifixion's pain and suffering, preferring to emphasize happy, hopeful possibilities generated by resurrection instead. Even the Catholic Church, by far the most popular home of stigmatics, remains uncomfortable with this directly physical participation in divinity, never counting stigmata toward the required miracles for beatification or canonization and, except in the case of Francis of Assisi (generally regarded as the first stigmatic), universally withholding judgment on the cause or source of stigmatic wounds.[3]

However, it is not the "truth" of the stigmata that concerns me here, but rather the roles they play among those who believe in them, including those who believe themselves afflicted (or blessed). That is: bracketing the question of the "truth" of stigmata just as we can the "truth" of their religious contexts, we can nonetheless inquire into what it is that they *do*, how they might be theologically understood, or what they suggest to us about the beliefs and practices in which they are grounded.

Like the more widespread passion for the sacred heart, the very possibility of stigmata may be traced back to early devotions to Christ's wounds (derived in turn from devotions to the Passion).[4] These wounds are traditionally numbered five, usually the feet, hands, and side, though I have seen divergent listings numbering the feet together as one and including the coronal stigmata (pinprick wounds around the head or on the forehead as from the crown of thorns) as the fifth wound. In addition to these classic locations, stigmata sometimes appear as tears of blood (exhibited by the famous stigmatic Therese Neumann), marks of flagellation on the back, or a raw place on the shoulder as from the carrying of a heavy cross-beam (the scapular stigmata). Others report cordlike marks, as from binding, on the wrists and raised or bleeding wounds in the form of particular emblems such as a cross on the chest or forehead.[5]

Devotion to the five wounds appears early and remains intense for centuries. A prayer from the medieval missal, debatably attributed to St. Gregory the Great, asks, "May Thy wounds be to me food and drink by which I may be nourished, inebriated, and delighted."[6] The connection of the bleeding wounds to drink is perhaps not terribly exceptional, though it becomes more disturbing the more seriously one thinks about it, but the image of food, despite its clear continuity with the Eucharist, makes the latter's overtones of cannibalism uncomfortably vivid: this Christ has bites taken out of him.

But this is less cannibalism than mutual consumption; the closing prayer to each set in the chaplet of the five wounds asks for wounding in return: "Holy Mother, pierce me through,/In my heart each wound renew/ Of my savior crucified."[7] This desire *to be wounded*, common in the early wound devotions, clearly suggests the stigmata (let *me*, too, bear the wounds of the crucifixion) as much as the more metaphorical desire to be wounded in the heart.[8]

In this more metaphorical sense, wounds—suggestively ambiguous in their belonging to human or God—are often attributed to love in medieval prayer. For instance, St. Columbanus (ca. AD 543–615) asks, "I wish for these wounds, O Lord. Blessed is such a soul which is wounded so by love. Such a soul seeks the fountain and drinks of it, but always desiring more, always drinking more, always thirsting for more of that which it drinks."[9] In fact, the number of prayers either devoted to the wounds or mentioning them centrally is impressive, particularly if we stop to think how odd an image this is for celebration.[10]

Finally, the wounds, particularly that in the side, figure frequently as places of shelter or refuge, further confounding their inherent violence.[11] Perhaps the best-known instance of this invocation in prayer is that of the Anima Christi, often attributed to Ignatius Loyola though in fact almost certainly written before him. The prayer asks,

> Blood of Christ, inebriate me
> Water from Christ's side, wash me
> . . . .
> Within Thy wounds hide me
> Suffer me not to be separated from Thee.

This lack of separation, though often conceived as union-in-fusion, might also be read as a still stranger loss of being in communication.

I have dwelt on the intense and widespread character of the devotion to the wounds for two reasons. The first is simply that this is the background to the discussion of the stigmata; it is only by realizing how centrally important these wounds have been in Christian devotion that we can hope to understand why they would reappear on other bodies. Second, we find here an almost gruesome focus upon Christ as victim, the insistence on the damage he suffers—on the very possibility that God too can be subject both to laceration and to sacrifice, and thus on the possibility that here too is a space for communication, a space often missing from the cleaned-up versions of contemporary Christianity.

The first human to manifest these wounds, at least the first of whom we know for certain, is St. Francis of Assisi, though there is at least one possible prior case, that of Blessed Dodo of Hascha, whose stigmatalike wounds were discovered after he was killed by a falling wall in 1231.[12] Francis' is an unusual case in a few respects (beyond the obvious one of being—probably—the first). The nature of the wounds themselves is unusual; rather than being open wounds or seepages of blood through the skin, they are dark, raised, and painful, resembling bent nails through hands and feet both. In the earliest account, Francis is meditating on the Passion when a seraph appears to him, then takes on the form of the crucified Christ: "Then after a long period of secret converse this marvelous vision faded, leaving . . . in his body a wonderful image and imprint of the Passion of Christ. *For in the hands and feet of Saint Francis forthwith began to appear the marks of the nails in the same manner as he had seen them in the body of Jesus crucified.*"[13]

These wounds remain constantly after their first appearance, rather than disappearing and reappearing as is much more common.[14] Francis is also a somewhat unusual stigmatic because of his gender; in one of the more authoritative counts of stigmatics, the total of 321 included only 41 men.[15]

In some respects, however, he is more typical. His strong asceticism and, still more, his visionary ecstasy are both near universals in stigmatic religiosity.[16] Rene Biot notes, "Very frequently, in fact almost always, stigmatics are also ecstatics," adding, "It is exceptional for the first impression of stigmata to be received apart from an ecstasy, but often this rapture takes place many times before the appearance of the bodily marks."[17] Ecstasy, the loss of time in joy, is a prelude to the loss of boundary in woundedness.

In other words, stigmatic religiosity is intense and corporeal, as we might indeed expect; it is, for those who are taking it seriously, communication with the incarnate passion of God. The opened space in the body is also the mark of the opening of a communicative space, a creation of community with Christianity's embodied divine. Bataille distinguishes the communication that links two beings from that in which being itself is shattered—communication with the beyond, the ungraspable, the sense of one's own death (OC 5:

388/G 139). Stigmata, communication by being-in-common with the pain of the passion, is fascinating in some measure because it insists upon both at once: communication with the person of Christ and the mutual beyond of agonizing death, in which God, too, "is" otherwise than being.

Bataille writes that communication requires laceration, a violent openness:

> The more perfect, the more isolated or confined to ourselves we are. But the wound of incompleteness opens me up. Through what could be called incompleteness or animal nakedness or the wound, the different separate beings *communicate*, acquiring life by losing it in *communication* with each other. (OC 5: 263/G 27)

And again:

> Incompletion, the wound, and the pain that has to be there if communication is to take place. Completion—the contrary of this.
>
> What's requisite for communication is a defect or 'fault.' Communication enters like death through a chink in the armor. What's required is an overlapping of two lacerations, mine and yours. (OC 5: 266/G 30)

Seldom, of course, is the laceration as literal as that of wounds opening in the skin. But the woundedness of the stigmatic is never "simply" physical in a reductive sense; rather, the physical suffering seems invariably to be accompanied by an intensity of spiritual or psychological "experience" that necessarily registers as agonizing.[18] Bataille too emphasizes not only the wound but also its painfulness (OC 5: 266/G 30); laceration is not the neatly anaesthetized opening of a surgical procedure. It is only thus that the wound cuts all the way through, from skin to self.

Pain is constant, a necessary attendant to the experience but also essential in itself, as the rending intensity of this communication necessarily exceeds the boundaries of pleasure; as pain functions both as a sign of this intensity and as a means of intensification. Rene Biot writes that suffering "is never absent, whatever the form of stigmatization. It is always intense."[19] Often the stigmata seem to hurt just as if the marks had been received by more evident means. Or, as in the case of nineteenth-century stigmatic Anne Catherine Emmerich, "a vision of Jesus appeared to her with wounds that 'shone like so many furnaces of light' and felt as if they burnt into her flesh."[20]

This communicative agony might seem an unlikely place for the sacred, given Bataille's insistence, "For those who understand communication as laceration, communication is sin, or evil. It's a breaking of the established order" (OC 5: 305/G 65). But it is important that this sense of "evil" is "a breaking of the established order," including the order of the profane and the sustainable hierarchy of the church (always threatened by ecstasy and charisma, both of which tend to be rather strongly manifested by stigmatics—think of the famous recent example of Padre Pio). The "apex of sacrifice," Bataille declares, is the "inexpiable crime" of the crucifixion; the body of the stigmatic blurs the boundaries of sacrificial priest and victim, as Christ's blurs those between the sacrifice offered and the god to whom that offering is directed: all of sacrifice bleeds together in the flowing of open wounds.

This sacrificial death of God, irredeemable except as self-redeeming (not after or despite, but *in* its mortal violence), opens the space for the movement beyond subjectivity into the opening of the self. The contestation of the subject, the ripping-open of the self, comes out of that subject's own agony of desire. The finitude of the self, the boundaries that make it, open to the infinity of the divine, shattering in flesh and blood the order of the profane—in imitation of the mortal wounds of the bleeding, dying, glorified God. Here the sacred is not the "set apart," but that which is neither apart nor contained.[21]

In this ecstatic opening, communication becomes possible. This "experience" wounds—opens—the finite creature: "ecstatic, breathless, *experience* thus opens a bit more every time the horizon of God (the wound): extends a bit more the limits of the heart, the limits of being" (OC 5: 122/IE 103–04). The horizon of God is the wound: so God too, at the limit of the divine, is wounded, and this indeed is the point upon which stigmata are based. The wound opened in the stigmatic skin bleeds out into the God who enters there.

Stigmatism belongs to a religious tradition emphasizing not only human but also divine desire, God's desire for entry into humanity, just as "No greater desire exists than a wounded person's need for another wound" (OC 5: 267/G 31)—the desire invoked in those prayerful pleas for God's wounding love. Communication requires not one wound but (at least) two, "an overlapping of two lacerations" (OC 5: 266/G 30). But to lacerate God, the only way to communicate, cannot be other than sinful;[22] hence sin and salvation are intertwined, again beyond a simple sense in which one pays for the other.

The more obvious, and in fact simplistic, versions of salvation would have stigmata be salvific in a sort of working-off-the-debt arrangement; suffer enough, as those who are wounded and bleeding surely do, and you get to go somewhere pretty and sit on clouds. I would like to suggest what seems to me a somewhat richer possibility, in which suffering itself is transformed, not merely for what one gets as a reward but inherently, in which mutilation transforms the possibilities of the self—by violently opening the space of divine communication. Bataille calls ascetic activity mutilation, but he adds, "If it is a question of salvation, let one mutilate" (OC 5: 36/IE 23). Thus one seeks to provoke anguish, itself a means of knowing; "communication still is, like anguish, to live and to know" (OC 5: 52/IE 39). This "knowledge" is not a set of facts, nor this communication their transmission; it is the knowledge with which we return to ourselves from our own ecstatic loss (OC 5: 67–68/IE 53). "Anguish assumes the desire to communicate—that is, to lose myself—but not complete resolve: anguish is evidence of my fear of communicating, of losing myself" (OC 5: 67/IE 53). Rapture or ecstasy occurs only in giving in, necessarily fleetingly, to self-loss.

Lack or incompletion, implied by the opening in a space that seems to demand closure, is likewise essential to communication; there must be a point of entry. God and human alike lack wholeness (OC 5: 135/IE 116), are lacking, and are thus, potentially at least, open to one another.[23] This connects us back to the shocking foundation of Christianity in the sacrifice of God: "There's a necessity for god to be killed: to see the world in the weakness of incompletion. The next thought to occur is that, come what may, the world has to be *completed,* although this is what's impossible and incomplete. Everything real fractures and cracks" (OC 5: 262/G 27).

Taking up Bataillean notions of communication and community, Jean-Luc Nancy and Maurice Blanchot understand community as the place in which the self becomes possible, not by isolation and boundary-marking but by exposition, by being open to others, to otherness, and by being held in memory. Finite and limited, we are not self-contained; as Nancy emphasizes, community is not a subsequent gathering of individuals but the very undoing of the absolute immanence that individuality suggests.[24]

As we have already noted, the space of communication demands for Bataille the violent openness of laceration, a woundedness linked directly to the possibility of speaking: "Should one sew my lips together," Bataille asks, "like those of a wound!" (OC 5: 81/IE 67). Nancy warns against a simple conflation of community and communicative laceration but notes that "what tears apart is the presentation of finitude in and by community."[25] And it is not one-self that is lacerated:

> What is lacerated . . . is not the singular being: on the contrary, this is where the singular being compears. Rather, it is the communal fabric, it is immanence that is lacerated. And yet this laceration does not happen *to* anything, for this fabric does not exist. There is no tissue, no flesh, no subject or substance of common being, and consequently there is no laceration of this being. But there *is* sharing out. . . .

> "Laceration" consists only in exposure: the entire "inside" of the singular being is exposed to the "outside."[26]

This openness to alterity is the space of community and communication for finite beings, so it might seem to have little place in an effort to understand divine communication (at least in a tradition that understands God as infinite). But stigmata emphasize the paradox of an infinite God made flesh, sharing finitude, vulnerability, even mortality (if God is not dead, the resurrection is at best a parlor trick) to emphasize that we are not only finite. They mark a sharing not in any customary notion of divine glory but in the degradation of mutilation and the ecstasy of suffering. Here, the stigmatic finds not "self" in the sense of individuality but the wounding of subjectivity past mortal limits, the laceration of self that opens self onto the unlimited.

Nancy in particular links community specifically to the Christian incarnational myth. Noting the dual and conflicting Christian myths of the *deus absconditus* and the familial, familiar human god, he writes that "the thought of community or the desire for it might well be nothing other than a belated invention that tried to respond to the harsh reality of modern experience: namely, that divinity was withdrawing indefinitely from immanence, that the god-brother was at bottom *himself* the *deus absconditus* . . . and that the divine essence of community—or community as the existence of a divine essence—was the impossible itself."[27] The impossible, of course, is precisely what draws Bataille's interest. The divinity evoked by stigmata is not absolute immanence any more than it is transcendence of the human condition; it is woundedness, opening, the refusal of closure. It is the desire to experience at once the fleeing of God, a God who seems to have forsaken the mortally wounded humanity of his son-self; and the God who returns and sustains, who without closing the wounds nonetheless lives again in the flesh. Thus stigmata mark at once the with-ness (the impossible necessity of community in the absence of self-sufficiency) of finite and vulnerable beings, and ecstasy, the opening of the self to the divine beyond finitude. "What community reveals to me," says Nancy apropos of Bataille, "is my existence outside myself."[28] But we may also think, with Blanchot, from the outside: what community with the divine reveals is the outside of my existence, myself otherwise than in (my) being.

In a seeming paradox that echoes this problematizing of inside and out, Bataille connects "inner experience," that famously contradictory state that defies the interiority of the experiencing subject, to community: "there cannot be . . . inner experience without a community of those who live it" (OC 5: 37/IE 24). Complete, whole beings would not communicate; they would be "isolated or confined to [them]selves" (OC 5: 263/G 27). Blanchot similarly notes, "A being, insufficient as it is, does not attempt to associate itself with another being to make up a substance of integrity. The awareness of the insufficiency arises from the fact that it puts itself in question, which question needs the other or another to be enacted. Left on its own, a being closes itself, falls asleep and calms down. A being is either alone or knows itself to be alone only when it is not."[29] A being seeks others not in order to fill its gaps and complete itself but in order to be exposed (opening the "inside" of the singular being), to be present to the other in a way that makes plain one's incompleteness—or even makes one's incompleteness. Thus one starts "being only in that privation that makes it conscious . . . of the impossibility of being itself, of subsisting as its *ipse* or, if you will, as itself as a separate individual: this way it will perhaps ex-ist, experiencing itself as an always prior exteriority, or as an existence shattered through and through."[30] Again, stigmata make this literally clear, rupturing the body, making the interior blood and fluid exterior, the interior pain visibly manifest, the existence shattered, the prayer *suffer me not to be separated* agonizingly fulfilled in open wounds, vivid welts, bleeding eyes.

The opening of stigmata, the moment of community, of the violent intimacy of communication, is thus the moment of laceration, of the self not merely wounded but torn apart by the ecstasy of the death of God. According to Blanchot, "Death, the death of the other, like friendship or love, clears the space of intimacy or interiority which is never (for Georges Bataille) the space of a subject, but a gliding beyond limits. 'The Inner Experience' says the opposite of what it seems to say: it is a movement of contestation that, coming from the subject, devastates it, but has as a deeper origin the relationship with the other which is community itself, a community that would be nothing if it died not open the one who exposes himself to it to the infiniteness of alterity, while at the same time deciding its inexorable finitude."[31] The subject desires to get out of itself, but this is self-loss; exposure to the divine is a devastating intimacy at the intensity of death, where alone community can exist.

Thus, in that moment of knowing ourselves to be alone—of participating in the passionate question *why have you forsaken me?*—we seek not to be, seek the shattering of our own existence, seek to put ourselves into question. Blanchot writes, "What, then, calls me into question most radically? Not my relation to myself as finite or as the consciousness of being before death or for death, but my presence for another who absents himself by dying. . . . to take upon myself another's death as the only death that concerns me, this is what puts me beside myself, this is the only separation that can open me, in its very impossibility, to the Openness of a community."[32] The stigmatic takes upon herself a very peculiar death, a death with life at its maximum of intensity—eternal or divine life—already bound up in it, an impossible death of a God in human flesh.[33] Thus too we find community at its maximum.

Blanchot writes, "What purpose does [community] serve? None, unless it would be to make present the service to others unto/in death, so that the other does not get lost all alone. . . . Georges Bataille writes: ' . . . a community can last only at the level of the intensity of death.' "[34] Community here become salvific so that we do not get lost all alone.

Nancy likewise links death (which we, even knowing ourselves mortal, can only encounter as the death of an other) intimately to community. "A community is the presentation to members of their mortal truth. . . . It is the presentation of the finitude and the irredeemable excess that make up finite being: its death, but also its birth, and only the community can present me my birth, and along with it the impossibility of my reliving it, as well as the impossibility of my crossing over into my death."[35] The reliving of the passion and crucifixion impossibly suspend the stigmatic between the moments of death and birth: "to not *reach an end* was one of the exigencies of Bataille's endeavor."[36] This is the realm of Blanchot's "unworking," beyond questions of "production or completion."[37] The deadly wounds of Christ perpetually reopen, unfinalized, incomplete, in the bodies of communicating believers, bodies asking the impossible; that is, seeking union, fusion, the completion of communication in another's death; in that death, by its peculiarly double and temporary character, is an infinity of life.

Community is inherently, necessarily unfinished, unclosed, and so at once finite—because it does not extend forever, but lasts only at the intensity of imminent destruction—and without defined limits, even opening the ecstatically wounded body to the limitless joy and suffering of the divine.[38] Stigmata represent a communicative pair, the stigmatic and Christ, less like the community of a society and more like what Blanchot calls the "community of lovers"; "love . . . exposes the unworking and therefore the incessant *incompletion* of community. . . . Lovers form the extreme though not the external limit of community."[39] But, complicating the distinction, stigmata occur disproportionately often in members of religious communities, pushing the community formed around the story of the incarnate God to the limit of recognizing that carnality within itself.

In the scar as a site of memory, I recently argued, one finds oneself where one was absent.[40] The site of the stigmatic wound may be more complex still. The wound is the opening of communication, the all-the-way-through laceration of body and spirit without the strict division that modernity will impose upon them as if it were self-evident. The edges of the stigmatic's blood-seeping wounds overlap with those of the perpetually wounded figure of Christ (even in stories of his resurrected body, the wounds remain unhealed) in a moment of impossible communication, the formation of an impossible community of self and God, a community in which neither stigmatic nor God is a being in the sense of self-containment, of definite, defined existent.

The stigmata form community as the Eucharist forms communion, at the moment of death with an emphasis on corporeality (this is my blood), but at the same time at a moment of life pushed to shattering intensity. "The quick of life would be the burn of a wound," says Blanchot, and so it is here, God and human sharing the ultimate vulnerability to death.[41] In the presence of one dying, the stigmatic seems to be taken over by a memory so somatic as to transform her identity into that of another. We may be assured that Francis' "fervour grew so strong within him that he became wholly transformed into Jesus through his love and compassion," as if a singular identity were constituted repeatedly in the bodies of stigmatics following Christ.[42] Yet this is not quite right either; it is not the case that now there are two of Christ and none of Francis or any other stigmatic, but rather that in this communication with the open space of the sacred, neither human nor divine retains the identity of presence. Rather, "identity" is shared in the space of absence, in the inside-out of "inner" experience, in the wound. *In the presence of one who is dying*—at the limit of vulnerability—the stigmatic does not merely reenact the passion and crucifixion of the sacrificed God but sacrifices herself in communication: and this, this ecstatic vulnerability, this violent intimacy, is what remains to us of the sacred after Christianity's ultimate paradoxical madness in the sacrifice of God.

Notes

1. For a concise summary of these explanations, see the entry "Stigmata," in *Wikipedia,* en.wikipedia.org/wiki/Stigmata.

2. On hysteria, see among others Nitza Yarom's analysis of St. Francis: *Body, Blood and Sexuality: A Psychoanalytic Study of St. Francis' Stigmata and Their Historical Context* (New York: Lang, 1992); for self-hypnosis and dermographia, Ian Wilson, *Stigmata: An Investigation into the Mysterious Appearance of Christ's Wounds in Hundreds of People from Medieval Italy to Modern America* (San Francisco: Harper and Row, 1989), 92, where Wilson is succinctly representative of widespread perspectives; for "florid sadomasochistic neuro[sis]" (the phrase comes from a description of St. Maria Maddalena [late 16th c.]), Wilson, *Stigmata,* 25; and for multiple personality, Wilson, *Stigmata,* 92.

3. On the other hand, the Catholic Church notes with equal caution, "If the progress of medical science and psycho-physiology should present serious objections, it must be remembered that neither religion or [sic] mysticism is dependent on the solution of these questions, and that in processes of canonization stigmata do not count as incontestable miracles." August Poulain, transcribed by William G. Bilton, "Mystical Stigmata," *Catholic Encyclopedia Online* (Arvada, CO: Knight, 2003), www.newadvent.org/cathen/14294b.htm. Originally in *The Catholic Encyclopedia, Volume XIV* (New York: Appleton, 1912).

4. The *Catholic Encyclopedia* attributes the rise of devotion to the wounds to St. Bernard, St. Francis, and "the enthusiasm of the Crusaders returning from the Holy Land" in the twelfth century and following. F. G. Holweck, transcribed by Michael T. Barrett, "The Five Sacred Wounds," *Catholic Encyclopedia Online*, www.newadvent.org/cathen/15714a.htm. Originally in *The Catholic Encyclopedia, Volume XV*.

5. Both the wrist marks and the cross over the heart were reported by Marie-Julie Jahenny, ca. 1873. In Wilson, *Stigmata,* 40. Forehead stigmata were reported in 1983 by Roberto Casarin of Turin and earlier by Soeur Jeanne des Anges of Loudon in the seventeenth century. In Wilson, *Stigmata,* 61

6. "I Beseech Thee, Most Sweet Lord," Michael W. Martin, ed., *Thesaurus Precum Latinarum*, 2005, http://www.preces-latinae.org/thesaurus/PostMissam/Obsecro.html

7. A special rosary devoted to the five wounds has been approved since 1823 (see "The Five Sacred Wounds"). The Passionist fathers have created a chaplet of the five wounds, in which each wound is the object of meditation. Catholic Doors Ministry, "Chaplet of the Five Wounds," http://Catholicdoors.com/prayers/chaplets/chap05.htm. The Sorrowful Mysteries of the standard rosary are a variation on these meditations. For the quotation asking for wounding see "Devotion to the Five Wounds," http://www.kensmen.com/catholic/5wounds.html.

8. Though expected as part of a chaplet or rosary, the invocation of Mary is startling given her usual image as gently maternal and the fact that the wounds, after all, were not inflicted by those particularly fond of her son. We are reminded both of how strongly the wounds take on a positive value and of how desperately the saints desire their own.

9. The prayer continues, "Likewise, the more a soul loves, the more it seeks that which wounded it. The more it is wounded, the more it is healed. May our Lord and God, Jesus Christ, the loving and healing physician, wound the depths of our souls with this healing wound- who with the Father and the Holy Spirit is one forever. Amen." "Thou Art, O God, Our All," Martin, *Thesaurus*, http://www.preces-latinae.org/thesaurus/Filius/TuEsDeus.html. In a similar vein, St. Bonaventure asks "Pierce, O most Sweet Lord Jesus, my inmost soul with the most joyous and healthful wound of thy love." "Prayer of Saint Bonaventure," Martin, *Thesaurus*, http://www.preces-latinae.org/thesaurus/PostMissam/Bonaventurae.html.

10. "Saint Clare's Litany of the Sacred Wounds," in Trinity Communications, *Catholic Culture,* 2005, http:..www.catholicculture.org/lit/Prayers/view.cfm?id=1120. From *Kyrie Eleison: Two Hundred Litanies,* by Benjamin Francis Musser OFM (Manchester NH: Magnificat, 1944). St. Clare of Assisi is responsible for this thirteenth-century litany of the sacred wounds, in which each wound is again addressed with a particular prayer. (See also "The Five Sacred Wounds.") More strangely still, St. Bridget of Sweden (or, more probably, one of her followers after her death), having apparently determined in meditation that Christ suffered not five but 5,480 wounds (a number based upon the multitailed, multiknotted whip with which Christ was flagellated), prayed fifteen prayers daily for a year, somewhat exceeding the wounds' calculated total. "Prayers of St. Bridget," Martin, *Thesaurus*, http://www.preces-latinae.org/thesaurus/Filius/StBrigid.html.

11. Nor is this image restricted to Catholicism; a seventeenth-century exhortation by the Puritan Andrew Gray asks, "Know ye the language of the wound in

his side? It says, Come, come; and the wounds in his hands say, Come, come. And who would not come then?" "A Word of Exhortation, by Mr. Andrew Gray, AT Kirklistoun, Upon the 12th of June 1653." "Andrew Gray: The Youngest Puritan," http://www.newble.co.uk/gray/exhort1.html.

12. Wilson, *Stigmata,* 20. Wilson cites *Acta Sanctorum,* March, vol. III (Antwerp: Societé des Bollandistes, 1643–1940), 751, as trans. in Herbert Thurston, *The Physical Phenomena of Mysticism* (Chicago: Regnery, 1952), 39.

13. Unknown author(s), *The Little Flowers of St. Francis,* trans. L. Sherley-Price (Harmondsworth: Penguin, n.d.), 165, quoted Wilson, *Stigmata,* 11.

14. Steven Connor, *The Book of Skin* (Ithaca: Cornell University Press, 2004), 122.

15. Poulain, "Mystical Stigmata."

16. Rene Biot, *The Enigma of the Stigmata,* vol. 57 of *The 20th Century Encyclopedia of Catholicism,* ed. Henri Daniel-Rops (New York: Hawthorn Books, 1962), 71, 72.

17. Ibid.

18. Biot, *Enigma,* 53; Wilson, *Stigmata,* 82.

19. Biot, *Enigma,* 53.

20. Wilson, *Stigmata,* 31.

21. Jean-Luc Nancy, "Inoperative Community," in *The Inoperative Community,* ed. Peter Connor, trans. Peter Connor, Lisa Garbus, Michael Holland, and Simona Sawhney (Minneapolis: University of Minnesota Press, 1991), 35.

22. Indeed, communication is necessarily sinful for Bataille; see OC 5: 305/G 65.

23. Bataille adds that, contrary to theology's claims of completeness (OC 5: 262/G 27) only for atheism is the world complete, without the anguish of insufficiency (OC 5: 176/IE 153).

24. Nancy, *Inoperative Community*, 3–6.

25. Ibid., 30.

26. Ibid.

27. Ibid., 10.

28. Ibid., 26.

29. Maurice Blanchot, *Unavowable Community,* trans. Pierre Joris (New York: Station Hill, 1988), 5.

30. Ibid.

31. Ibid., 16–17.

32. Ibid., 9.

33. I have commented on this reading of the crucifixion and resurrection in "Touch," chapter three of *Word Made Skin* (Bronx, NY: Fordham University Press, 2004), 49–70.

34. Blanchot, *Unavowable Community*, 11.

35. Nancy, *Inoperative Community*, 15.

36. Ibid., 21.

37. As described by Nancy, ibid., 31.

38. The question of who suffers on the cross turns out to be theologically tricky. The simple answer "God" is generally regarded as heretical, making of the

persons of the Trinity simply aspects of one divinity. (This is Sabellianism, with Patripassianism the heresy particularly concerned with the suffering of God the Father.) At another extreme, some versions of Gnosticism deny the reality of divine suffering at all; the heresy of aphthartodocetism likewise denies that God could suffer. I am working here from the perspective that at least Christ suffers fully, in divinity and humanity inseparably.

39. Nancy, *Inoperative Community*, 38.

40. MacKendrick *Word Made Skin,* "Cut," 137–60.

41. Maurice Blanchot, *Writing the Disaster,* trans. Ann Smock (Lincoln: University of Nebraska Press, 1986), 51.

42. L. Sherley-Price, trans., *The Little Flowers of St. Francis,* 165, trans. of *Fioretti*, as cited in Wilson, *Stigmata,* 11.

CHAPTER NINE

A Blood Altered in Its Own Sense

Marc Froment-Meurice
Translated by Jason Kemp Winfree

1

"Altered in his own sense" (*altéré de son sens*)—I take these words from the *Mémoire des Héritiers*, cited by Bataille, concerning Gilles de Rais: "Everyone knew that he was notoriously extravagant, having neither sense nor understanding, since in effect his senses were often altered [he was altered in his own sense], and often he left very early in the morning and wandered the streets entirely alone. And when someone pointed out that it was not fitting, he responded more in the manner of a fool and a madman than anything else" (OC 10: 280/TG 15). "Notoriously extravagant," Gilles likes to give. But his gift is the gift of death. It will therefore be necessary to bring into relation unrestricted expenditure and the killing of children: the same absolute pleasure (*jouissance*) of the unlimited gift, which goes as far as to consume itself in an exorbitant way. The child's eye pawned to the devil . . .

"He wandered the streets all alone" is repeated again at the end of the first chapter, "The Sacred Monster," repeated as confirming the "perhaps" of a hypothesis that is itself equally insane, that Gilles is bound to the ultimate sense of Christianity and its "pressing demand for crime." At bottom, fundamentally insane, barbaric, archaic, violent, sacrificial in the manner of the Aztecs, irreducible to "reason" or common sense, which is always shared. Utterly alone, Gilles wandered the streets of the world alone, without the slightest reason, without the slightest end or goal or intention. He wandered astray in search of prey or whatever pleased him. He is the Sovereign. From this point on, it is necessary to let him wander all alone, let him go altered in his own sense.

2

Gilles de Rais is a figure whose historical existence is evidenced by documents from the trial, which Bataille scrupulously edited in the translation made by his friend, Pierre Klossowski. It is necessary to begin by reading all the depositions given by witnesses, by accomplices and victims alike, all the accounts from the hearing, all so clearly horrific. It is necessary to read—if it can be read, intolerable as it is—the double confession of the accused to the sovereign religious authorities, both in secret and in public, in order to understand a "phenomenon" Bataille calls a "sacred monster," perhaps the monster of the sacred, or the sacred as monstrosity, up to the very point of no longer knowing how to speak about a proper sense. "Gilles de Rais owes his lasting glory to his crimes. But was he, as some have said, *the most abject criminal of all time*? In essence, this speculative affirmation is barely defensible. Crime is a fact of the human species, a fact of that species alone, but it is above all its secret aspect, impenetrable and hidden. Crime hides, and by far the most terrifying things are those that elude us. In the night marked out by our fear, we are bound to imagine the worst. The worst is always possible; and also, with crime, the worst offers the last possible meaning" (OC 10: 277/TG 13). The empire of the worst—such is the ultimate and eschatological sense of humankind, of the animal species that Bataille tells us is the only one to make crime its distinctive mark, its proper signature, indeed, the *law* of its being. To be human is to be capable of the worst, to the point where there is crime only with humankind. Can we, then, even speak of crimes against humanity without immediately sinking into flagrant contradiction? Is such talk not obviously inane, monstrous?

Let us imagine, for a moment, this trial unfolding before our very eyes, a bit like those instituted by the International Court of the Hague. Gilles would appear there, like so many other warlords of our day, indicted for crimes against humanity. Now it would be even riskier to affirm that he is or was "the most abject criminal of *all times*." For the thesis of the worst, of a final degree of evil, absolutely and not relatively superlative, carries the emblem of evil beyond history and therefore beyond all possibility of judgment. It leads it straight into the impenetrability of the non-sense of which evil may well be "the last sense," the end, and even the ends of sense. At the same time, without this thesis, which posits death as the final sense (and redeemer) of evil, the same notion of "crime against humanity" loses all sense, all meaning, and consequently, not only crime, but also humanity itself.

But would Gilles himself even be judged criminal? A criminal intentionally commits the acts deemed "criminal," acts prohibited and pronounced such by the law, which alone establishes and defines crime as violation of the law (a logic Hegel takes to its limit, making the law itself a unique criminal). And Gilles ignores—royally—every law. Still he is perhaps not altogether without faith or law, since he "believes," at least, in the existence of an evil principle, which he pursues fiercely and unrelentingly (relentlessness that calls for the slaughterhouse) yet without any success and even recognizing the absurdity of his quest, the futility of calling on the devil to reestablish his fortune. In any case, Rais never stops or hesitates even for an instant before the consequences of his acts. In the eyes of common sense, he behaves like a child. And one cannot judge a child, even for taking pleasure in the deaths of other children. He can be exorcised or excommunicated; he can be burnt as an example but only as a monster.

If Gilles de Rais passes for an extraordinary and uncommon criminal within history, he could not but be transformed into the Bluebeard of legend, since the absolute of crime is better represented in literature than in real crimes, which are always limited and imperfect because they are always too human, always marred by finitude. "We can never forget that it is the legendary aspects of crime alone that have ordained the truth of crime," writes Bataille (OC 10: 270/TG 13). Evil reveals its truth only in fiction, the paradoxical thesis established in *Literature and Evil*.

3

The last book to occupy Bataille's attention, *The Trial of Gilles de Rais,* generally goes unnoticed, partly because it is taken as a "purely" historical work, based merely on archival reading and interpretation. But it is above all because of Bataille's incredibly harsh and hypercritical tone with respect to Christianity, and in general every religion founded on sacrifice, that sets this book apart. Like the accursed share of a thought with no other destiny than illuminating the most obscure and disturbing depths of existence, a bright and directing light inaccessible to the *lumen naturale* of reason, *The Trial of Gilles de Rais* has been overlooked, dismissed, and above all, avoided. The gesture linking Christianity—which Gilles de Rais shows in its anxious archaism and its unbearable, inconceivable violence—to the fury of the Berserkers, the Germanic warriors thirsty for blood and intoxicated by death, such gesture gives the proper measure of the book, and hence the vertigo I always felt in reading Bataille, and Bataille alone.

The present history of the world proves him right. But this is not because history conforms to a legend that alone has the power to evoke that which in the crime is not reducible to the limits of the intelligible world, as Bataille puts it explaining the transformation of Gilles de Rais into a Bluebeard (with whom he had nothing in common, if only for the crude reason that Gilles was not attracted to women; and besides sexual pleasure is secondary in this "tragedy"). Consequently, contrary to what Bataille asserts, the legend has rather the opposite effect of reducing the mystery to the "limits of the intelligible world." By transforming the sexual and generational deviance into a mere detail of hair color (Gilles was beardless), the popular legend covers with a modest veil what the Church and the religious art from this time incessantly wanted to unveil, since it is an essential part of revelation. The monstrosity at the bottom of humanity, the evil embodied in Satan, prince of this world, has always been necessary for the economy of salvation. In a world dominated by evil and at each instant doomed to perish by the fire of an apocalypse (the very end of the world, its being destined to disappear, so as to reveal its Creator), Gilles was in no way an Antichrist or even a Mephisto. Rather, as Bataille had to concede: "Even though he invoked the demon and expected from him the reestablishment of his fortune, up to the end he was naively a good and devout Christian" (OC 10: 281/TG 16). And this flat and depressing fact scandalizes Bataille. He cannot imagine how a hardened criminal who took pleasure from his young prey could really be afraid of the devil: "His tragedy is that of a Doctor Faust, but an infantile Faust. Before the Devil, in fact, our monster trembled. Not only did the Devil—our criminal's last hope—leave him trembling like a leaf, but Gilles de Rais was ridiculously, devotedly afraid of him. The Devil reduced him to begging. The monster was covered in blood, but he was a coward"(OC 10: 280/TG 16). Being from the start and above all a warrior, Gilles de Rais was not scared at the sight of blood. He was a savage afraid of nothing except loosing his soul. But is not the supreme ruse of a deranged Christianity the invocation of the devil in order to frighten, in order to occasion the experience of conversion?

In this case, forcing the criminal to pray for the salvation of a "soul" that is strictly unknown to him (for he knows only bodies, so weak)? As long as the original sin weighs on mankind—and its abolition would clearly mean emptying Christianity of its substance, if not its sense, since at bottom it is senseless—the devil has his intimate necessity in the economy of salvation. What sort of blood, then, did Bataille have in mind? Is it possible that he touched, without really measuring the extent of it, the very strength of Christianity, its inexhaustible resource: that the "blind faith" that impels the "faint-hearted" Gilles comes from the same fascinating power awakened by the mere "sight" of Christ's blood, so much like Gilles' victims, the earthy images, the human simulacra closest to the figure of the Savior: children, and even beautiful little "angels."

4

"Perhaps Christianity is above all bound to an archaic humanity, one unrestrainedly open to violence?" (OC 10: 281/TG 16) This question carries more than one trace: atonement, anguish, indeed, fear and trembling. In any case, it points toward a primitive Christianity, one whose possibility we in our anemic age wish to avoid. Yet all the evidence is there, beginning with those who first testify to the new faith, those justly called "martyrs," which is to say in Greek, witnesses. What is the difference between the blood of children shed by the "sacred monster" and the blood of Christ? While invoking Satan, "with astonishing impudence, Rais imagined saving himself to the end, despite his abominable crimes, and escaping Hell's flames, which for him were the object of a coal-seller's implicit faith." But what is amazing in this "impudence," as if Rais constantly plays a double game, is the origin of a "perhaps" still more audacious, a monstrous hypothesis, which Bataille formulates almost tepidly: "Perhaps Christianity is even fundamentally the pressing demand for crime, the demand for the horror that in a sense it needs in order to forgive" (OC 10: 280/TG 16). But one can only forgive the unforgivable, since otherwise, if evil is in itself forgivable, it would not need the forgiveness, which is just *given*, completely unjustified, as a divine favor, providential and always excessive in proportion to what is humanly and reasonably permissible. And Bataille is right to emphasize, "It does not seem to me that Christianity above all requires the rule of reason." On the contrary, it is in league with violence, or more exactly, "it makes *allowances* for violence," announces violence and shares it out, the accursed share of evil necessary in every economy of salvation (OC 10: 281/TG 17).

In this regard, it is necessary to recall a troubling coincidence, one Bataille barely addresses, and the history of "France" still less: what schoolboy today knows that Gilles was the companion in arms, the second in command to Joan of Arc in the liberation of Orléans? To be sure, the virgin did not spoil herself on the open stomachs of cute little lambs, and the voices she claimed to have heard did not come from the choir children engaged in the service of the chapel of the glorious *sieur* de Rais, marshall of France at the age of twenty-five. But serving the same cause, they both ended up on the stake. Of the two, only Joan of Arc has been canonized, but only Gilles has kept his body more or less intact, preserved in the consecrated earth. This is significant because Gilles' closest relatives, due to the nobility of their blood, were able to recover his body, which had not been completely charred, and indeed recover it for a Christian burial (you see, he was almost forgiven). By contrast, nothing remains of the corpse of the "Saint," fatally excommunicated for heresy and sorcery.

All this bears upon the very sense of sense. For who can endure that God could speak to a young peasant girl, practically illiterate, a nobody, and, infinitely aggravating this, for him to order a sacred mission that is above all political? For what reason did a peasant girl prefer one king to another? Like Gilles, Joan has been transformed into a legend, but even more terrifying than that of Bluebeard, because she ultimately sanctifies the bourgeois political fiction of the *nation*: to a certain extent, it is Joan who crowns Charles at Reims, anointing him and at the same time performing the last rites of the feudal nobility, the benediction of the "people." Blood is not enough. It is earth that prevails or at least constitutes an exigency as essential as birth. Such is the profound sense of the sacred mission entrusted to this peasant: to sanctify nationality and consecrate the nation itself, the nation in its suave integrity, immune and exempt from everything strange or foreign. It is necessary to drive the English out of France, not because they are worse than others but just because they are foreigners. Is it really surprising that today the National Front celebrates Joan as its patron, even if nobody any longer would think to take up arms against the hereditary enemy?

By contrast, Gilles de Rais does not defend any cause. He has no political sense, no strategy, and if he relies on the devil, it is as a last recourse, in desperation, as he himself says. But, in itself, invoking the devil is not as insane as claiming to hear heavenly voices. In both cases salvation is at stake, either that of the community or that of the individual. In truth, though, it is perhaps less natural, at least at the time, to try to enlist God in the service of a temporal sovereign than to ask Satan, prince of this world, to procure that favor thanks to which he rules the world: gold. Is it not an absolute sacrilege to address God for the sake of riches? Is it not because of the religious prohibition concerning money that princes and the bourgeois alike owe their recourse to the Jews? But if there is a difference between this recourse to the Jews and Gilles' invocation of the devil, we must not forget that Gilles is kept from signing any commercial contract with the devil, and in this way never wagers his soul. On the contrary, Gilles remains free to go back on his word, which he never gives in person but always through a third party, one who knows how to play on his credulity (one will even go so far as to inflict upon himself real blows and injuries to persuade Gilles). All the same, a deal with the devil is more suitable than the Pharisees of the Christian Coalition would maintain with their God of war: the devil "in person" remains desperately absent, and perhaps this very fact is how he steals from his creator his unique privilege.

5

"Write with blood, and you will experience that blood is spirit."[1] Or blood becomes sense, which is what Nietzsche "believed."

> [A]nd he, the witness, saw among the archives of the said Gilles, the accused, five or six leaves of paper with large borders, on which there were crosses, red signs, and red writing in the hand of the said Gilles, the accused; which writing he, the witness, presumed and suspected had been done with human blood, considering what he had heard previously: that the said Gilles, the accused, had children killed for their blood to write books with. (OC 10: 511/TG 219–20)

> according to public rumor . . . the said Gilles de Rais was killing a large number of children, and having them killed, and that he was writing a book in his own hand with their blood. (OC 10: 510/TG 218)

What book? What book did Gilles write? Did he even write? Or rather does this rumor not translate in a subterranean way the popular expression of an absolute terror of Writing, what is always associated with death, with blood, and evil? Because every writing (above all to an illiterate) is incomprehensible, secret, and so forbidden? Even the Holy Scriptures demand the mediation of interpreters, priests, or better still professors, at least if they are to become comprehensible for the common people. Was there a book written by Gilles in secret, written in the blood of those who have themselves never even written? A book in powdered bones? A papyrus of skin and blood shed in order to write this very book? What book? "The Book," the only book, toward which the whole world is directed?[2]

6

Gilles de Rais is not Oedipus: he gouges the eyes of those who have nothing (i.e., nothing except their eyes to cry, nothing but their tears). And he seems to take pleasure in his torture, the only motive that can be proffered, a pleasure that will be called perverse, even though it remains to be seen if all pleasure is not so, at least all pleasure which has no other end than itself, serving no greater purpose. But is pleasure ever legitimate other than by serving a sovereign good? Gilles reveals something else entirely, something that is even the very Thing itself (*la Chose même*) (the Thing I love [*la Chose m'aime*]). If Gilles is "altered of his own sense," it is because his proper sense (and the sovereign pleasure that he takes or that has its source in him) refuses to let itself be altered by *common* sense, of which he clearly has none. Nevertheless, he is so sensitive to the danger of excommunication that it is the absolute weapon, even more so than torture. More than mortal danger, Gilles is concerned with his very salvation, so he confides an exhaustive confession without restriction. No doubt, the logic here is difficult to follow, since our conception of what constitutes a human being rests on entirely different foundations, a completely different thinking of the "body" as "altered" from the start: the body is first of all the dead body, or rather the dying body, but promised resurrection by what is endured and shared in the death of Christ. The body is therefore in "substance"—consubstantially and transubstantially—the body of Christ, and it is his blood (shed "in memory," in memory of blood shed, of the original and originary crime) that cements the community in the communion whose sense, at bottom, Gilles has reversed, making it his alone. But this concerns the *same* sense, the same blood . . .

All the more, it concerns sovereignty, which in the last instance is perhaps "nothing," as Bataille says. This expenditure without reserve (this exhaustion of foundations) never consumes "better" than in the worst and most extreme instance, never better than in pure loss: for the sake of its proper loss, and because the pure is attained only in loss. Pure loss of the pure father: perhaps the supreme resource of sacrifice (and disinterestedness is not far off) resides in the nonsense of its cause (or its Thing, the *Sache selbst*[3], it is the same thing). Recognized as such, this nonsense would be "sacred," serving only to reinforce the origin of sacrifice. It goes so far as to sacrifice its own interests, all proper sense, and consumes itself in order to make its Thing, the heart of the matter, triumph in an apotheosis and an apocalypse without reserve, a total and complete holocaust of sense, but a proper sense that goes so far as to sacrifice itself in order to manifest the purity of its intentions is only more sacred and therefore absolutely inaccessible to every other sense (and above all to the "common" sense). This non-sense is given in the nudity of the bodies that precisely give nothing else to be seen, and this alone touches on the secret of the body proper (against all symbolism of what it might otherwise be). Its nakedness grants access directly to that which remains absolutely inaccessible even in its exposure, indeed, inaccessible because it is completely exposed. Thus, it passes through a sort of sixth sense, that of the "without," about which one could say that it drains its sense or its source like the blood in our veins. It does without sense because its only sense is of this passing, once and for all [*une fois pour toutes*], a faith for all [*Une foi pour toutes*].

Perhaps we are only now beginning to turn toward the dark night of Gilles, the night where all bodies hide at the very moment they are exposed, utterly without resistance (and not a single example of any of the victims can seriously be challenged, in part because each has already placed his fate in the hands of the all-powerful Lord). They withdraw more than they expose their nakedness; but even as torture victims, they are no less out of reach. But it is only about bodies. Anyway, bodies will always lie around, thrown bodies, rejected in the world [*monde*] as unclean [*immonde*] (see Jean-Luc Nancy[4]). In these somber days, wherein still today our same and not same world remains submerged, life counted for nothing, less than nothing. And this without even considering the evil, which in addition to everyday misery, overwhelmed all these animals who are unreasonably called reasonable: religious and infectious diseases, wars and spoiled harvests, measures of permanent insecurity, not to mention the new virus that was beginning to surreptitiously ravage the city, namely, banks.

Life is worth nothing, especially the lives of those who are wasted. But for whom does expenditure matter, the expenditure whose Lord (whether in a good or bad mood but always well born like Gilles) never even notices, never takes responsibility? Nobody! Or perhaps it concerns, by default, a poor devil who will never leave his room. Certainly, it is here that Rais fascinates but also irritates Bataille. How can one believe these tired old wives tales? How, in the same vein, could one be afraid, as if this puppet takes hold of life like a marionette, a Bluebeard in the hands of an autistic child? Likewise, how could Gilles attack a clergyman with his bare hands after having liberated France with God's virgin, Joan of Arc? "Gilles de Rais is possessed, a loose cannon in the church who roars: 'Ha, ribald, you beat my men, and extorted from them; come outside the church or I'll kill you on the spot!" (OC 10: 287/TG 21). But what a monumental error this is, ridiculous stupidity, childish bragging! Gilles was in fact unaware of the realities of his time. He failed to anticipate the decline of knighthood and chivalry in the profit of the vulgar bourgeois, withdrawn into their empty shells, counting their money. Gilles had no political sense (either tactical or strategic). And for these reasons, he appears to Bataille as a simpleton, a thick-headed idiot, in short, an acephalic brute who does not even think to save himself.

Gilles is disturbing. He is completely insane, entirely unreasonable. But is he really the most abject criminal of all time? Is he even really a criminal? For that, it would be necessary to attribute to him responsibility for his acts. It is not just a matter of recognizing the crimes he committed, as he does without flinching: he will confess them all; it is he and he alone who envisages them and carries them out. He is not encouraged by anyone, not even the devil (whom he never saw nor understood, to whom he will gladly pass off a promissory note on the sly, committing him to nothing in the end). And it is this that will leave his confessor so astounded and incredulous, as if confronted with a miracle: that this simpleton could have acted of his own accord, when he is so clearly lost, confused, out of it. "Following his imagination and his thought, without the advice of anyone, and according to his own sense, solely for his own pleasure and carnal delight, and according to some other intention or for the sake of some other end" (OC 10: 288/TR 22). It is the moment of truth in his confession—obtained "freely," but we might also say "by force," since it was under the threat of torture (legal at the time). What Gilles did and carefully hid from the eyes of the world (that which is all the same a prowess, even though the thick castle walls of the time make the more modern "high security" prisons pale by comparison, their dungeons swallowing entirely the memory of those who disappear, reducing them to ashes), he brings to light in a confession, at first private, but repeated publicly as documented for the trial and judgment. He brings to light his very birth as the crime for which he is inexplicably held accountable, as if he had ever asked to be born Gilles de Rais! "[N]one are pure of sin in your presence, not even an infant of one day upon the earth."[5]

Altered in his own sense, it is the alteration that makes sense. And what alteration is more radical and intense than the passage of life into death? Just his sense, then, nothing more, but an altered sense, corrupted, satisfied only by new blood. The most surprising move on the part of Gilles, though, consists in sovereignly denying this sovereign change: sovereignty does not differentiate between life and death; it denies the limit that makes possible every transgression, such that it could be said to transgress transgression and in this way serves only to go along in its own sense: Rais wandered about altered in his own blood. He does not see the break between life and death, and this is even why he can bid farewell to his companions, assuring them that they will soon see one another again. If his mind is always altered in a theater of illusions, the blood itself is true, and even the sole truth in this ignoble world: that life holds little sense. Similarly, it is not even clear that Gilles has differentiated God and the devil. He knows obscurely that they are two extremes of a spectrum, but why not hold them together? Without the one, the other has even less chance of gaining victory. At bottom, they split quite well the roles and the places, the high and the low, except that in the middle, right here, on earth, they are nowhere to be found. For the here-and-now is neither a place of justice nor of measure on this earth, and in any case, not a middle ground between heaven and earth. Satan waits and keeps us waiting. Gilles burns (with fear) to force the devil out into broad daylight or even back into his stronghold. Prince of this world, he is the angel who carries the light as dark as the blood that flows on the battlefields where men measuring their truth, that is to say, their death, are delivered from every scruple and from all religion: for Gilles no one (not a single human being) is sacred, and that is his sacred evil. Fundamentally, nature gives no reasons, this being its only noblesse or the nobility of the Unique, never answerable to anyone. To remain inborn, innate, without anybody, neither god nor father, like the inside of a tomb, the tomb of "without."

7

The constant recourse (particularly with Luther, first unfounding father of Christianity) to an original spirit of Christianity whose purity has supposedly been perverted over time, and above all with the Church, found its stopping point [*point d'arrêt*] in Rais. Gilles could not be farther from Kant, who claimed to see in Christianity the universal moral religion to come. At the archaic basis of Christianity, already announced in its hatred of nonbelievers and other philosophers succumbed to the "folly of the world" (Paul), the call of Christ cuts with a double-edged sword: the persecution of the father who sends his son to the devil, so to speak. This original violence is what Bataille sees in Gilles. But Bataille will not forgive him for committing evil without intending to do so. Human being differs from the animal only by the sense of evil, that is to say, because he alone suffers from the malady of having been born, as if this were his original crime, an indelible defect. Gilles certainly has no control over his stars, so to speak (what we call his "instincts"); he is excited only at the sight of blood, recalling that only the blood of Christ can save from the *bad blood* at the heart of birth. The fall at the beginning shows clearly the origins of Christianity: at bottom an empire [*empire*] consumed by the worst [*pire*], the catastrophic birth of a universal moral religion created by and for slaves. The fact that the entire crowd accompanied Gilles to his torture appears scandalous for Bataille, who could explain this fact to himself only as a moment of collective disorder and frenzy, as if everyone had been, like Gilles, altered in its sense. Take the Mysteries, the only moments of play authorized by the Church, which otherwise excommunicated actors: these famous Mysteries gave place to endless processions, where the "Passion of Christ" was revived and relived in twelve or thirteen frames or tableaux. Gilles, at bottom, is staged as a sort of Antichrist more Christ than Christ himself, up to the point of burning the stage with his life.

At this point, one can ask if the fascination that Gilles radiates like sulfuric gas does not come down to the same thing, namely, that it makes no difference: the indifference being as sovereign as death, which never differentiates in the least between its victims, not even sparing the children, who have been left to the grace of God, that is, to their own forces, which by definition are so limited.: One can legitimately conclude that Gilles kills children only to accomplish the divine will! In any case, he embodied Christianity in the monstrosity of the congenital idiot, saved by his own imbecility: resembling so strongly the entire "actual" world (Christianized-globalized).

Gilles is the monster of Christianity as Flaubert is the village idiot of literature. Everything in him attests to an archaic mentality: born in blind chance and early on left to himself, which makes him see the world as obscure, indifferent, chaotic, dangerous, but above all, *exciting*. We can, of course, denounce the silliness of Gilles. But this does not avoid the inverse silliness, which leads the enlightened in their naïve belief to be able to triumph over uncertainty by the good will (of the righteous) without dying of boredom in the perpetual peace of the Father. In a sense (in a sense altered in its own sense), Gilles rejoins the tragic Greek sense where human being is characterized by monstrosity (*deinon*).[6] He can transgress his proper limits precisely because he never even encounters them at all.

As many modern historians have shown, childhood is a recent invention practically unknown to the Middle Ages. As soon as the child has reached what one calls the "age of reason," it is no longer fundamentally different than any other sinner. Gilles too, therefore, had his chapel, and it is always in thinking of the heavenly voices of the children's choir that he will tear out the hearts of other children, joyfully listening to the voices of the victims he lays to waste, sending them immediately to their deaths. It is here that it is difficult to follow him. But Gilles did not understand himself any more than does a child, as he said and confessed. In this sense, Bataille was correct: reason is baffled here, insulted; more than defeated, it is ignored, rendered null and void. Bataille does not use the word *stupid* (*bêtise*) but prefers *simpleton*, since the stupid echoes the beast (*bête*) and effectively tends to see in Gilles a beautiful blonde beast thirsty for blood. However, it is difficult to speak of "pure" animality or bestiality here. For Gilles does not throw himself indifferently on the first-comer: he takes precautions, and he even succeeds in keeping his secret with an admirable tenacity up to the end. His plan is almost more audacious than that of the Marquis de Sade, since his castle walls never hid him at the end of the world but, on the contrary, extended everywhere in order to dominate the country, the entire peasant population terrified of all those "at the top." His crimes were not the fruit of an imagination or machination nurtured by a blood perverted by decades in prison. Moved by an incontrollable force, his crimes were perpetrated on people of real flesh and blood, blood that he loves to see run from the throats of his decapitated angels. Contrary to the heroes of Sade, Gilles does not reason. He does not want to prove anything. He is content to be what he "is." And he does not know, he has never known, and perhaps will never try to know that.

Does this unknowing make him a monster? But then we all would be more or less in the same condition. And we forget that to kill children, for such a lord, is almost just a detail in times where children died like flies from diseases, misery, or forced labor. In any case, it is not a crime answerable to religion any more than is the murder of animals. Rightly understood, as soon as Gilles has encroached upon divine law—already in carrying arms into a church, a place of sanctuary and refuge from violence—it is inevitable that his abominable sodomy be imputed to diabolical influence. And are children not the most effective acolytes of the devil, having no moral sense? "Morality is a weakness of the brain," the child Arthur (Rimbaud) will say.[7] But, to the extent that Christianity makes criminals of us all in our very origin, it is impossible to distinguish what would be a high crime and our being born criminal. Consequently, the Church could never but pardon all real criminals whoever they are, even the genocides, such that they attain the height neither of the first nor last crime, the crucifixion of Our Lord. Beside a similar event (unique and yet repeated each time for faith itself) the crimes of Gilles are but a speck of dust, but nevertheless evidencing the elementary archaic abjection whereby Christianity plants its roots like talons in the body of its prey.

8

"[H]e had burned and turned [them] to ashes to eliminate any trace of his crimes and to avoid disclosures by the said children" (OC 10: 568/TG 283). Ashes do not speak, nor do children.

Reasoning in three steps: One, man is capable of the worst. Two, God alone can pardon the worst. Three, provided there is regret, the slave pays for having dared "to do" something of his own. (It is understood that God has already given and no longer *does* anything but watch his creation disfigure itself.) Man is indebted in this regard to God, who gives him forgiveness so that man accrues even more indebtedness. Forgiveness is the invention of the genius who transformed the gift into debt; it is the very formula of credit and of the fiction that goes to make of Christianity the most reliable vector of evangelical capitalism. God created man capable of the worst, that is to say, capable of God.

Taking another example (always filicide, since the reverse would go against nature), is it any more reasonable for Abraham to sacrifice his only son according to faith in a divine voice, the source of which no one ever sees? Gilles actually seems more frank and honest: he never invokes a sacred mission in order to justify a simulacrum of sacrifice whose sense is at bottom nothing but a sordid commercial contract cloaked under the habit of faith and allegiance. One can also ask what really distinguishes Isaac and the children murdered by Gilles and his stooges: is it because Abraham's sacrifice is stopped, thus ultimately inconsequential? But this is no less a sacrifice, and although it is perhaps sacred, it is no less abominable; or perhaps it is even more hateful still, since the blood transubstantiated in spirit is whitened, washed, purified, and made innocent, thus being without consequence. In his intention, in thinking, Abraham is just as much a dangerous, insane criminal, and no less altered in his sense than Gilles, a sense equally incommunicable, equally absent foundation or reason: the sense "without," the absolute dissolution of sense (which is given only *as* divided or shareable).

The logic of expenditure requires that it be unlimited, heading toward inevitable self-destruction. It establishes its limits as their very absence. "The" religion ("universal" Christianity) always rests on this postulate: life is or has an absolute value only if it values infinitely more than the "simple" life.

> Sometimes they severed the head from the body with dirks, daggers, and knives, sometimes they struck them violently on the head with a cudgel or other blunt instruments, sometimes they suspended them with cords from a peg or small hook in his room and strangled them; and when they were languishing, he committed the sodomitic vice on them in the aforesaid manner. Which children dead, he embraced them, and he gave way to contemplating those who had the most beautiful heads and members, and he had their bodies cruelly opened up and delighted at the sight of their internal organs; and very often, when the said children were dying, he sat on their bellies and delighted in watching them die . . . after which he had the children burned and their cadavers turned to ashes. (OC 10: 488/TG 196)

At this point it is impossible to contain Gilles de Rais in the simple limits of reason or "moral" religion. Huysmans[8] and all the aesthetes of Satanism have only followed the "common reaction." They are stupidly blind and captivated by the majesty of a fictional character: "There is in the evidence of monstrosity a sovereign grandeur which does not contradict the humility of the wretched man proclaiming the horror of the crime," writes Bataille in contrast to Huysmans' simple praise. Bataille then adds in a note: "Reciprocally, would not the ordinary man assume, in his conception of sovereignty, that it has an equivalence to crime?" (OC 10: 300/TG 32).

Not only is sovereignty in the crime carried to this monstrous level, but there is a crime in the sovereignty itself, as if the latter harmed, precisely, the community and above all the equality of those who are alike. Gilles is no longer human like the others but rather is set apart, separated, infinitely other, and in that he is put on the same plane as the sacred, put in the place of the sovereign which no one takes without immediately being reduced to ashes. And yet, in revealing the complete extent of his crimes he allows the two classic ingredients of tragedy, terror and compassion, to bring about the final scene of purification (expiation in the flames). Gilles is therefore an inverted Christ, even more so than an Antichrist, but in this way he manifests the troubling ambivalence of sovereignty, his always possible conversion from one extreme to another, as if the two absolutes of Good and Evil touch at an unimaginable digressive point, which is necessary in order that one triumph over the other. It is thus necessary that there be communication of one with the other, even as each wants itself undivided and absolute.

The secret of Christianity resides precisely in this reversal of the lowest and the highest: " 'Enough to kill ten thousand men!'[9] How could anyone display more pride or humility?" (OC 10: 289/TG 23). But at this limit it is no longer possible to distinguish between pride and humility. *De profundis clamavi!*[10] The nerve center of Christianity, the ignoble is its foundation, its *basso continuo*, and that is why it is impossible to put it down (*mettre à bas*): it went down to the point of making its degradation (which it baptizes "humility") its supreme grandeur. The question of the absolute (the Unique) turns at once to martyrdom as soon as it requires absolution from the hands of another absolute, one with which it nevertheless should share nothing. Straight to the tomb—empty, of course, of any body. Now if the body—"He had killed a large number of small male children, whom he had burned and turned to ashes to eliminate any trace of his crimes and to avoid disclosures by the said children" (OC 10: 567–68/TG 283). —is to be vanquished, like death, it is still destined to be sublated in the glory of Christ, in his example, in a resurrection which hides the body to itself in order to reveal or sublate its mortal base.

9

For Bataille as for any reasonable being, the "faith of the coal-seller," which animates Gilles, appears all the more monstrous because it is not feigned, and moreover every fiction seems here to have been banned (including from the Gospels, thus rendering them unreadable). Yet the image of the coal seller seems ill-suited for this extravagant lord who parades around as much as some monarch, only with more splendor. Does not his ostentatious taste accord secretly with the obscurity of the castle walls where he commits his "abject" crimes in the absolute secret of a tomb? Gilles' life is consumed, burning at both ends of the candle: throwing gold out the windows in broad daylight simply to dazzle and blind, and thus to be able to freely abandon himself to his darkest desires, the onset of night. Crime wants night, writes Bataille. Yet, it wants the day as well, the revelation and the avowal that in bringing the crime to light will alone dissolve it, reducing it to powder like the disemboweled, burned, consecrated bodies of children.

Thus, "This monster is before us like a child. We cannot deny the monstrosity of childhood." The child is a monster by nature. He is the monster of Nature, although he is not physically monstrous. Altered in his own sense, Gilles leaves early in the morning, tracking his own self and falling onto another one, another whose blood will quench his thirst up to the point where death follows—indeed, the death of sense. The monster does not even know how to properly speak, though, so it is necessary to forgive him. He is only a child. No one risks becoming this child. He is the only one, he and he alone, alone without God, without even the need for God. He becomes nothing, has always been and will always be the same child—sterile, unformed, inborn, without kinship or family. The child is the monster, at least in the eyes of reason, since, "Reason alone defines monstrosity" (OC 10: 290/TG 24).

An atheist pure and simple, Bataille saw the horror at the basis of Christianity as the archaism of sacrifice, but at the same time he saw further that this very Christianity persists all the way up to and into the pure violence of the Berserkers, "going berserk" ("*fou furieux*" in French, which does not really have a word for this). It would be necessary then to speak of an arche-Christian impurity that has come to contaminate the sublime purity of the rite of communion, even stemming from the basis of an absolute purity flowing from the source: pure prodigality, blood shed for nothing, certainly not to save humanity. Gilles is not only the monstrous criminal; he is "the foolish prodigal" who is consumed in this total gift without return, the gift of death. Gilles not only throws money away on lavish feasts but also in lust and crime, so much that in a certain manner, death always has the advantage over life, since it is more hospitable and generous. Lacking all half-measure, death gives without calculating that noblesse that has the sense of a violence unconcerned with anything, and before which there is nothing that would not surrender. The sovereignty of Gilles holds to his *indifference*, sovereign indifference because life does not count for him, and less still the difference of one life from another.

Bataille holds to the control of reason, no doubt due to his fundamental Hegelianism (the sublation or mediation of Spirit). According to the "laws" of (the science of) experience, the conversion of the negative into being operates on the basis of the recognition of the other and therefore first requires the acceptance of death as absolute master of all. Sovereignty has to disappear, lose itself, or alienate itself (share itself) in order to leave place for the world of work, which is to say division, since division is the labor of sense, producing the sense of history: enlightenment at the end of the night and in order to finish with its terror (without which nevertheless there is no "proper" pleasure).

Likewise, Bataille scorns the sort of secret society (by no means Acéphale, of course) that Gilles created around himself. Yet it functioned "as one man alone," and no one betrayed its secret. Moreover, it is Gilles himself who exposes it, incurring the wrath of God by carrying arms into the Church and threatening a clergyman in a manner that still stupefies us: "I will kill you on the spot!" (OC 10: 287/TG 21) He is the same one who will not hesitate to carry to his companion, Prelati, "hand, heart, and eye perhaps, of a child. He was so eager to see the devil!" (TG 59) But then why does Bataille attribute "human" sentiments to him: "Gilles could not dissemble what was unforgivable and repugnant in the sacrifice of an innocent, of a miserable child to the 'unclean spirit'" (OC 10: 354/TG 59; tm). How did he not see the logic at the heart of the sacrifice, the horror at the heart of this nauseating sacred heart? The more the crime is unforgivable (the child is the one closest to the sacred, and the Christ promises his kingdom to the children first), the more it must be forgiven, in the name even of the very worst that has already taken place, the crucifixion. To sacrifice filth, a criminal or conman, is no sacrifice at all! Only innocence can respond to the enormity of sacrifice, which it designates according to a schema whose sinister consequences we endure daily: all the victims of terror or counterterror are "innocents" by definition, as if only the innocent can be victims.

Gilles interests Bataille for reasons diametrically opposed to those of Huysmans, for whom the "sacred monster" attested to the sublime (inaccessible to the decadent bourgeoisie), to a perhaps Christian nonsense, but at least living and sovereign . . . thus, "noble." Educated, reading Nietzsche, Bataille does not commit the error of aestheticizing archaic origins in order to remedy present decadence. Indeed, it is difficult to sublimate a figure as brutal and violent as Gilles. And to stagger under his fascination is at bottom to commit the same crime and to evidence the same stupidity at the base of every myth of "primitive strength" (the Aryan myth is not far from the *berserker*). Gilles concentrates all the recalcitrant contradictions of archaism: expenditure without reckoning but capable of unchained destruction and unlimited terror, life and death linked once more in their very coming apart. Never to be truly known, it is still here, in this difference, that indifference is made sovereign and sovereignty indifferent: to laugh at nothing, to laugh as I say, "lovely as the tail of a rat," so as to expire.

"And certainly I know that the intimacy of M., who is dead, was like the tail of a rat, *lovely as the tail of a rat!* I knew already that the intimacy of things is death" (OC 3: 136/I 54).

Notes

1. Friedrich Nietzsche, *Thus Spoke Zarathustra*, trans. Walter Kaufmann (New York: Penguin, 1975), 40.

2. See Mallarmé, "*Quant au Livre*" *Œuvres complètes*, vol. 2, ed. Bertrand Marchal (Paris: Gallimard, 2003), 214–28. Partial English translation in Stéphane

Mallarmé, *Selected Poetry and Prose*, ed. Mary Ann Caws, trans. various (New York: New Directions, 1982), 77–84.

3. "*Cause*" and "*chose*" both come from the Latin "*causa*." But "*la chose même*" translates the German "*die Sache selbst*."

4. Jean-Luc Nancy, *The Sense of the World*, trans. Jeffrey S. Librett (Minneapolis: University of Minnesota Press, 1997), 9.

5. Job 14:4–5, quoted by Augustine, *Confessions* I, 7. Saint Augustine, *Confessions*, trans. Henry Chadwick (Oxford: Oxford University Press, 1998), 9.

6. See Antigone's chorus (lines 332–75) giving the Greek "definition" of man as "deinotaton," which Heidegger translates, in *Introduction to Metaphysics*, as the most *Unheimliche*. Martin Heidegger, *Introduction to Metaphysics*, trans. Gregory Fried and Richard Polt (New Haven: Yale University Press, 2000), 156.

7. Arthur Rimbaud, *Œuvres complètes*, ed. Antoine Adam (Paris: Gallimard, 1972), 110. *A Season in Hell and the Drunken Boat*, ed. and trans. Louise Varèse (New York: New Directions, 1961), 65. One can also invert the formula and say that weakness is the morality of the mind, so much the morality is made by and for the weak. But Christianity has made this weakness ("fortunate weakness of the spirit" and all the moralizing of the "Sermon on the Mount") its inexhaustible strength: who does not defend the weak? Would it not be the privilege of the strong to protect the weakest? Like the hateful feudal lords who prevail on three quarters of the earth?

8. See Joris-Karl Huysmans, *Là-bas* (Paris: Flammarion, 1993).

9. Translator's Note: Gilles replies to Pierre de L'Hôpital's query as to how he conceived his crimes without anyone's assistance: "Truly, there was no other cause, no other end nor intention, if not what I've told you: I've told you greater things than this and enough to kill ten thousand men" (OC 10: 289/TG 22).

10. Translator's Note: This is the Latin translation of Psalm 130, as well as the title of a poem by Baudelaire.

CHAPTER TEN

Bataille: Discerning Edges in the Art of Lascaux

Edward S. Casey

> The first sketch on the walls of caves founded one tradition only because it was gleaned from another—the tradition of perception.
>
> —Maurice Merleau-Ponty, "Indirect Language and the Voices of Silence"

Few would dispute that the art of Altamira and Lascaux is largely an art of the line: it is linear art in some significant sense. But what kind of art is *this*? Somehow the art of these ancient caves seems more than mere sketching yet less than full-fledged painting; but it is also not located exactly midway between these extremes. Georges Bataille's discussion of such art raises basic questions: What kind of art is it? Primitive? Presciently premodern? Is it art at all, given that it seems to have been employed primarily for ritual purposes? What does it communicate? What are its communitarian dimensions, and how are these pertinent to the contemporary world?

Let us agree that these paleolithic works, whatever else they may be, are works of the edge: *edge works*. They exist at the southern edges of European civilization as its concealed underedges: at once underground and under the tumultuous world to emerge on the surface many centuries later. They are spatial edglings of times to come. The caves themselves involve an intricate interplay of edges; however ancient their origins, they still take edges to new places—places novel to us today as we reflect on them anew. By attending to them more closely, we may be able to understand something new about edges—and something different about art—as well as something about Bataille's fascination with these mysterious works as forms of communication and as intimating an alternative conception of community.

I

Edges come in many forms—many formats. They occur as falling-off places; as rims and peripheries; as limits; as borders and boundaries; as precipices; as created and given; as geometrically determinate (i.e., as convex dihedral angles); and as radically indeterminate. But three senses of edge are actively at stake in works such as those we encounter in the caves of Lascaux (to which I shall here confine attention): edge of the surface; edge of the material medium; and edge of line as such. Let me comment briefly on each of these:

1. *Edge of the surface*—the works on which Bataille comments so insightfully cling to the surface of chambers in limestone caves of very early geological formation. The works constitute the outer edges of the inner linings of such caves. These are not sharp edges. On the contrary: they are spread out on the stony surfaces, disparately and in dispersed fashion. The paleo-artist or thaumaturge took express advantage of the contours and patterns inherent in such surfaces, following their lead by fitting into their naturally given fissures and fracture lines—while also infusing independent pictorial forms into them. The result is a dense dialectic of the given and the contrived that observes the logic of the "rift-design," their *Riss* in Heidegger's term. As rifts, the edges of the surfaces are already established by entirely natural means—long before the artist or ceremonialist entered the scene. As designs, however, they are the devising of this tribally sanctioned person—what he felt he had to add to the scene to make it at once more striking and more lasting. The edges that result are a complex commixture of the given and the meant, their subtle *Deckung* (in Husserl's term for the convergence of the intended and the provided). The scene is double-edged.

2. *Edge of the material medium*. The first sense of edge is that of the outer surface of the cave wall, which offers itself *from below* as it were; on the basis of this offering, the rift design of the

imagery sits upon the surface as such: situates itself there, deftly guided by the artist-practitioner. But any particular image has *its own* edge: the place where the image runs out and comes to an end. This coincides with the termination of the paint or charcoal as the material medium employed by the artist: *its* edge as such, where it gives out. Heidegger might designate this as the *Umriss*, the "common outline" as this term could be translated. We can also call it the "contour" of the image, its profile—that by which it is most readily perceived and recognized. It is where the image begins and ends. If the paradox of the first kind of edge is that it belongs both to the surface and to the image that lies upon it, that of the second sort of edge is that it is where a given figure stops and starts—*both at once*. For it is indifferent whether our eye moves from the external edge into the figure for which it is the edge or the same eye moves out from the heart of the same figure toward its outer limit and its surroundings. These are simply two directionalities of vision which the spectator can assume at his or her volition (whether the original participants in cave rites had the same visual freedom will be forever moot).

3. *Edge of the line as such.* I say "the line *as such*" in order to emphasize that it is a matter of *any* line, whatever exact form a given line may take: distinct and separate, merged and continuous with a visual mass (as in a "border-line"), thick or thin, colored or black, etc. In all of these line formats (and there are still more: dotted, straight, sinuous, etc.), there is the undeniable fact that in each case *the line is itself an edge*: this is the corresponding paradox of this third avatar of edge. A given visual phenomenon of this sort is equally well characterized as "line" or "edge." In view of this dual characterization, the very phrase "edge of the line" becomes pleonastic, and we could just as well speak of "the line of the edge": that is, the line at least implicitly formed by a given edge. The fact is that by tracing out an edge we are very likely to produce a line of some significant sort.

This points, if not to a coincidence between edges and lines, at least to their extremely close alliance. I say "extremely close" rather than "exactly equivalent," as the relationship between lines and edges is certainly two-way or reciprocal yet not precisely symmetrical. That is to say: although every line is an edge, not every edge is linear. Some edges are so blunted or smooth that it is difficult to find for them an adequate linear representation (examples include cartographic symbols for the slopes of mountains and other precipitous but nonangular geological entities: such symbols are typically gridded or shaded in suggestive ways). But in the instance of the images at Lascaux we witness a strong overlap between edges and lines: the pictorial line that limns a given animal or human being not only represents the edge of that animal or human: it *is* its edge, it embodies and materializes it. It is grasped as both at once—both the edge of a recognizable figure and the line that presents that edge, the two together in a single act of perceptual recognition.

A corollary is that edges as lines are not just depictive but in effect "lines of force" in Deleuze and Guattari's term for that aspect of lines that carries with it a special vectorial directionality—an intentionality of the line, as it were, by which it seems to aim itself somewhere in particular and even at a certain implicit and nonquantifiable velocity. Deleuze and Guattari themselves add that forceful lines open up a new dimension of space by means of their energetic trajectories. Without endorsing this description as such—which would require a careful discussion of what "dimension" signifies—we can agree that lines of force are not merely delineative or depictive, that is, they are not "representational" in the sense of being pictorial icons of certain preexisting actualities. They have their own *élan*—their own vitality. This is just what so many experience in viewing the animal and human figures at Lascaux even if these are conveyed solely by photographic images. (See figure 10.1.) Modern and postmodern viewers alike find these figures not so much "lifelike" (that is, accurately representational) as being in vital movement, seemingly generated by the very lines by which they are drawn or painted—which is to say, by their bare edges.

II

In "The Birth of Eros," the first part of his last book *The Tears of Eros*, Georges Bataille proposes a distinctively different sense of edge than any we have so far considered: that between death and eroticism. Meditating on the enigmatic scene in the pit room of Lascaux, Bataille is struck by the fact that the man with a bird's head (or a bird's head mask) has an erection as he stands before the dead or dying bison, its entrails streaming out of its stomach. (See figure 10.2.)

Whether the human figure is a shaman or not—the bird on a stick below him may be a talisman—and whatever the state of mind of this figure (in a trance, dying himself, exhausted from the kill, etc.), he does seem to be in some kind of ecstasy, to be carried away. Bataille speculates that this is a scene in which sexuality and death, normally (i.e., in post-Cartesian thought)

Figure 10.1. Frieze of Swimming Stags. Lascaux Caves, Périgord, Dordogne, France (Art Resource, NY).

Figure 10.2. Scene of the Hunt. Lascaux Caves, Périgord, Dordogne, France (Art Resource, NY).

considered antithetical, are brought together—seen as sharing a common edge. Indeed, they appear to penetrate each other's edges, much as the spear that has killed the bison resembles the man's erect penis. Reminding the reader of the signification of "*la petite mort*" as an epithet for orgasm, Bataille comments: "[T]o judge from appearances, eroticism is by all accounts linked to birth, to a reproduction that endlessly repairs the ravages of death. . . . To the contrary, it is because we are human and live in the somber perspective of death that we know this exacerbated violence of eroticism" (OC 10: 586/TE 33).[1] "This exacerbated violence of eroticism": violence, then, is what links sex and death. It is what leaps over the edge between these two states, otherwise so seemingly disparate. It is striking that within the image in the pit, there are in fact *two* weapons, one shown as still piercing the bison's body and the other lying below the human figure and almost at his feet. Taken together, these vehicles of violence frame the bison and the hunter from below—in an inner *edge of violence*, as we could consider it: or better yet, of *violence already enacted*. The arms have here done their deadly service, presumably only shortly before the moment of the scene itself. We are witnessing a pause, a time of suspension between life and death—a temporal edge that supports the spatial edge between live and dead bodies as they are juxtaposed in a scene of battle.

The edge between human and animal, too, is at stake, visibly so in the manifest identity of the images themselves. In the text of "The Birth of Eros," Bataille returns again and again to the theme of the animal/human distinction. He is not concerned with the visible differences between the two (or rather, several) species but with what activity sets humans apart from animals. His first answer is that this activity is a form of *work*: "[I]f it is true that work is our origin, if it is true that work is the key to humanity, human beings, through work, ended up distancing themselves completely from animality" (OC 10: 591/TE 42).[2] The distancing, then, is not only from animals per se, those "other" living beings with whom we share the earth, but from *our own* animality, as Bataille makes clear in this passage: "Of course, it is work that separated man from his initial animality. It is through work that the animal became human. Work was, above all else, the foundation for knowledge and reason" (OC 10: 591/TE 41).

In addition to work, human beings also play, and Bataille does not hesitate to invoke play in his efforts to hold animals and humans apart. In fact, play is even more crucial than work in establishing this apartness—especially when it is allied with the creation of art: "In the end, it is not work, but *play*, that marked the advent of art and the moment when work became in part, in genuine masterpieces, something other than a response to the concern for utility. Indeed, man is essentially an animal who works. But he also knows how to change work into play. I would emphasize this in the context of art (of the birth of art): human play, truly human play, was first of all work, work that became play" (OC 10: 594/TE 46–47).

Nevertheless, even in the most engaged work and creative play (and in their fusion in art), the separation of humans from their "initial animality" is never complete. The violence of eroticism is a symptom of a residual animal force within even the most civilized human beings. It is what continues to bridge the gap between man and beast. Moreover, art is linked to sexual passion, expressly so in paleolithic caves: "[I]n the charged atmosphere of these caves it was seduction, the profound seduction of [erotic] play that was no doubt preeminent . . . these somber caverns were actually consecrated above all else to what is, at bottom, play—play as opposed to work, play whose essence is above all to obey seduction, to respond to *passion*" (OC 10: 594–95/TE 48).[3] It is play, then, that ties eroticism to passion—especially the "voluntary play" of foreplay and the "calculation of pleasure" (OC 10: 593/TE 45) that mark the transition from stolid work to sexual activity. Such play is the bridge between eroticism and work.

In this way, then, Bataille points to various forms of edge: edges between human and animal, sexuality and death, work and play, eroticism and work. These edges acts as gaps, yet none is absolute; each is bridged or bridgeable by an intermediate term, whether this be violence (in the hunt, in art, in the sacred), by erotic activity considered as a form of play, or by art itself. The bridging of the gaps is not lasting, nor is it part of a larger dialectic as in Hegel; it is closer to momentary leaping or spanning since it *leaves the gap intact* and must be *continually reenacted* (albeit in different times and in different cultures).

The bridging is more of a "stop-gap" measure than a permanent solution or ideal type. It is subject to dissolution; what works/plays effectively in crossing over the edges of a gap may not be effective at all the next time around. The gap presents itself in ways that must be respected for their own sake. The implicit embrace of the gap can sustain many bridges set over it. The gap precedes history; indeed, it precedes prehistory. It is for this reason that the figures at Lascaux were effective in a certain way (magical? religious? practical?) for the prehistoric people who created and admired them; if they do not work in the same way for us, this is only because the way we span the gap has changed: Bataille himself proposes a specifically erotic interpretation of these figures and others from the same period. But the gap from which the figures stem is not subject to historical vicissitude; it arises from "the free-play of space-time" that precedes all determinate interpretations in its radical status as an ultimate "in-between."[4]

The cautionary remarks I have just made remind us that in the end we are dealing as much with an enigma as with a merely "problematic situation" (in John Dewey's revealing term). Bataille agrees. He links the "inaccessible depths"[5] of the paleolithic caves, including the pit room that is so difficult to find and enter, with the permanently veiled state of the artwork they contain. In these caves, we have to do with the lost, the hidden, the unknown, the mysterious, but also with the revealed, with that which *shows itself* from within the veils, however briefly and ambiguously: "Thus, in this barely accessible crevice [i.e., of the pit] stands revealed—but obscurely—a drama forgotten for so many millennia: it re-emerges but does not leave behind its obscurity. It is revealed, but nevertheless it is veiled. *From the very moment it is revealed, it is veiled*" (OC 10: 597/TE 52; em).[6] This is to follow the ample logic of the edge, all edges, above all those that serve as gaps between things or terms, at once obscure and manifest: they shield their content from the plain light of day, and yet they also show it. Otherwise put: edges occlude, but they also envelope.[7] This duplicity derives from the basic dihedrality of their structure: the fact that at least two lines stream back from every edge, thereby allowing for concealment to occur between the lines or around them. Such is the material-geometric condition for their being simultaneously apparent and dis-apparent. We are here dealing with the coeval character of revealing/veiling.

This means in turn that this doubleness is redoubled in the case of the caves of Lascaux—or any comparable circumstance. A cave is a first edge: it is a crevice in the earth; and the artwork on its walls constitutes a second set of edges, just as much veiling-cum-revealing as are the depths of the cave itself, only now at the level of the image and its specific content, edge within edge, veil within veil—just as the animal is within the human, play is in work, passion is in art.

III

And folds within folds! Folds are still another sort of edge, one that eschews sharp angularity in favor of more mellow shapes: curvaceous, rounded, umbelliform, often following the lead of that around which it is wrapped. Folds are less in our face than are edges; in contrast with the brash and forward character of many of the latter, they are experienced as receding, as moving back and down. Folds are "pleats of matter" in Deleuze's phrase, "invaginations" in the flesh of the world (Merleau-Ponty). Whatever their exact topological properties—and they are complex, as one learns upon trying to draw them—folds are, at their most basic level, folds in the earth or folds in human flesh (the third major kind of fold, that found in clothing, is intimately related to the latter). Let us consider the first two types of fold as they characterize the speleological situation of cave art.

First, a cave can be considered a pleat in the earth's surface, an in-folding of this surface inward and downward. A concrete sense of this is given in the well-known photograph of the first exploration of the caves at Lascaux in 1940. There the fold takes the form of a hollow—a double hole opening into the earth's interior from its surface. The humans are shown beginning to descend into the depths: presumably the two youths who came upon the cave by accident and the two adults who were assigned to investigate them. There is something both inviting and threatening about the double entrance—this unexpected incursion into the earth, where, deeper down, the scene we have examined and others were found, having been lost from view for more than twenty thousand years.

Second, the human body consists of folded flesh, and in this respect it can be regarded as an "earth-body."[8] The tie between the human body and the earth has been pursued by sculptors from time immemorial—indeed, it is buried in the very etymology of "human"—and it is especially evident in the figures discussed by Bataille in several of his later books. He is particularly struck by the Lespugue Venus, now at the Musée de l'Homme in Paris. (See figure 10.3.)

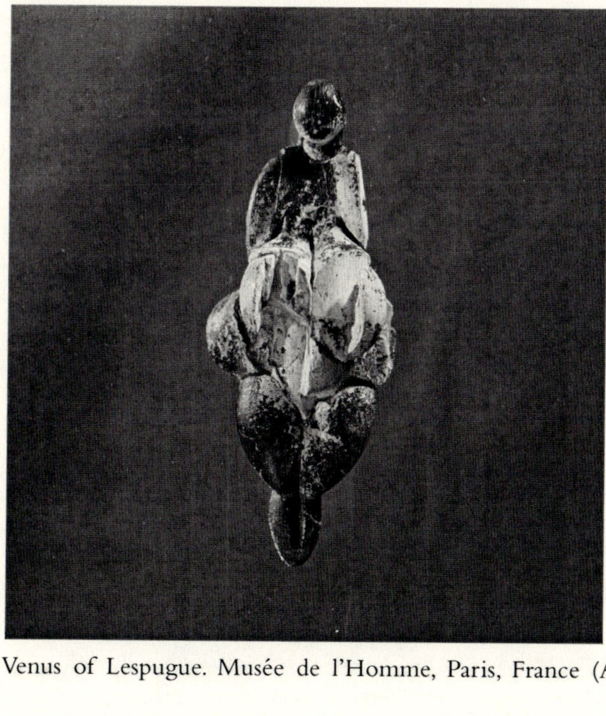

Figure 10.3. Venus of Lespugue. Musée de l'Homme, Paris, France (Art Resource, NY).

In an essay of 1958 on this celebrated statue, Bataille found in it a "paradoxical beauty"[9] because it combines awkward deformity and apparent obesity with a highly suggestive eroticism. This latter is linked directly to the folds of flesh it possesses. Remarking on figures of this same type that have been unearthed in Europe from the Upper Aurignacian period of the Paleolithic, Bataille writes: "There is a blossoming of the genitalia manifested by the enlargement of the pelvis and the breasts, a blossoming of sexuality in the abounding folds of soft flesh" (OC 9: 348/CH 112). The Lespugue Venus has notably flattened breasts—in contrast with, say, the Willendorf Venus[10]—but its buttocks and genitalia are immense, intimating both arousal and fertility. On Bataille's reading, the front view is of open genitalia that have become engorged with sexual excitement.

An even more direct representation of sexuality is found in this image in bas-relief from Laussel. (See figure 10.4.)

Bataille interprets this object as a man and a woman (identified by her breasts in the upper part) who are having intercourse, each being flat on their backs but with the man entering the woman from below. However this may be, what are undeniable are the remarkable enfoldments of this image: it presents intertwined folds of human flesh, the interfolding of

Figure 10.4. Laussel bas-relief: Deux personnages têtes bêche. Musée d'Aquitaine (Mairie Bordeaux, photo).

human beings in close proximity to each other. It gives us "fold over fold, one upon the other"[11] in a formula of Deleuze's that is meant to describe the Baroque obsession with folds but that prochronistically describes the bas-relief of Laussel.

Confronted with the guileless spontaneity of an image such as this, we are tempted to believe that stone taken from the earth has *folded itself* in such a way as to embody the equivalent of human flesh—as if the earth's rocky furrows had given birth to such flesh—highly charged, ecstatically expressive flesh. The world's body generates a human body, and it does so entirely by means of edges that form folds. For folds here furnish the integument, the interface, between two otherwise antithetical substances, stone and flesh, just as folds in the earth create caves in which human beings are inspired to represent the flesh of humans and animals in a relationship that is at once erotic and lethal. In both cases, the link between the flesh of the world and human flesh is intense; they are deeply implicated in each other.

Other stones in other places also suggest the human body, as for instance in these photographs from Sand Beach in Stonington, Maine. (See figures 10.5 and 10.6).

From the distance of photograph 10.6, we can make out a recumbent figure with more or less coherent body parts, including phantom fingers of

Figure 10.5. Photograph of Sand Beach, August 2006 (Edward S. Casey, photo).

Figure 10.6. Photograph of Sand Beach, August 2004 (Edward S. Casey, photo).

a stony arm. Closer up, the same set of stones is no less fleshlike. Here we are brought close to a gigantic rocky hand in the midst of folds of stone that could not be more fleshlike were this to be taken of a living human being. Is this a matter of pure coincidence, a product of sheer fantasy? Let us just say that folds have the uncanny capacity to bring the most diverse natural substances together in one convincing display—a manifestation that can be interpreted with equal ease as human or nonhuman. Such is their expressive force, their inherent lithic power.

These reflections suggest that between body and earth there is a deep affinity, an alliance that amounts to a very special, and a very deep, form of community. I refer to a body-to-body confederation between earth-body and human-body, a collusion that is as ancient as the caves at Lascaux. One set of folds, that belonging to human flesh, is affine with another, that belonging to the world, to "the flesh of the world" (in Merleau-Ponty's phrase). This is a communitarian relation that precedes any known form of political alliance, yet that makes the latter possible in the first place—the very first place. It is a matter of a primeval natural contract between human bodies and the body of the earth on which they live and move. Thanks to this contract, human beings—and other animals, along with plants—are no strangers on earth.

IV

What are the folds of stones, whether those of cave walls or a rugged seashore, attempting to communicate? Do they have something to say to us? What would this be? Is it a message—as most theories of communication presume—or does it take another much less determinate yet no less significant form?

In *Lascaux ou la naissance de l'art* (1955), Bataille gives his most complete account of the caves on which we have found him commenting in other texts. Here he proposes that the paintings they contain are to be understood as acts of communication. But what does this mean?

On the very first full page of the text, Bataille suddenly announces: " 'Lascaux Man' " *created, and created out of nothing, this world of art in which communication between individual minds begins.* And thus Lascaux Man communicates with the distant posterity today's mankind represents for him" (OC 9: 12/L 11). This statement is more complicated than it may seem at first glance. For one thing, it states that the protoartists did not themselves stem from an earlier tradition of cave painting; instead, they created the Lascauvian images from whole cloth—"*de rien* [from nothing]," and not just these images but the very idea of what counts as an artwork. From this idea they produced works that communicated with a "distant posterity" that is in effect "present humanity." These protoartists created the very fact of humanity itself. Bataille finds a "close connection between the initial coming into being of the work of art and the emergence of humankind" (OC 9: 9/L 7). For the appearance of these artworks meant that animality was transformed in one stroke, so to speak—in a "miraculous dawning (*éclosion*) of human being" (OC 9: 9/L 7; tm). This occurred in a moment when "at one point night gave birth to day and the daylight we find at Lascaux illumines the morning of our human species" (OC 9: 12/L 11; tm).

These are extraordinary claims to make. They are based, in part, on Bataille's conviction (said to be held by the leading artist of his day) that "nothing finer has been done since them" (OC 9: 9/L 7).[12] Since these paintings are fully accomplished—not just legible but supremely skillful and sophisticated as well as highly suggestive—they can be taken at face value. We need not look for their predecessors. Indeed, as far as we know, there are no predecessors. The "miracle" of Lascaux (OC 9: 9/L 7) is that its art arose with apparent autonomy—that is, "from nothing." Bataille does not deny that predecessor works may someday be found, but he is speaking from the moment of *his* "present humanity," that is, in 1955, fifteen years after the discovery of the cave itself. By then, caves at Altamira had long been discovered, but Bataille dismisses them as filled with less impressive images that are, in any case, imperfectly preserved in contrast with those at Lascaux. The intensive focus on Lascaux allows Bataille to make a very strong case for his major thesis—that the birth of art (*la naissance de l'art*: the subtitle of the book as a whole) is simultaneous with the birth of humanity.[13] Otherwise put: if art emerges, humanity must also be there. The minor premise of this syllogism is that art is symptomatic of humanity—art being humanity's most distinctive, even if not its exclusive, expression.

I shall not contend with this most basic claim. It is not only highly controversial; it is essentially unfalsifiable. Too many ideas are presupposed in it for us to be confident of its truth without further questioning: for example, that humanity can arise instantaneously rather than having to evolve gradually; that art is the emblematic sign of humanity (what of language? or human community?); that no apprenticeship preceded the achievements of Lascaux; and most important, that art might not be autonomous but autochthonous: "born from the earth," as I have suggested in the last section. Instead, in keeping with the aims of this volume, I shall concentrate on the issue of communication in the case of the images from Lascaux: first, on what is communicated by them; then, on how it is communicated.

At one point Bataille implies that what is communicated is the "inner life," as in this statement: "[B]efore Lascaux, we never attain the reflection of the inner life (*cette vie intérieure*), of which art—and art alone—assumes the communication, and of which it is, in its vibrancy, if not the imperishable expression (these paintings and the reproductions we make of them will not have an unending duration) at least the durable survival" (OC 9: 12–13/L 12). This claim is not convincing, and for the major reason that the inner life—by which we must understand the life of thought and emotions on the part of individuals, that is, "the solitary life of the soul" as Husserl calls it—could not, by itself alone, effect the miracle he sees in Lascaux. The domain it inhabits is too self-enclosed to bring about the "fundamental revolution" that the paintings at Lascaux represent.[14] Indeed, it is so confined that others have no access to it except through a perceptible communicative vehicle that converts it from the privacy of solitary experience to forms accessible to others—e.g., gestures, words, and other semiotic activities: in short, to something properly *expressive* of the thought in question.[15] It is revealing that we often call such a semiotic vehicle "a communication." It is required if interior experiences are to become accessible to others (and sometimes to ourselves, as when we don't fully understand what we feel until we put it into words). We need this vehicle to communicate not only inner thoughts but also intense emotions felt within our subjectivity. Thus it does not help greatly to say that "these paintings before us are miraculous, [for] they communicate a strong and intimate emotion" (OC 9: 14/L 13). Perhaps, but if so they still require the materialization of paint, wall surface, and a room for display—otherwise, we would never know what their paleolithic creators were feeling or thinking.

Not that we know this unambiguously; but with visible manifestations such as are found at Lascaux we have something to start with, specific images we can interpret and discuss. I take Bataille to be referring to this public manifestation as well as its essential ambiguity when he points to "this deep but enigmatic communication that is a detached artwork" (OC 9: 14/L 13; tm).

If what is communicated is not only and by itself a privately held thought or emotion, what can it be? Could it be the effort or "work" of the artist who created these extraordinary images? Sometimes Bataille speaks this way, as in his discussion of these "times when man, with a perfect slowness, disengaged himself from animality through work, attained consciousness by degree, made works of art, and, from that moment at least, came to resemble us in every way" (OC 12: 515/CH 176). Here we are taking recourse to something that can be considered the very converse of the inner life—that is, to something wholly external, a matter of bodily labor that is public in status. If the move to the inner life was a matter of moving into the inaccessible reaches of the subject (hence requiring a semiotic vehicle), the reference to work takes us too far outside this same subject—to his or her immersion in the life-world of labor, that is, the domain of the instrumental, the environmental, the world of work. From the extremity of the private sphere we have only fallen into the embrace of another extreme, that of the public realm.

But if what is communicated is neither a subjectively held emotion or thought nor a matter of objective work, we are left in perplexity. What, then, *is* communicated? For Bataille the answer can only be: the idea of humanity, which is neither subjective nor objective but transtemporal, something that happens across or over time—something that is not subject to time's depradations. However, this is to overlook the deeply spatial origins of paleolithic art: its enfolding in the folds of the earth.

How is the idea of humanity communicated—that is, in what form? One obvious answer is: as a *message*. If the art of Lascaux is meaningful as bearing the idea of humanity, perhaps this meaning is embedded in a message, that is, in a statement or the equivalent of a statement. A message has determinate content, determinate enough to be expressed in words even if it is not itself in verbal language. Its meaning, in other words, is of the order of *Bedeutung*, a kind of meaning that is intrinsically allied with language—that cannot be understood without recourse to words. Bataille's own commentaries on the art at Lascaux can be taken as a case in point: the fact that Bataille, one of the leading intellectuals of his generation, could find so much to say about these works, both in speech and writing, might seem to signify that they yield to a semantic analysis that requires language for its explicitation: in short, that they have a message (e.g., the idea of humanity) that can be spelled out in so many words.

Yet Bataille himself would be the first to question this assumption. The communicative power of these images, a power on which he insists, does not consist in the sort of expressivity that finds its fit form, much less its necessary nisus, in verbal language. He does not claim that a message that would betray the secret intentions of its creator is here at stake. Instead, he proposes that the communication is of something considerably more general: the idea of humanity or (as a variation thereon) the transition from animality to humanity: that is, "the effacement of man before the animal, at the very moment when the animal within him became human" (OC 12: 262/CH 60).[16] In other words, Bataille maintains that though a certain general signification is immanent in the images at Lascaux, this does not occur at a level that would amount to a message that could be translated into a definite verbal formula. Hence his many reformulations of this general signification, indicating that it is polyvalent in character. It is certainly not a message with a univocal meaning that, once found, could be made explicit and repeated indefinitely in exactly the same verbal format. If a message is in play in this communication, it is not just contingently but essentially ambiguous. Since the core sense of the idea of humanity will never be found, any search for it will be inherently futile.

Yet to say that this sense is equivocal is not to say that it is meaningless. On the contrary, it is quite meaningful—but in a sense of meaning that refuses reduction to any single noematic nucleus or determinable X.[17] This sense is sense itself: *Sinn* in Frege's term for endemic signification, only now as enriched with other layers (as is set forth in Husserl's *Ideas*, Book One), or as given peculiar powers (as on Levinas' reading of *sens* in his *Otherwise than Being*).[18] These powers allow the bare sense of a phenomenon to extend into new reaches of signification that have ever-augmenting semantic resonances. This is just what happens with the images at Lascaux: their intrinsic sense radiates outward in continual emanation from the day of their first discovery—that is, through perceiving and remembering them, ruminating about them, and re-expressing them (as occurs precisely with Bataille's writings on these images). We have to do here with what Gadamer calls *Seinszuwach*—modulated into what we could call *Sinnszuwach*: "the augmentation of sense." This augmentation is radially ramifying, ever increasing, ever reaching out beyond the last level attained. In this way there is brought forth a signification that is purely expressive and sheerly communicative, both at once, the two together. Any effort to hold them apart must founder.[19]

V

If we press further and ask ourselves exactly what *form* communication takes in art—especially in the paleolithic art under discussion here—we soon encounter a factor that brings us back to our starting point: the *edge*. It is

Bataille himself who suggests this move. Although he sometimes refers to the cave works at Lascaux as "paintings" and "images," in a more analytical spirit he describes them thus: the cave artists were "indifferent to the cave wall after a drawing [had been made] . . . let's imagine before the hunt, on which life and death will depend, this ritual: an attentively executed drawing, extraordinarily true to life, though seen in the flickering light of the lamps, [is] completed in a short time [and brings forth] the drawing that provokes the apparition of the bison" (OC 9: 327–328/CH 50–51). Remarkable here is the use of the term "drawing" to refer both to the ritual of its execution and to its deposition on cave walls. A moment's reflection shows that a drawing is a congeries of lines—thus a concatenation of edges. For lines and edges exist in intimate proximity with each other: lines, as I suggested earlier, *are* edges—to see a line is to see an edge—and they also create edges, as in the very action of drawing a line. By assimilating the images at Lascaux to drawings, Bataille is in effect claiming that these artworks are edge-works.

However ancient in origin, these works configurate and intrigue our perception in the present. "The traces of their distant humanity that these men left," writes Bataille, "reach us after tens of thousands of years" (OC 12: 262/CH 60). This is to say, they create a special visual community of people who will likely never know each other in person. Anyone looking at these murals, including their reproductions in a photographic format, belongs to this same open community. Such a community, in its character of descent in time, contrasts with the *horizontal community* that existed between the hunter depicted in the pit scene and the bison, who belonged to a simultaneous present world in which hunter and prey were once co-present (both in an actual hunt and in the act of depicting it). In contrast, those who are linked over millennia form part of a *vertical community* that comprises all who witness the depicted confrontation over the course of time, however discontinuous or distended the temporal interval may be. Such a community is an instance of *communitas* in Victor Turner's sense of the term—a gathering of people who come together in ritual events. To enter a genuine *communitas*, one must pass over a threshold, a *limen*, of some determinate sort, and by means of a certain ritual. Just as the original paintings at Lascaux involved a ritual of preparation for a forthcoming hunt—such is Bataille's own hypothesis[20]—so we late onlookers must also undergo a liminal experience of our own, crossing a threshold in the concrete form of entering the caves ourselves or else (if we are limited to looking at photographs of the images) imagining ourselves doing so. Real or imagined, this threshold is a boundary—itself a distinctive kind of edge.[21]

Rendering the vertical community of artist and viewer possible, literally supporting it, is the artwork itself. *Through* it, the link between two (or more) human beings arises—the edges of their respective lives intersect.

Across it the *communitas* of artist and spectator is formed. Serving as a *truchement* ("go-between"), the artwork is not just a neutral third term or a mere mediator; it is distinctive on its own terms and has a force and identity of its own, however schematic it may be in appearance or unknown it is in origin. Physically, it has to be robust enough to remain intact on cave walls over entire epochs; psychically, it has to be an image striking enough to catch the attention of those who are willing to let it sediment itself into their memories and flourish in their fantasy life after it has been perceived. When this latter process happens, we can say with Merleau-Ponty that artworks of this kind have, from the moment of their conception, "almost all their life still before them."[22]

They still have such a future insofar as there are many still unborn who may well become its admirers. Even if the physical work were to be destroyed, its descendents will continue to proliferate—in photography and commentary, in memory and in imagination. Unlike scientific communities, these emerging vertical communities will not converge on a single settled signification—as on Peirce's model of the evolution of scientific truth—but will, instead, diverge in opinion and judgment even as the immanent sense of the original work remains in force. Once more, we have to do with an augmentation of sense.

These divergent but concordant communities constitute a "we" that is drawn together around a shared item of aesthetic admiration: the artwork as the communitarian bond. The cynosure it forms embodies the ramifying sense that is experienced diversely on each different occasion yet stays coherently the same throughout the vagaries of the history of its reception. We—you and me, Georges Bataille and his many readers, but also the aboriginal artist and those who discovered Laxcaux and saw the frescoes for the first time and the numberless viewers of their photographs who see them for the nth time—cross the threshold of sharing the sense of something experienced in common: the sense arising from the traces themselves: that is, from schematized images, amulets of admiration. It does not matter that this same sense was to begin with focused on the hunt-to-come, acting as propitiation and auspicious anticipation, and later became an aesthetic object in Dufrenne's sense of this term: the artwork as perceived (and amplified in imagination and memory) in the various viewings on which it is perforce dependent.[23] Despite these major vicissitudes, it exhibits *the same expansive sense throughout*, whether this is the idea of humanity or some other still more viable candidate. For this very reason, it places all those in the vertical *communitas* that streams forth from it into the *the same world*—the world of the work, the world that makes those who are affiliated with it members of an ongoing community. We are there together, there at the origin of the work, in its incipience, inspired and sanctioned by it—even if we ourselves are located at a much later historical moment. The prehistory of the work is carried forward in the posthistory of its deferred perception; its creation and reception are epicenters of one and the same ramiform communitarian experience.

In this community, all are active members, creating thereby a distinctive communalism of participation. The belated perceiver partakes of the aboriginal artwork, albeit at a different historical moment and in a different visual modalization and doubtless to a different practical effect than for those who first viewed it. Communication is rife in this silent polylogue—a communication across epochs of time but also by means of the edges of space, the two intertwining intensely in a nexus of attention and creation, projection and remembrance, feeling and image—all of this held intensely together by the various lines and folds we have found to be at work in the work, bringing forth the drawing of its images and the filling out of its schemata, and constituting at once the aesthetic object and the world of the work of art.

※ ※ ※

And the import for edges? The augmentation of sense that serves as the basis for community and communication alike intimates a new sense of edge: edge as ever–opening, extending itself beyond its previously delimited perimeter—opening into earth as into world. Just as we earlier witnessed the spontaneous collaboration between body and earth—their coeval status—so we have now come to recognize the affinity between sense and world. Where the bond of the previous dyad is the nexus of in-folding that exists between the body of the artist and spectator and the earth common to both, so the union of sense and world is found in the opening outward of a radiating and reverberational semiosis. The edges shared by sense and world are out-folded, reaching beyond the limits of matter, location, and origin in the continual emergence of new vertical communities of appreciation and understanding. Every such edge is a reaching-out and a self-surpassing. To the three forms of edge discerned at the beginning of this essay—edges of surface, of medium, and of line—we can now add a final and fourth form: that of the expansive edge of sense itself.[24]

Notes

1. The reference to *la petite mort* is at OC 10: 576/TE 20: "How can I fully *live* the 'little death' if not as a foretaste of the final death?" Cf. also OC 10: 592/TE 45: "The 'little death' has little to do with death, with the cold horror of death. But is the paradox [not] altered when eroticism is in play?"

2. See also the discussion of tools at OC 10: 591/TE 41: "[T]he making of tools and weapons was the point of departure for that early faculty of reason which humanized the animal we once were. Man, manipulating matter, figured out how to adapt it to whatever end he assigned to it."

3. Bataille explicitly links passion and eroticism in the next sentences and refers to "a female figure who is quite obviously expressing desire" (OC 10: 595/TE 48).

4. These phrases come from Martin Heidegger, *Mindfulness*, trans. Parvis Emad and Thomas Kalary (New York: Continuum, 2006), 85. Heidegger continues: space-time is "the unassailable, intimately swaying fullness of the '*in-between*' that, while holding unto the ab-grund, grounds every nearness and remoteness, every refusal and gifting, every concealing and clearing, and is neither in man's discretion as power of representing, nor in the discretion of beings as the form of appearances" (85; em).

5. "What can one say about this striking evocation [of the image of the hunter and bison], buried for thousands of years in these lost, and, so to speak, inaccessible depths?" (OC 10: 587/TE 35).

6. On the pit as a "crevice," that is, another kind of edge, see OC 10: 596–97/TE 51.

7. As Merleau-Ponty put it: "the enigma [of depth perception] consists in the fact that I see things, each one in its place, precisely because they eclipse one another, and that they are rivals before my sight precisely because each one is in its own place. Their exteriority is known in their envelopment and their mutual dependence in their autonomy," "Eye and Mind," trans. Carleton. Dallery in Maurice Merleau-Ponty, *The Primacy of Perception*, ed. J. Edie (Evanston: Northwestern University Press, 1964), 180.

8. I borrow this term from Glen A. Mazis in his book, *Earthbodies: Rediscovering Our Planetary Senses* (Albany: State University of New York Press, 2002).

9. "The Lespugue Venus" (OC 9: 344–52/CH 105–19), 347/111. Bataille underlines "beauty."

10. See the reproductions of this famous statue on TE 30.

11. Gilles Deleuze, *The Fold*, trans. Tom Conley (Minneapolis: University of Minnesota Press, 1992), 3. The more complete statement is: "[T]he Baroque trait twists and turns its folds, pushing them to infinity, fold over fold, one upon the other. The Baroque fold unfurls all the way to infinity." The prehistoric, though equally preoccupied with folds, has no interest in pursuing them to infinity, being content to keep them within the confines of human figures. "Pleats of matter," a phrase I used earlier, is the title of chapter one of Deleuze's perceptive study, whose allusion to labyrinths as constructed from folds is especially pertinent to Bataille's analysis of the caves at Lascaux: "A labyrinth is said, etymologically, to be multiple because it contains many folds. The multiple is not only what has many parts but also what is folded in many ways" (3).

12. This artist is Picasso.

13. Bataille says this in effect in this hypothetical clause: "If we envision the birth of art (better yet, the birth of man himself)." ("The Passage from Animal to Man and the Birth of Art," OC 12: 260/CH 57; Bataille italicizes "birth").

14. On this notion, see Bataille's essay "Unlivable Earth?" (OC 12: 514–17/CH 175–78), 515/176.

15. See Husserl's analysis of communication in his discussion of the "solitary life of the soul" in *Logical Investigations*, 2 vols. ed. Dermot Moran, trans. J. N. Findlay (London: Routledge, 2001), vol. 1, Investigation 1, section 8–15.

16. We shall look at another variation of this claim below in the next section of this chapter. I take these avatars of the basic signification at stake in the transition from the animal to the human—a signification to which Bataille returns many times in his writings of the decade 1951–61.

17. These latter terms are those of Edmund Husserl in *Ideas Pertaining to a Pure Phenomenology and to a Phenomenological Philosophy: First Book,* trans. F. Kersten (Dordrecht: Kluwer, 1983), part 3, ch. 3.

18. See Husserl, *Ideas.*; Emanuel Levinas, *Otherwise Than Being or beyond Essence*, trans. Alphonso Lingis (Pittsburgh: Duquesne University Press, 1998), 162–65. I thank Megan Craig for this reference.

19. See my own earlier effort to separate communication from expression: "Expression and Communication in Art," *The Journal of Aesthetics and Art Criticism* 30: 2 (Winter, 1971): 197–207.

20. "Let's imagine before the hunt, on which life and death will depend, the ritual: an attentively executed drawing, extraordinarily true to life, [is being created]" (OC 9: 328/CH 51). See also Bataille's remarks on "festival" in "Unlivable Earth" (OC 12: 514/CH 175).

21. See my unpublished essay, "On Borders vs. Boundaries Considered as Edges."

22. "Eye and Mind," 190.

23. On the aesthetic object, see Mikel Dufrenne, *Phenomenology of Aesthetic Experience*, trans. Edward S. Casey et. al. (Evanston: Northwestern University Press, 1973), chs. 4–6 ; on the dependency of the artwork on human perception, and thus its "heteronomous existence," see Roman Ingarden, *The Literary Work of Art*, trans. George G. Grabowicz (Evanston: Northwestern University Press, 1973), part 3.

24. I would like to thank Andrew Mitchell and Jason Winfree for their careful reading of, and constructive suggestions concerning, an earlier draft of this essay.

Appendices

APPENDIX ONE

What We Have Undertaken . . .

Georges Bataille
Translated by Stuart Kendall

What we have undertaken over the past few months, we have undertaken in agreement on a point that it was impossible for us to discuss with much precision. We well knew where we started from, and we also knew that it required us to turn our backs on those who had already been more than surpassed. But we did not know where we were going or how we could find out. The only publication that has served as a sign of our activities responded, incidentally, in keeping with these conditions: it had the merit of signifying—even in an apparently brief and absurd way—the departure that we took from what seemed to have engaged us up to that point.[1] But it envisioned nothing that could offer satisfaction, however weak, to those who demanded that action have a precise goal. The only valid response that we were able to oppose to irony—a valid response, incidentally, to the extent that we kept it to ourselves—is that action as we understand it cannot have a limited goal.

Today I am no more in search of a more encouraging path than I was a few months ago. I am on the contrary haunted by the idea that the path that we are following could be more repulsive, that to advance as we have is to encounter rigorous demands. When I reflect on the occasionally frightful and often lacerating demands to which human beings have everywhere been able to respond with a kind of shattering joy, I am struck to observe how little it is possible to obtain from us. If we can only serve to testify to the exhaustion of contemporary existence, it would be better that beings such as ourselves had never lived. . . . I wish that oneday we could live with a resolution so explosive that the life of a Trappist would make us laugh. The Trappists "exist" without any doubt, Tibetan hermits "exist" . . . [2]

But this is not to want to make things easy any more than it is to admit a limit to our present attempt to specify the directions in which we find ourselves engaged.

Besides, it is less a question of establishing principles than of defining a state of fact. Amidst the current decomposition, it can only be a question, effectively, of rediscovering the conditions of affective communal life through arbitrary decisions or by being elevated by inspiration. We cannot tolerate maintaining a link to a past of any kind. Nothing can contradict the fact that each of us, in isolation, has never recognized any external guide other than science. Science is the only authority to which we will submit. This means, among other things, that we have admitted nothing above us that might drive us to blasphemy or laughter.

The objectivity of science does not cease to exist in us at the moment when we take a position against rationalism in general. And since our attitude is irrational, since it results directly from impulses that we have not jointly devised, we can refer this attitude and these impulses to a group of facts whose consequences and antecedents are known. The consciousness that follows from an understanding extended from the different possible forms of affective life is one entirely new element in an elaboration of collective, impassioned forms of life, a paradoxical element that offers precisely one exact figure, one particular direction for all of our possible activity.

In this way, mythology inserted itself into our understanding from the beginning as an arch key to a science of society, perhaps even as a game of enchanting images given as nourishment to our disquiet. Here is a condition that should seem irreconcilable with a religious attitude to which only the unconscious and naiveté would offer a course. But it suffices to oppose this pessimistic thought with a representation of everything about contemporary life that is different from life during the first years of Buddhism and Christianity. Buddhism and Christianity found themselves equal to their times; they were naturally inspired within the history of thought in their day. "The Gospel according to Saint John is a laughable testimony." It would be senseless today because communal exaltation should be recovered, but the secret is lost in the Gospel and seems to belong to the past, imagining only regressive forms as possible. The religious exigency, whatever acid it can reveal from one day to the next, does not demand that anyone *risk* mystics or prophets. It is true that Nietzsche, paralyzed by the impoverished forms of life of his day, had necessary recourse to the fiction of Zarathustra in order to express himself completely. But Nietzsche did not express himself only in the voice of Zarathustra—even though Zarathustra's burning passion is essential to his teaching—and, since then, everything in the world has been so profoundly shaken that it is possible to chew with one's own teeth, to burn in one's own bones: to escape from one's clothes in order to exist completely is a necessity that belongs to a state of things still more degraded than ours, an extinct state.

Every aspect of modern activity is spread out before our eyes, and there is nothing there that creates malaise. The traditional forms of poetry and mythology are dead. To the extent that this can speak to human will, this world has become the outskirts of a great city: at least the outskirts of great cities with their factories and their formless houses represent the only human social fabric that can be produced indefinitely. Independently from our disgust for drama, we know that one does not enter into a world as empty as this with the distant contempt of a sage but with that of a surgeon, which is to say with the most active, the most caustic in fact of contemptuous sympathies. The disintegrated human material to which we address ourselves—in order to subordinate that material to values that escape it—can only be cut down by lucid men.

I do not even imagine that such a hope could be conceived so precisely if we were not in the position to bring lucidity to its apogee. In the eyes of those who cling to what is immediately visible, there is nothing to hope for. He who sees human beings at risk around him, who, in anguish despite himself, keeps a close eye on his private conversations, if, as is natural, he has the fever of something more, there remains for him only to accept prostration. But if there is something analogous to icy contempt and scientific aggression in him, all these vague movements of bones and lips are no more than a mask to tear off, a mask that hides nothing more than inner combustion. Behind the ashes and the waste, he perceives a motion that is difficult to detect, but with all the more reason to catch his breath, all life in slow formation, revealing its incandescent marks and its ceaselessly broken structures bit by bit, more like a mortal wound, a greedy scream, than everything that the strange lacerations of poetic inspiration have permitted to us suppose across the night.

It is true that I am speaking of a vision that is not yet accessible. But I am speaking about it precisely because I understand that the inaccessible nature of *this reason that human beings exist*—this could not be designated with greater precision—is the obstacle that should be overcome *by us*, it is the fog that should be cleared so that this impious promised land can reveal itself in the light of day. But the obstacle at stake here is not among those that can only be reached and overcome after a long wait: the promised land is still inaccessible, but, that it may become so—and this should be said in categorical terms—very little is now necessary. The effort that is incumbent upon us in particular is limited, and its short limits are not our choice but result from the present state of knowledge. Methods of investigation have been elaborated that have led to a precise understanding of the affective structure of primitive societies. These societies appear to have been constructed mythically and ritually, to the extent that a human being does not exist within them like an isolated brick. The images and the rites of primitive and savage communities, heavily charged with affective value, represent for us the fabric of these communities. And, to the extent that we move to a philosophical interpretation of these facts, we will admit that these myths and rites compose the being of these communities. The methods that have lead to these capital representations have not yet discovered their essential point of application since they have never had as an object anything but forms of human existence distant from us: with a few rare exceptions, no one has wanted to make contemporary society, the society that we "live," the object of a structural analysis.

It is possible that a kind of tacit taboo strikes such a temptation (or "attempt"). However, until recently, difficulties that were not at all religious were in fact opposed to it. The existence of the social community was profoundly disintegrated, everything that could be designated by the name *structural fabric* presented itself as a holdover from the past, not as a truly living tissue, still less as a form in formation. But for the last twenty years the communal existence in which we participate has undergone transformations that count among the most rapid that our historical understanding permits us to perceive across the threads of time. The facts that we can analyze directly—because they are present—represent an unexpected richness of material for analysis, and this richness is opposed to the exceptional poverty of the first years of the twentieth century. The fabric that forms the social structure has proliferated before our eyes with a stupefying vigor, and the principles that have been established in decomposing societies have found themselves marked, in a certain case, as a waste deprived of life. This new fabric is precisely of the same nature as that of primitive societies: it is mythic and ritual; it has shaped itself vigorously around images charged with the strongest affective value; it has formed itself in the vast movements of crowds regulated by a ceremony introducing symbols that subjugate them.

Incidentally, our chance holds that Freud already introduced a facility for the specific interpretation of these facts. The analysis of the affective structure of the army and of the church, as Freud set it out in his *Group Psychology and the Analysis of the Ego*, is perhaps one of science's most surprising and most consequential revelations about the nature of life, for it is not only an introduction to the comprehension of great forms that unite their members. Having acquired knowledge of the facts about primitives, the premises of Freud's analysis open the way to a general understanding of social structures of all kinds, whether it be of a church or a religious order, an army or a militia, a secret society or a political party. And if Freud himself was not able to practice a general analysis of living forms, this is not to say that he did not leave the possibility of crossing that divide open to those who follow him. And not only the analysis of what is, is henceforth open in several senses, but it has become possible to envision experience itself, which is to say the attempt to pass from understanding into action. Facing the great formations—those that unite living beings—that have brutally closed and fixed existence in other countries, attempting a religious movement or perhaps more precisely a "church," that in response to the immediate needs of a composition of forces, will not only unite existence but will also to set it free.

Here it is necessary to cleanly and even brutally indicate how these possibilities present themselves. I began by speaking of science. Now I am speaking of experience. But it is obvious that the vocabulary here will introduce a misunderstanding if something was continued from this subordination of experience to the science that goes along with it when it does not concern human life. Experience, in the case we are imagining, dominates in so imperious a way that it would be laughable to compare such a situation to that of medicine. Medicine imagines effectively only the middle terms, the organs, the functions, that could be indispensable to life but that do not constitute the goal or end of that life. Sociology—and more precisely mythological sociology—on the contrary imagines only the *goal or end* of man, which can only be found beyond him.[3] Myths are even more than the spaces in which individual existences come together: they are the reason a human being can offer that which is most precious to him, his blood. Here and here only existence accedes to the *totality of being* and in this dizzying and weighty moment everything that is still only a function—science itself—enters a region of silence. Because even if it becomes the only means to which we can appeal to discern in the shadows exactly *what it brings us*, this means of discernment can only be confused with what is revealed. All that we should be able to affirm from the outset is first, that in the case in which we place ourselves science cannot push us to discover in its object the values that it is reduced to observing without being able to ground them rationally; and second, reciprocally, there is no preexisting affective predetermination in us that might be able to soften the cold objectivity of science within us.

And undoubtedly this final point is essential precisely at the moment wherein I should be able to insist on the necessity of moving to a choice. Two radically opposed methods of experience appear in effect possible *a priori*. Following one, we would proceed to whatever experience is possible, which is to say that one would have no other goal than to create a common existence, a "church" that could definitively be no more than a party; following the other, one would set out from some principles revealed by a transcendent authority. There is a way to avoid both of these solutions equally. There is a goal that can be determined in advance without the intervention of any revelation: this goal is that of finding or recovering *the totality of being*. I do not think it should be necessary or even useful to have any other limitation intervene, but to this alone such an ambition excludes a great number of possible experiences. Undoubtedly something of an immense freedom subsists, something that has not ceased to preside over the formation of human bonds: because particular beings are always available for more than composition. But in the given circumstances, the search for the totality depends on the ensemble of alterations to which the life of man is subjected: precisely at that moment. Totality, moreover, always demands what human beings reject under the influence of what they call "good sense," which is only a kind of aging: totality demands that life reunite itself and this is to say confound itself in an orgy with death. The object of experience ought therefore to be to pass from a certain fragmented and empty state of life liberated from the concern for death to this kind of brutal and suffocating refusal of all that is, which undoubtedly takes place in numerous agonies.

Beyond these considerations or similar ones, room should be made for freedom! Myths—or to speak in a more precise way—the mythic images that are available to us do not refuse to speak. I mentioned the Trappists a few minutes ago. It is not a question of us becoming Trappists; we have nothing to do with Christian greed. We are free beings: a limitless generosity and a Greek, which is to say happy naiveté and even peculiar movements of humor . . . the kind of puerile avidity with which we approach the tragic place where our existence offers itself, risks itself, will lack the generosity of a new Christian greed. Something the myths destroy amongst themselves, distend, and hate. That they resemble the stupid saints of fountains rather than Christ! And that they can do this, facing a universe emptied of its servile function, emptied of God; that they make human life into a festival equal to so free a game of chance!

I know that I have once again said only a part of what is necessary: I believe that I can communicate, truly communicate what I see, and at the same time, bear what I experience in the presence of what I see; a lightening, a liberation, a need to act and to agitate others, a patient and terribly joyous need will necessarily follow for those who understand me. But it is clear to me that whatever I do, I can make this need only a little less obscure for others. I would only like to add what I feel profoundly: in everything that I experience like this, I fade as far as a very short scream.

Notes

Bataille delivered this lecture to members of the secret society Acéphale during the spring of 1937. The group then included Georges Ambrosino, Jacques

Chavy, René Chenon, Henri Dubief, Pierre Dugan, Henri Dussat, Imre Kelemen, and Pierre Klossowski, many of whom had followed Bataille from Boris Souvarine's Democratic Communist Circle into the short-lived movement Counter-Attack, and now into Acéphale. Patrick and Isabelle Waldberg, Jean Rollin, Michel Koch, Taro Okamoto and others would join Acéphale over the next two years, some members joining as others left. André Masson, Laure, Michel Leiris, and Michel Carrouges were only occasional participants in the group, if they participated at all. At the very least Bataille shared his thoughts about the group with them and invited them to participate on several occasions. Masson, Klossowki, Jean Rollin, Jean Wahl, Roger Caillois, and Jules Monnerot contributed to the journal *Acéphale*, which reflected the thought of the secret society without being a direct adjunct to it. Bataille was the only consistent participant in both the journal and the group.

During these same months, Bataille, Caillois, Ambrosino, Klossowski, Monnerot, and Pierre Libra (an unknown), founded the College of Sociology, with an initial lecture in March. The lecture series would not begin in earnest until November. Also during these months, Bataille, René Allendy, Adrien Borel, Paul Schiff, and Michel Leiris, among others, founded a society for the study of collective psychology.

Bataille was, in short, active on several fronts—indeed in several *disciplines*—at the same moment. His was active in the fields of religion and myth, psychology and sociology, and he saw all of this as an extension of his previous political activism. All of these agendas commingle in this lecture, which was addressed to Acéphale alone.

The text here translated was found among Bataille's papers deposited at the Bibliothèque Nationale after his death. Published for the first time with an introduction by Francis Gandon in the *N.R.F.* 537 (1 October 1982), 163–73, it was reprinted in OC 11: 559–63. Another version of the text, with minor alternations, was found among Pierre Andler's papers and published in Marina Galletti, *L'Apprenti sorcier* (Paris: Editions de la Différence, 1999), 367–78. Our translation follows the version published in the *Oeuvres complètes*.

1. Translator's Note: The publication Bataille references here may be the journal *Acéphale*, the first two issues of which had been published by January 1937, or it may be the internal "journal" of the group, written by Bataille and circulated in February 1937 (see Galletti, *L'Apprenti sorcier*, 336–41). During these same months Bataille drafted his manifesto piece, "The Sorcerer's Apprentice," which would be published in the *N.R.F.* the following year.

2. Translator's Note: In his early twenties, Bataille pursued a religious vocation. Later, having abandoned his faith, he studied Chinese, planning a trip to Tibet.

3. Translator's Note: The term *mythological sociology* will obviously be replaced with *sacred sociology* within a few months. Sacred sociology will be the central concern of the College of Sociology.

APPENDIX TWO

Silence and Literature

Georges Bataille
Translated by Stuart Kendall

There is a bad joke in comparing Maurice Blanchot to Wells' "invisible man." First off, the author in question never wanted to reveal the nothingness that Wells' specter revealed when he unwrapped the bandages that covered him. Yet, on another level, silence is revealed in the sentences that Blanchot's novels undo or develop, if you like. Nevertheless, in this distinction I find an exact image. Blanchot's works have a single object, silence, and it is true that the author lets us hear this silence in almost the same way that Wells lets us see his invisibility (what the film drawn from this story unveiled so terribly and so perfectly).

The joke, all told, is interesting for this reason: it is difficult, through this comparison, to suggest the role that Blanchot gives to literature in his works; it is more difficult still without it. The author, it is true, explains himself on this point in his critical writings, but a tangible representation is not bad.[1] I should offer this corrective without waiting: there was something troublesome about the Wells image, a kind of unhappy aggressiveness, a terrified terror, that created—still more than a trap holding us—the stupid mishap of suffering. In Blanchot's novels, there is neither trap nor capture, and the image of a final silence beneath the words, if it is no less striking than that of nothingness visible beneath clothes, if it is troubling and if it even appears contrary to all repose, it is nevertheless neutral, being entirely incapable of intention; leaving us in the end—perhaps—with only a sense of distant friendship, distant complicity.

Friendship? Complicity? This is precisely where the paradox of Blanchot lies. I fear that to most of his readers, his name suggests a world of anguish or of the reflection that anguish encloses. I should recognize, effectively, that the author's manner of expressing himself nourishes such a feeling. In fact, a literature like this is made to disappoint in every way. It imposes itself with a mastery that literature rarely attains, but it is to be feared that once this mastery has been recognized the reader complains of not seeing it, the better to absolutely fail to see what the author wants to say. This impression is not justified. But it is inevitable.

I should on the contrary insist on the fact that Maurice Blanchot's "récits" do not share in the almost de rigueur depression of our times. Not only is *When the Time Comes* a happy book, but there is no other book that offers such a description of happiness. If such a book still invites confusion, it is because the author's mode of expression introduces into literature a kind of perfect reversibility, in a way similar to that of the movement of a horse on screen, if one suddenly reverses the film. This is what my first image attempted to indicate in a less precise way: pulling back the bandages reveals the void. For the author, nothing is comparable to silence. He is profoundly absorbed in silence, effortlessly, without misfortune: effort and misfortune only begin at the moment when he begins to speak.

How can one bring too much silent attention to the author, saying (that which, in a kind of brusque and monstrous tearing, draws from language something other than language, that which language brings to an end):

> My only strong point was my silence. Such a great silence seems incredible to me when I think about it, not a virtue, because it in no way occurred to me to talk, but precisely that the silence never said to itself: be careful, there is something here for which you owe me an explanation, the fact that neither my memory, nor my daily life, nor my work, nor my actions, nor my spoken words, nor the words which come from my fingertips ever alluded directly or indirectly to the thing which my whole person was physically engrossed in. I cannot understand this reserve, and I who am now speaking bitterly towards those silent days, those silent years, as towards an inaccessible, unreal country, closed off from everyone, and most of all from myself, yet where I have lived during a large part of my life, without exertion, without desire, by a mystery which astonishes me now.
>
> I have lost silence, and the regret I feel over that is immeasurable. I cannot describe the pain that invades a man once he has begun to speak. It is a motionless pain that is itself pledged to muteness; because of it, the unbreatheable is the element I breathe.

> I have shut myself up in a room, alone, there is no one in the house, almost no one outside, but this solitude has itself begun to speak, and I must in turn speak about this speaking solitude, not in derision, but because a greater solitude hovers above it, and above that solitude, another still greater, and each, taking the spoken word in order to smother it and silence it, instead, echoes it to infinity, and infinity becomes its echo.[2]

The problem of silence could not be posed with more precision: the problem of silence is a question of *speaking*, silence being the last thing that language can silence, and which language cannot nonetheless take as its object without a kind of crime.

First off, a crime against language, in regard to which the writer who chooses silence as an object stands as in incest before the law, is also a crime against silence itself. I do not know of a better way for a writer to enter the inextricable pathways of scandal, a better way for a writer to rise up against the weight that regulates the conduct and judgment of all men. And how can one conceive of a possibility of escape? The inevitable trickery is at the same moment the impossibility of trickery, since the demand to which we must respond is our own. Of course, each of us remains free to speak, but since one cannot enter into this kingdom where one would know what language does not reveal, that about which Maurice Blanchot has spoken in his books, through a kind of prodigious and frightening effort, wherein failure is only offered at the limits of one's forces, which is in the end tolerable only on one condition: ceaseless deliverance to the judgment that loss betrays.

To speak of the one who speaks of silence, I can only play the game in my turn with increasing difficulty. But this is not without compensation. I have retained a latitude. . . . What I say is perhaps provisional, and it is at least permissible for me to simplify. If I should speak of *When the Time Comes*, I can still say of this apparition, not being or at least not right now being linked to the desire for silence, that unrolling the bandages has revealed what silence undoubtedly and alone reveals: that it has the feeling of happiness (in distinction from the image of Wells' man, and despite the fact that it did not, on the contrary, arise from a less frightening moment). Of happiness *and* of *nothing*; of happiness exactly what no premeditation can attain, and what the premeditation of its duration would instantly change into *nothing*.

One might suspect me of dulling what rigor alone . . . Effectively, happiness seems to fade . . .

But I would like to show less vaguely that if this happiness, arisen from the extended desert of silence, followed from a story conforming to the ordinary rules of language, it would remain unknown to us. I should be able to summarize the story as it proceeds, or so it seems to me. A man comes looking for a woman, Judith, after a certain period. He says of her, "[T]here was clearly such an accumulation of events between us, excessive things, torments, incredible thoughts and also such a depth of happy forgetfulness that it was not at all hard for her not to be surprised by me."[3] But she lives with Claudia at the time; Claudia is "the same age . . . and her friend since childhood, but backs her up more like an older sister with a strong character."[4] Claudia inserts herself between Judith and the narrator. Claudia is not beaten but in some way drowned by the narrator's absence of premeditation; he finds Judith freely. Sometimes and as if by chance, the récit follows the easy course of a convincing reality, arising nevertheless from the half-sleep of reality."The fire had probably gone out. I recalled that fire with a feeling of sympathy—it had allowed itself to be lit so easily a short time before, and during a snowfall. The flakes had been followed by powder, and the powder by an attractive, radiant outdoors, something too manifest, an insistent appearance, almost an apparition—why that? Was the day trying to show itself?"[5] But between the images that follow one another, there remains a kind of void, created by the absence in the récit of any tissue tightly linking one group of events to another, essentially lacking the concerns and the intentions of the characters who are only given to us to the extent that the present instant possesses them. If these intentions are delimited in the meantime, it is as if negated, rendered in the lightness of the moment.

> Each of them had her own household duties. "I'll do this." "I'll do that." These duties were just as important as the large projects of the future, they were solemn decisions that referred to another world. "I'll go buy some wood!" "I'll go to the laundry!" "I'll speak to the concierge!" All this flew over their two cups, in the morning, like eternal vows. "The vacuum cleaner!" "The leak!" "The blocked up garbage chute!" And the conclusion, the dismal end of every venture: "Madame Moffat will get rid of all that." The doors slammed, banged. The chilly air, ferreting about, ran behind them wherever they went, busy, idle, with no other role but to wrap their comings and goings in a fringe of cloth.[6]

But nothing ever meshes with a hope for the future any less disinterested than these "deep snowy masses," this snow "becoming once again a gloomy depth," this "so somber (infinitely if uselessly white)" time. Never in these successive moments do the past and the future escape from what is uncertain, useless, and stifling about the present. Nothing however is more eventful, dazzling, or gay. But in the end that which puts thought to sleep is, in this muffled world from which an animal's cry occasionally escapes, the image of happiness that only silence would know how to suppress (and which no one would have expressed if it had not first been part of the silence that has no end).

> At that instant, there was no day, no night, no possibility, no expectation, no uneasiness, no repose, but nevertheless a man standing wrapped in the silence of this speech: there was no day and yet it is day, so that this woman sitting down there against the wall, her body half inclined, her head bent toward her knees, was no closer to me than I was near her, and the fact that she was there did not mean that she was there, nor I, but the conflagration of this speech: now it is happening, something is happening, the end is beginning.[7]
>
> Forgetfulness has not passed over things, but I must say this: that in the brightness where they glitter, in this brightness that doesn't destroy their limits, but unites the unlimited with a constant and joyful "I see you," they shine in the intimacy of a new beginning in which nothing else has a place; and as for me, through them I have the immobility and inconstancy of a reflection, an image wandering among images and drawn along with them in the monotony of a movement that appears to have no conclusion just as it had no beginning. Perhaps, when I get up, I have faith in the beginning: who would rise if he didn't know the day was beginning? But, even though I am still capable of taking many steps, which is why doors slam, windows open and, the light coming in once again, all things are also in their places, unalterable, joyful, definitely present, with a presence that is firm and even so definite and so constant that I know they are indelible, immobile in the glittering eternity of their images. But, seeing them there, where they are, slightly distanced from themselves within their presence, and transformed, by this imperceptible withdrawal, into the happy beauty of a reflection, even though I am still capable of taking many steps, I too can do no more than come and go in the tranquil immobility of my own image, bound to the floating festival of an instant that no longer passes. It may seem astonishing that I should descend so far from myself, into a place one could, I think, call the abyss, and that I should only have surrendered me to the joyful space of a festival, the eternal glitter of an image, and I would be surprised by this too, if I had not felt the burden of this indefatigable lightness, the infinite weight of a sky in which what one sees remains there, where the boundaries sprawl out and the distance shines night and day with the radiance of a beautiful surface.[8]

In such a language whose abundance is a kind of dizzying fall, mastered nevertheless, how can one not see that the meaning is to reveal what is already a nothingness, the instant alone being the dazzling burst, that which, in the world of duration (and of intentions), is only the void without which this inner state would be less intense.

Notes

This review of Maurice Blanchot's *Au moment voulu* was originally published in *Critique* 57 (February 1952): 99–104; reprinted in OC 12: 173–78.

1. Maurice Blanchot, *Faux pas* (Paris: Gallimard, 1943); *Faux Pas*, trans. Charlotte Mandell (Stanford: Stanford University Press, 2001); *Lautréamont et Sade* (Paris: Éditions de Minuit, 1949); *Lautréamont and Sade,* trans. Stuart Kendall and Michelle Kendall (Stanford: Stanford University Press, 2004); *La Part du feu* (Paris: Gallimard, 1949); *The Work of Fire,* trans. Charlotte Mandell (Stanford: Stanford University Press, 1995).
2. Maurice Blanchot, *L'Arrêt de mort* (Paris: Gallimard, 1948), 64–65. *Death Sentence*, trans. Lydia Davis (Barrytown, NY: Station Hill, 1978), 32–33.
3. Maurice Blanchot, *Au moment voulu* (Paris: Gallimard, 1951), 8. *When the Time Comes,* trans. Lydia Davis (Barrytown, NY: Station Hill, 1985), 1.
4. Ibid., 25/9.
5. Ibid., 81/34–35.
6. Ibid., 73/31.
7. Ibid., 145–46/64.
8. Ibid., 158–60/70–71.

APPENDIX THREE

The Political Lie

Georges Bataille
Translated by Stuart Kendall

In our day lies and the indignation that they provoke have assumed an important role in the political scene. Action delays the drawing of weapons as little as possible: one hopes to convince before using force and finds an advantage in distortion, sometimes silencing the truth.

No one is surprised that it should be this way. But, they tell us, the cause of freedom and justice cannot adjust to lies. Lies can be a natural weapon in the oppression of the weak, in the abuse of power. Would someone lie if they were not seeking to force us to do something? Undoubtedly it is easy to object that lies easily occasion social constraint, that one does not lie to slaves, that the history of politics is that of an advance in the art of lying. (Has Christianity not proven the inviolability of a world wherein every participant sees, naked and uncompensated, the brutality of institutions? Has it not decidedly engaged the progress of mores along the path of a necessary dissimulation?) But the debate about lies has its place in the world of intelligence, between those who make a profession of speaking and maintain their raison d'être in their use of language. The political lie can be necessary in another way: it ruins not only free speech but free discussion where the "intellectual" moves and encloses him or herself. Hence the insistence on protesting against the political realism of communist rulers.

I do not want it to be understood that I think the edifice to which I am now contributing is vain. . . . But the question of the lie is posed in a debate that exceeds legitimate preoccupations linked to the exercise of thought.

Today a conflict opposes the communist world to the capitalist world. This conflict is not in a violent phase, and until the new order it will unfold in the form of a moral debate: it is even, undoubtedly, the sharpest debate in the moral history of humanity, because in the end it poses ultimate questions without refuge (the questions are no longer posed to an abstract humanity, whose life is already assured: man must struggle for life and death). Having laboriously raised ourselves to the height of moral interrogation, we would certainly understand finding it unpleasant to encounter an individual who is oppressed, crushed, shaken with anger, who lacks the leisure necessary for reflection, who has come to us for an accounting, we who without the aid of his sweat would have to sweat in his place. The encounter with communism, which is not only a system of ideas but generally the irruption of real force in the system of ideas, could have been accommodated by thought as a possibility. Most adherents to the movement who are foreign to human reflection have another reaction, but this is not to hold them in contempt but, on the contrary, to invite them to reflect more profoundly, to forget the concerns that are their own and that leave most men indifferent.

Could they not say to themselves, these men, if it disturbs the laws that found the life proper to the intellectual world, that it is incumbent upon their thought, first, to seek reasons, rather than to respond to passion with passion, and to respond to a force that they believe is blind with an indignation that they believe is not?

Here I cannot examine the question of knowing if the communists are liars, or to what extent they are. But supposing that they are, and that their lies exceed the "authorized" margin (and this debatable opinion at least appears to be reasonable), I wonder if it is not light, contradictory, and, for the vigor of intelligence, deleterious to expressly stop our reflection about communism at the question of lies.

"The lie, it is said, is the leper of the soul" (Marc Bloch, quoted by Roger Stéphane in his questionnaire about communism). I believe I am as moved as anyone else is by a love of the truth; and I do not really know what we owe to Marc Bloch's memoir. But this affirmation made in general is unreasonable, because if it is the case, all action is leprous. I should say: I am not really interested in action; the supreme value that is attributed to it seems very debatable to me (to the extent that after the fact one can say that an action is in a sense a necessity, of the same order as a bitter remedy or the payment of a debt). But I cannot compare a man of action to a leper. For the man of action, lies are evidently no less necessary than speech. And moreover, if he refuses to lie, I could only look at him with an astonishment nuanced by irritation: asking myself if he had been carried away by hysteria or by his unconscious. Those who *speak* of action *speak* of not lying. But those who act, and know how to act, lie to the extent that

that their lies are effective. Action is *struggle* and, to the extent that there is struggle, the diverse forms of violence are unlimited, nor is there any limit, beyond efficacy, to lies. Every other way of seeing things is idealist and as such is the true leper of the soul: it is the incapacity of seeing right, the weakness that diverts the eyes for fear of being unable to endure.

One cannot insist too strongly on this: to act is to struggle reasonably. Strategy is the rational rule of combat: it opposes the naïve practices of savage warriors, who wanted to display their bravery first; it is the art of obtaining a supplementary efficacy through a game of force, using or provoking errors on the part of one's adversary. Transposed into the ideological struggle, the strategic principle demands that one reject the truth, but this is likely to conquer the resistance of those who hesitate or to overcome the lassitude of supporters. Of course, it is not certain that the lie does not return in kind. The lie is bad if the listener is wearied. An ideological expression does not intend isolated results; it intends to create a lasting link between those who speak and their listeners. In particular, if one intends to fight oppression and to establish justice, the efficacy of the lie is limited. *But again it is a question of efficacy: the moral question cannot be posed.*

We will undoubtedly see in this position a manner of lessening a debate that some maintain at the height of naïve sentimentalism. But it is not doubtful that despite appearances, horror of the lies aroused by communist propaganda has a brief meaning. The "intellectuals" cannot bear the fact that speech, which is their goal, should be treated as a means in propaganda. Here it must be said precisely that the use of speech toward the goals of propaganda—of ideological strategy—places the foundation of the intellectual edifice in question. If the dominant authority is efficacy, the conditions that permit the relative autonomy of thought are no longer present. Therein lies the most serious problem; one would not know how to negate the role of autonomous thought in the development of man; one would also not know how to dissociate autonomy from this development, often purchased by cruel sacrifices: in principle, man identifies his destiny with that of his spirit. But if the question of communism has the importance that I give it, does it not belittle it by limiting it to the particular problem of the intellectual world? The communist question is elsewhere; it is intimate in other ways, and this puts in its place an *external* preoccupation that holds it to the naïve vituperation of lies. I think, on the other hand, that a formal protestation against principles that are fatal to thought paralyzes no less profoundly the movement of thought that will not perform a rigorous application of these principles themselves.

The thought that naively asks reality (in the hands of political power) to respect the laws that direct it—without which it would not exist—is comparable to the proper mother who cracks her stubborn kid's head in order to resolve his problems. Undoubtedly, the human spirit is in atrophy if immediately restrained to efficacy. Thought cannot be subordinated: that of men of action who live in necessity is never anything but embryonic (that of Marx is a tribute, if not to Hegel, to his own developments, preliminary to his *Theses on Feuerbach*). But inaction, ineffectiveness, if you will, is no less inevitably harmful to *liberty*. In the end, would propriety and logorrhea be any less foreign to thought than constraint?

But leave thought to the side: thought is always developed in very bad conditions; its greatest danger would be to offer it what it would choose. One can say nothing that would put communism or its methods in an awkward position if one refuses to get to the bottom of them. If one envisions the methods of communism, they are quickly revealed to be effective. It may be that they betray an initial intention: that is something else. But if one denounces this betrayal, one is thereby charged with responding effectively. It does not suffice to say: current communism is far from real communism. . . . One can say nothing of the kind without action—*with consecrating one's entire life* to effective action. The loss, on this level, would have the value of a negative demonstration. Marxism is not a pure theory: it is the enactment of possibilities given by history. But no one is held to be Marxist (even in the U.S.S.R., where one can silence oneself or lie). No one is held to speak of true communism. I do not think it is necessary to envision the always debatable consequences of a doctrine here. I am only trying to clearly define the inevitable problem that Marxism and the U.S.S.R. pose to humanity today.

It cannot be doubted that there has been oppression in the world and that we are only partially enslaved. To the extent that we are oppressed and enslaved, we are no longer human beings but rather things. We cannot lucidly accept being things. To the extent that we feel reduced to things we are *engaged* in the destruction of those who reduce us in this manner.

We cannot escape reduction individually, other than in what is still a doubtful way. In fact, for this we must integrate ourselves into a world wherein human beings are basically treated like commodities. At least through complicity, we must make our neighbors commodities. To truly escape we must continually destroy the effect of our integration, pushing us beyond things, violently affirming our individuality. But we will cease to be things only in the affirmation that separates us from humanity in general. Our individuality aggressively acknowledged (*against the others*) is not treated as a commodity; the simple humanity in us is never recognized for what it truly is—*entirely other than a thing*. We only affirm the repudiation of the human community. We are traitors insidiously.

But if we refuse individual flight, and if we affirm the human community—if we accept not being things while at the same time and to the same extent as the others, *we must first accept being things*. It is only when humanity as a whole will have ceased being oppressed, when no commodity-man remains anywhere to be sold that we can ourselves escape reduction. Only there, at the level of the available thing, at the level of debased humanity, must we contribute in the field to an immense labor of liberation.

We must even envision troublesome refinements. The development of science is by nature intended to permit a marked reduction of human nature to a thing. The "political lie" is itself the first work of a science that will generally make man into a field of experiments to which science will respond rationally. Pedagogy and biology, for their parts, are susceptible to suppress with an increasing perfection man's resistance to the activities of the state. It is thus of a decisive importance that the state itself not surpass in any way the principles of the thing, that it holds sovereign only the name, that it should be subordinated without reserve to the individuals that it subordinates, being itself only an instrument and a soulless object.

At that moment, man will be free!

And we can no longer speak of it.

But it is in this way that it becomes a pure object in the limitless functioning of operations, that the question of humanity is posed with a sufficient rigor. From that moment, man's repudiation of human community takes on another meaning; it is no longer the careless repudiation that the strong make of the weak nor the puerile flight of conscience. The *individual* distances himself without seeing the one who effaces him (who in return is ready to efface him). The man of objective society should on the contrary grasp his own humanity in the consciousness of his reduction to a thing and in the consciousness of the limits of that reduction.

Naturally it is unfortunate in a sense that everything has taken place at night, that communism cannot offer assurance, and that it seems at first to stray radically from the goal that it is in its essence to pursue. It is not natural to eliminate errors, misunderstandings, or wars. It is true that they only apparently depend on man. It is certainly sad that the result can be hoped for only at the end of the conflagration—at the point when it is certain that we will not escape the horror, but it is doubtful that the result will elude us.

This would not know how to exempt us from perceiving in the reproached reductions of communism more than a derangement of intellectual tranquility: the troublesome radical position, arousing the fundamental problem to the ultimate degree. Man cannot be taken for a thing. And it is for this reason that he is a communist. (But it must be added: communism can only initially complete, generalize the reduction of man to a thing, and it is for this reason that man must fight communism to the death.)

Claude Aveline, Jean Cassou, André Chamson, Georges Friedmann, Louis Martin-Chauffier, Vercors, *L'heure du choix* (Paris: Editions de Minuit, 1947).

> From the fact that they are not members of the communist party but simply sympathizers, the authors of the studies gathered in this collection discuss certain political positions. They specify that in their eyes the U.S.S.R. is an *example* not a *model*. French communism might pursue independent ways and recognize limits to the necessities of propaganda. One must account for the fundamental political facts of the present period: to know it is vain henceforth to envision the possibilities of an enterprise beyond a war. Whatever the obstacles on one side, some foreigners on the other, whatever these essays owe political realism, it would be vain, it would not conform with *political realism* itself, to forget that these positions are held by most members of the French communist party.

Roger Stéphane, ed. *Questions du communisme*, a special issue of *Confluences* vol. 8 new series, n° 18–20 (1947). Including responses from R. Aron, J. Beaufret, J. Benda, R. Caillois, M. Collinet, J.T. Desnati, J. Domarchi, I. Dorgot, J. Kanapa, H. Lefebvre, S. de Madariaga, J.-J. Marchand, G. Martinet, R. Maublanc, E. Mounier, A. Patri, P. Pia, G. Picon, D. Rousset, A. de Soras, S. Spender, R. Tavernier, Tran-Duc Thao, R. Vaillard, and Vercors.

> The rare communists who responded to this inquiry did so not without humor. Roger Stéphane's questionnaire cites Malraux and Sartre effectively, and naturally speaks of lies and of liberty; it engages the discussion in the direction of individualism and morality which underscores the disorder resulting from contradictions between the immediate actions of communism and its distant goals.

Notes

This article originally appeared in *Critique* 25 (June 1948): 561–66; reprinted in OC 11: 332–38.

List of Contributors

David B. Allison is professor of philosophy at the State University of New York at Stony Brook. He is the author of *Reading the New Nietzsche* and coauthor (with Mark S. Roberts) of *Disordered Mother or Disordered Diagnosis: Munchausen by Proxy Syndrome*. He is editor of the groundbreaking *The New Nietzsche*, founding editor of *New Nietzsche Studies*, editor of *Sade and the Narrative of Transgression*, and editor and translator of Derrida's *Speech and Phenomena and Other Essays*.

Edward S. Casey is Distinguished Professor at the State University of New York at Stony Brook, where he teaches as well as at the New School for Social Research and at Pacifica Graduate Institute. He was chairman of the philosophy department at SUNY, Stony Brook, from 1991 through 2001. He is has recently been elected president of the American Philosophical Association, Eastern Division. His books include *Imagining; Remembering; Getting Back into Place; Representing Place in Landscape Painting and Maps; Earth-Mapping: Artists Reshaping Landscape*. A new book, *The World at a Glance,* has just appeared. It is soon to be followed by *The World on Edge.*

Marc Froment-Meurice is professor of French at Vanderbilt University. His publications reflect a wide scope of interests in theory, art, and literature. His authored books include *La Disparue* (récit, Gallimard, 1987); *Solitudes, de Rimbaud à Heidegger* (Galilée, 1989; trans. SUNY, 1995); *La Chose même* (Galilée, 1992); *Tombeau de Trakl* (Belin, 1992); *C'est à dire: Poétique de Heidegger* (Galilée, 1996; trans. as *That Is to Say: Heidegger's Poetics,* Stanford University Press, 1998); *La Chimère. Tombeau de Nerval* (Belin, 2001); *Incitations* (Galilée, 2002).

Chris Gemerchak received his PhD in philosophy from Katholieke Universiteit in Leuven, Belgium, and was a member of the philosophical research group CLiC. Along with a number of articles on Hegel, Marx, Freud, and Lacan, he is author of *The Sunday of the Negative: Reading Bataille Reading Hegel* and editor of *Everyday Extraordinary: Encountering Fetishism with Marx, Freud, and Lacan.*

Stuart Kendall is the author of *Georges Bataille*, a critical biography published by Reaktion Books, and the editor and cotranslator of two collections of writings by Georges Bataille, *The Unfinished System of Nonknowledge* and *The Cradle of Humanity: Prehistoric Art and Culture.* His other editions include works by Paul Eluard, Maurice Blanchot, Jean Baudrillard, and Guy Debord. His articles and reviews consider modern and contemporary art and design, philosophy, poetry, and theology.

Alphonso Lingis is Professor Emeritus of philosophy at Pennsylvania State University. He is the author of numerous books, including *The Community of Those Who Have Nothing in Common, Abuses, The Imperative, Trust*, and *The First Person Singular.* He is the translator of a number of the most influential works in French philosophy, including Merleau-Ponty's *The Visible and the Invisible*, Klossowski's *Sade, My Neighbor*, and Levinas' *Existence and Existents*, *Totality and Infinity*, and *Otherwise Than Being.*

Karmen MacKendrick is professor of philosophy at LeMoyne College. Her research interests center on questions of language, corporeality, and temporality, primarily in relation to theology and religious studies. She is the author of *Word Made Skin: Figuring Language at the Surface of Flesh, Counterpleasures*, and *Immemorial Silence.*

Andrew J. Mitchell is assistant professor of philosophy at Emory University, specializing in the work of Heidegger and the Continental tradition. He is the author of essays on Heidegger, Nietzsche, Derrida, Fassbinder, and Joyce. He is cotranslator (with François Raffoul) of Heidegger's *Four Seminars.*

Jean-Luc Nancy is professor of political philosophy and media aesthetics at the European Graduate School in Saas-Fee, Switzerland. He is the author of a number of books, including *The Inoperative Community, The Gravity of Thought, The Sense of the World, The Muses, Being Singular Plural*, and *The Creation of the World or Globalization.*

Kalliopi Nikolopoulou teaches comparative literature at the State University of New York, Buffalo. She has written on philosophical aesthetics, European modernism, tragedy, and the relation of ancients to moderns.

Jason Kemp Winfree is associate professor of philosophy at California State University, Stanislaus. He specializes in continental philosophy and has authored various articles addressing problems of history, writing, and difference, among others.

Index